Enacting the Worlds of Cinema

Enacting the Worlds of Cinema

STEFFEN HVEN

OXFORD
UNIVERSITY PRESS

OXFORD
UNIVERSITY PRESS

Oxford University Press is a department of the University of Oxford. It furthers
the University's objective of excellence in research, scholarship, and education
by publishing worldwide. Oxford is a registered trade mark of Oxford University
Press in the UK and certain other countries.

Published in the United States of America by Oxford University Press
198 Madison Avenue, New York, NY 10016, United States of America.

© Oxford University Press 2022

Library of Congress Control Number: 2022901455
ISBN 978–0–19–755510–1 (hbk.)

DOI: 10.1093/oso/9780197555101.001.0001

1 3 5 7 9 8 6 4 2

Printed by Integrated Books International, United States of America

Contents

Contents

Acknowledgments

This project has been long underway and has been supported by a number of research grants. I would like to express my deepest gratitude to the Fritz Thyssen Foundation (A.Z. 40.16.0.001.KU) for awarding me a postdoc scholarship, the Bauhaus Research School for awarding me a Bauhaus-Postdoc-Stipendium, and to the Deutsche Forschungsgemeinschaft (DFG, German Research Foundation, Research Project Reference: HV 8/1-1) for awarding me a research grant that enabled me to spend fifteen months as a visiting postdoc fellow at the University of Chicago.

I would like to thank my editor at Oxford University Press, Norm Hirschy, for excellent editorial work on the manuscript. I would also like to express my gratitude to two anonymous reviewers. Their dedication, critical perspectives, and constructive feedback have sharpened and refined the arguments of the book, and I am deeply grateful for all their thoughtful comments.

My deepest gratitude to Lorenz Engell and Christiane Voss, the directors at the Kompetenzzentrum Medienanthropologie (KOMA) at the Bauhaus-Universität Weimar, where most of the research for this project was conducted and where its formative ideas have taken shape. I would like to thank all the doctorates at the research center, whose lively discussions at the colloquia have given so much fuel to the project as my own ideas were developing. I would particularly like to thank Friedlind Riedel for pointing me in the direction of contemporary German atmosphere research.

The final and most critical stage of the project was conducted during my stay at the University of Chicago. My heartfelt admiration and acknowledgments go to David Rodowick and Daniel Morgan for being such excellent hosts at the Department of Cinema and Media Studies (CMS). Both have in their own unique ways guided me through the final phase of this research project, and I am deeply grateful for them always being such indulgent, critical, and kind readers. All shortcomings are mine alone.

So many colleagues and friends in the world of film studies and beyond have contributed in one way or another, be it through their excellent writings; warm discussions, suggestions, or advice at conferences, workshops, or colloquia; or all of those at once. I would in particular like to thank Maria Poulaki, Steven Willemsen, Miklós Kiss, Adriano D'Aloia, John A. Bateman, Kate Rennebohm, Tyler Parks, Rebecca Sheehan, Blandine Joret, Martin Siegler, Franziska Reichenbecher, Johanna Seifert, Lena Serow, Christoph Carsten, Malte Hagener,

Johannes Bennke, Leander Scholz, Katerina Korola, Dominique Buhler, Allyson Nadia Field, Gustavo Jardim, Noa Merkin, Yuri Tsivian, Traci Verleyen, Antonio Somaini, David Bordwell, Carl Plantinga, Torben Grodal, Michele Guerra, Vittorio Gallese, Michael Wedel, Hermann Kappelhoff, Matthias Grotkopp, Jan-Hendrik Bakels, Eileen Rositzka, Mathias Korsgaard, Jakob Isak Nielsen, Volker Pantenburg, Christian Kassung, Andreas Gregersen, Johannes Riis, Birger Langkjær, Karen Pearlman, Murray Smith, Pia Tikka, Jelena Rosic, Daniel Yacavone, Patricia Pisters, Francesco Sticchi, Ruggero Eugeni, Rasmus Greiner, Luis Rocha Antunes, and Joe Kickasola.

Finally, all my love goes out to my family. Especially my children Emma and Jonathan for always accompanying me while I was (trying) to write this book during months of staying at home. I am particularly indebted to stimulating suggestions such as "zcvxbxvnsjon" or "fmrkmfpqnji0." This book is dedicated to you.

Introduction: Worlds Enacted

In the beginning of Lars von Trier's *Dogville* (2003), the narrator provides a literary description of the diegetic space that contrasts with its minimalist set design. The narrative, we are told, takes place in a small township in the Rocky Mountains "near the old, abandoned silver mine, where the road comes to an end." This is a township of modest means and "most of the buildings were pretty wretched; more like shacks, frankly." Visually present, however, are not shacks but chalk lines drawn on the concrete floor of the hangar building that provides the background to the film's ascetic scenography. Due to this lucid play with the affordances of both literary and theatrical forms of mediation (i.e., the narrator's exposition and the staging as black box theater), it has been argued that *Dogville* turns cinema into a "literary" experience (Badley 2010, 104).[1]

While it certainly relies on literary expressive means to counterbalance its frugal approach to set design, the opulent visual imagery of *Dogville* exhibits the powers of the cinematic medium to draw us into its worlds. Its persistent, almost exhibitionist insistence on its artificiality challenges the notion of the filmic world as a self-enclosed space that exists beyond its material manifestation in the film and the embodied act of its reception. *Dogville* neither rejects the formation of a coherent storyworld (e.g., *L'année dernière à Marienbad*, directed by Resnais 1961) nor restrains the emotional or affective appeal of its performances and events (e.g., *Pickpocket*, directed by Bresson 1959). In producing its diegesis, it underlines it as a fragile, ongoing gestalt that materializes on the basis of the specific employment of the medium's affordances (e.g., its use of a naturalistic sound design or camera movements and framings to create the sensation of space) and the cognitive and affective investments of the spectator that transform the film's minimalist design into an "environment."[2]

It would be an error to regard *Dogville*'s anti-mise-en-scène as merely an obstacle for our feeling of being immersed in its world when it in fact contributes to its complexity and aesthetic appeal by allowing for a unique cinematic interrogation of space as mediator of the entanglement of the individual and the collective. In a key scene of the film, Chuck (Stellan Skarsgård), one of Dogville's residents, rapes Grace (Nicole Kidman), the female protagonist, who has sought refuge in the small mining town and paid back the community by performing all sorts of (affective) labor. Moments before the township's growing abuse of Grace's generosity culminates in rape, the camera closes in on the discomfort revealed on

Enacting the Worlds of Cinema. Steffen Hven, Oxford University Press. © Oxford University Press 2022.
DOI: 10.1093/oso/9780197555101.003.0001

her face to evoke the sensation of being entrapped in a tight space. The film then cuts to a two shot that includes Chuck, whose growing hostility unveils his cruel intentions. As Grace realizes what is about to happen, the camera again moves in on her and rotates around her to create an atmosphere of mounting despair. These are all fairly conventional cinematic techniques for framing the narrative space and for charging it affectively. This is, at least, the case until a new cut opens up the space with a series of zooms and framings that integrate into the scene the villagers, who remain oblivious to the malicious act that literally occurs just before them. The open set design leaves an imprint of the villagers as willfully ignoring not just Chuck's but the whole township's abuse of Grace.

The lack of frames and boundaries implicates the whole community in the rape. The borderless, minimalist Brechtian stage design of the film thus provides a stunning visual anticipation of the collective sexual assault still to come, while providing exposition of the film's central narrative theme.[3] Through a modulation of the medium's affordances, i.e., its absence of a conventional set design, *Dogville* is capable of narrating with meticulous precision its story of communal guilt. The film contains a complex duality, where the naturalistic soundscape and the voice-over narration aid to the imagination of what is visually absent (e.g., the township's wretched shacks and the mountainous scenery), while the lack of set design is simultaneously exploited to present a fluid, borderless, and transformative narrative space designed to visualize the theme of the thin lines separating individual from communal guilt.

The textual legacy of film studies has taught us to think of the diegesis as a container of the narrative events, characters, and actions, where the elements of the film fall logically into the categories of either inside (diegetic) or outside (nondiegetic) the illusory space of the film. *Dogville* does not defy this logic, as much as it renders it hermeneutically ineffective. The film is staged so as to provide a direct perception of the characters as being both *inside* (corresponding to our immediate visual impression) and *outside* (corresponding to the film's illusory play with spaces) the space of the sexual abuse. Even if the film's suggestion of the villagers' implication in the crime is not "diegetic" in the textual sense, our direct, visual perception of the diegesis certainly suggests this.

To think about narratives as affectively charged environments or affective ecologies is to challenge the borders of what is internal and external, be it in the biological and psychological proposition of the co-constitution of environment and animal in the tradition that goes from Jakob von Uexküll's concept of *Umwelt* to James Gibson's ecological theory of perception, or the cognitive-phenomenological tradition of embeddedness from Martin Heidegger's philosophy of being-in-the-world to the symbiosis of brain, body, and environment in cognitive enactivism or the overcoming of modern versions of Cartesian substance dualism in affective and cognitive neuroscience.

This book is about the reciprocal relations of the filmic spectator and the narrative world. It involves a rejection of the disembodied semiotics that have dominated our thinking about cinematic narration from structuralist-linguistic semiotics to cognitive formalism. Rather than capture the diegesis as the sum of the film's denoted text (semiotics) or the mental representation of its cognitive cues (cognitive formalism), it shall be argued that the diegesis emerges in the embodied act of perception.[4] The main thesis to be explored in this book is that the spectator's cognitive and affective investments are inextricably woven into the fabric of the diegesis, not solely to be located *in* the embodied organism as mental representation nor *in* the film as text. Instead, the diegesis emerges as a function of their structural coupling in the film experience. The diegesis is thus no mirror onto reality; it provokes a unique mode of existence. A central term thus becomes that of the "diegesis," which will be used in the sense given to it by the French filmologists (Souriau 1951, 1953) rather than in its more common use in ancient Greek poetics, where it is structurally paired to the notion of mimesis.[5] Understood in the broad fashion as the "world of the film," the diegesis does more than duplicate, simulate, or imitate an external reality; it shadows, extends, reshapes, creates, and transforms it.

Where the diegesis has predominantly been captured in representational terms (e.g., the diegesis is *about* something), the way it both shapes and is shaped by the organism's capacities for thinking and feeling has been left underexamined. Needed is the development of a film narratology that not only understands the diegesis as emergent on the basis of the spectator's cognitive and affective capacities for sensemaking (turning the film material into a felt environment or affective ecology), but also how being embedded in media ecologies modulates not only our affective and perceptive capacities but also our general thoughts, feelings, and disposition. Examined will then be how the affective and narrative arrangements of films provide us with an experience of how it feels like to inhabit, perceive, and live in the narrative environment of the film.[6]

Films therefore do more than represent a world to us; they conjure it up and attune the way we think and feel about it. And cinema has the power to do so, even with nothing but chalk lines drawn on the floor. We therefore need to take into account the atmospheric nature of cinematic spaces. Yet, it is not enough to pose atmospheres (or moods) as filters that color the already constituted narratives in particular feeling tones (the position of cognitive theories of moods in film). Instead, cinematic perception needs to be understood as necessarily atmospheric perception.

This conception of the diegesis runs counter to the dominant aesthetic principle of classical Hollywood cinema, which relied on an unobtrusive style and narrative motivation. It has often been argued that this style developed and gained prominence because it had been designed in congruence with our cognitive capacities.[7] Much film theory and history have been written on the scheme of classical Hollywood cinema versus any kind of placeholder of a non-classical style. Perceiving the diegesis as environment, however, allows us to re-gard classical Hollywood cinema as merely one mode of diegesis construction that can be studied alongside other modalities such as cinema of attractions, German expressionism, neorealism, nouvelle vague, film noir, New Hollywood cinema, mumblecore, or even non-cinematic forms of world construction. Each of these is characterized by how they use or alter the affordances of the medium available to them within their specific socio-historical, cultural, and technolog-ical context to produce mediated environments.

Viewing the diegesis as environment thus allows us to compare cinema's modalities of producing the diegesis with those found in other media; even those that are not specific narrative media such as social media, television news, or talk shows (cf. Elsaesser 2004). All these accommodate the affordances of their medium to create environments that proffer specific kinds of social interactions (e.g., talk shows create environments for conversation, debate, or cozy chitchat); the broadcasting, discussion, and reflection of events (e.g., news shows or social media); or the telling of fictional stories.

In reinterpreting the diegesis as environment, the represented narrative is thus no longer the unavoidable conceptual starting point but an effect of the worldmaking capacity of its medium. Considering the diegesis in relational terms according to the coupling of spectator and film thus requires us to part with its textual conceptualization as an "objective" external universe cut off from the organism's capacities for shaping its Umwelt. Once conceived as a dis-embodied text, the diegesis re-emerges as the product of the "transmission of affects" that flow between spectator and film.[8]

Over the last decades the bodily, sensorial, material, and affective aspects of the filmic experience have become increasingly pertinent, and the cinematic ca-pacity to stimulate viewers in a direct, corporal, and sensorial fashion has been the growing subject of attention.[9] Unfortunately, this body of work has been conducted in relative isolation from studies that examine the narrative powers of cinema. In contrast to the field's general move toward embodied, visceral, and material forms of expression, film narratology has remained conceptually rooted in the communicational-representational paradigms of structuralism, linguis-tics, semiology, and cognitive formalism.[10]

Film narratology's disembodied, textual commitments have still to be thor-oughly investigated as part of the field's turn to the body and the material. In fact, it appears that many scholars are content with the dominant notion of the narrative as the film's representational site. This has made it possible to situate embodiment and affect as what transgresses or exceeds the film's demand for narrative according to an all-too-familiar dichotomy that separates the cognitive, intellectual, and analytical from the sensorial, visceral, and intuitive. This schism has its way of sneaking in through the back door even in works that argue for the conjunction of the visceral and the cognitive such as Vivian Sobchack's *Carnal Thoughts* (2004), whose back cover declares the intention of the book to provide a study of "our corporal *rather than* our intellection stimulation with cinema." In *The Skin of Film* (2000), Laura Marks explains, "haptic media encourage a relation to the screen itself before the point at which the viewer is pulled into the figures of the image and the exhortation of the narrative" (187–88). This corresponds with the affect-theoretical proposition of an immediate bifurcation in the response between the bodily autonomous domain of affect and the sociolinguistic fixation of emotions, cognition, language, and narrative (Massumi 1995, 85). The "affective" is thus conceived as nonrepresentational, nonlinguistic, bodily autonomous, nonsemantic, and nonnarrative.[11]

Even if it can be argued that it merely reinstates the crude separation of affect and cognition that was the problem to begin with,[12] "affect theory" (Clough and Halley 2007; Gregg and Seigworth 2010b) has envisaged a radical break with the homogenous focus on the semantical, representational, and disembodied textualism of linguistic, structuralist, and poststructuralist thinking. Theories of embodiment and affect from Deleuze to Massumi and Shaviro have demonstrated the neglected potential of cinema's manifold nonrepresentational capacities for producing immediate forces or intensities that move, act, alter, and produce rather than merely represent.

Concurrently, the continued influence of linguistics, semiotics, and the cognitive sciences on narratology means that the term "representation" is so widely used in defining narratives that this way of understanding narrative is one of the few methodological constants of narratology (Rudrum 2005, 196). In a field that is currently rethinking the chronological-linear models of its history (e.g., media-archeology), its visual bias (e.g., film sound studies), the cognitive foundations of spectatorship (e.g., embodied film studies), and the role of things, objects, and probs as material agents operating also outside their communicational/representational function in the text (e.g., nonhuman or posthuman agencies), film narratology's fixation on the causal-linear organization of the text, its disembodied communicational model, its binary logic (e.g., story/discourse, syuzhet/fabula, diegetic/nondiegetic), its reduction of narrative meaning to propositional content, and its insistence on representation makes it the last brigade hanging onto the once dominant metaphor of thinking the film as a text.

Even if structuralism, semiotics, or cognitive formalism are no longer *en vogue* in what is becoming an increasingly dynamic and heterogenous field, the conceptual heritage of film studies remains deeply entrenched in the premises of these formative schools of thought. This is most explicitly evidenced by the continuous influence of the most important legacy of textual film studies, namely, the idea that the film can be treated as a text. Once we begin to examine the most basic and pervasive comprehension of the filmic storyworld, we find that even recent "embodied" works on film operate with what is a textual comprehension of the diegesis as reducible to its literal meanings, its basic plot elements.[13] This reduction of the diegesis to the sum of its textual propositions is rooted in Christian Metz's reappraisal and subsequential popularization of the filmological concept of the diegesis as corresponding to the discursive and denotative level of the film.[14]

What is implied, or simply taken for granted, is that film narratives contain a representational core of textual meaning that is separable from the embodied and affective act of its reception. This idea has further been enforced by cognitive formalist film theory, in particular, the ascription of narrative comprehension to cognitive processes such as schemata application, the reorganization of the film material into a causal-linear sequence of events, and the spectator's inferential elaboration of the gaps of the film text. Within this framework, the affective, sensorial, and embodied nature of the cinematic experience is elicited in *parallel* to the film's representational dimension. The experiential, embodied aspect can thus relate to, comment on, be in contrast to, or contradict the narrative textual core, which it, however, never can establish, produce, or be part of. This is a fundamental assumption in the cognitive narratologies of David Bordwell (1985, 1989, 2008) and Edward Branigan (1984, 1992, 2006) that has continued to inform cognitive-oriented scholarship on embodiment, emotion, and affect. It would thus be misleading to argue that the affective and emotional aspects of the cinematic experience are sidestepped or ignored by cognitive film theory, as the works of Ed S. Tan, Carl Plantinga, Greg M. Smith, Murray Smith, Torben Grodal, and others bear witness to. What needs to be targeted specifically is how affective and emotional processes are perceived as *responses* to the already constituted cognitive, narrative, representational, and propositional "cinematic text." Cognitive theories of discourse thus isolate a "text base," the propositional representation of the narrative, from emotional responses and assume this text base to be the starting point not only of narrative comprehension but also our emotional response to films.[15]

This assumption continues to guide the dominant understanding of cinematic moods as "filters" onto the narrative world, the already formed text base. Similarly, most extant theories of film sound readily endorse the proposition advanced by the narratological musicologist Claudia Gorbman (1980, 1987) that the distinction between diegetic (intra-worldly) and nondiegetic (extra-worldly) music is the epistemological starting point for understanding the narrative role of film sound.

This book sets out to argue that our continuous insistence on understanding the film's narrative world according to its basic propositional text is no longer

compatible with the field's general movement toward nonrepresentational, affective, embodied, material, media-archeological, media-anthropological, and
nonhuman frameworks for understanding the phenomenon of cinema. The difficulty, however, lies not in pointing out this incompatibility. Far more challenging
is the introduction of a viable alternative that is a facilitator of new venues of
research to be explored rather than a stumbling block for established practices.

I believe that shifting our basic understanding of the nature of the film world
from the notion of text to that of environment is capable of achieving this. In
contrast to "cognitive-embodied" theories that base their theories on the cognitive narratology advanced by Bordwell,[16] this book argues for a more definitive
break with the disembodied assumptions to be found not only in cognitive film
theory but also in those which, it shall be shown throughout this book, are deeply
engrained in the tools, concepts, and methodologies of film theory (cognitive or
not). The aim is thus to radically break with the assumed primacy of the representational narrative text and challenge the disembodied conceptualizations of
the diegesis whether these are based on textual decoding or cognitive-inferential
elaborations.

In emphasizing the affective and material foundation of cinematic narratives,
this book proposes a post-textual narrative theory, whose major intervention in
current debates is the reframing of the narrative film world in environmental
terms. This has several consequences for how we think of the cinematic narrative. For instance, rather than thinking of the narrative space as a passive container of the events, situations, characters, and actions of the film, it is conceived
as an affectively charged environment that does not host events as much as it
generates them. Such a reorientation of the narrative space resurrects all the
nonrepresentational and nonreferential elements that had been stocked away in
the cabinet of textual narratology: the experiential, the atmospheric, the kinetic,
the multisensorial, the material, and the affective.[17]

The aim of this book is thus not to dispute the representational and communicational nature of cinematic narration, but to argue that these aspects of the
film do not operate *despite* or in *parallel to* but *on the basis of* the affective distribution of movements that attunes the spectator to the film. To properly address
a film's *aboutness* (representation), we first need to understand the contexts of its
worldmaking. Needed is thus an understanding of how cinema produces its distinctive affective media ecologies by reconfiguring, displacing, and altering the
spatiotemporal coordinates of experience.

Unlike literary art works, where our relation to the diegesis is entirely mediated by symbolic communication, the film material requires an embodied act
of perception to surface as a world of significance. Where it is possible to study
media environments without taking an interest in their narrative aspects (just as
we can have nonnarrative media environments), my contention is that we cannot

think about cinema narratives in isolation from their materialization within a specific media ecology. Many of the core concepts of film studies, including the diegesis, are still premised on the classical narratological assumption that the narrative can be reduced to its "literal skeleton," i.e., a series of narrative propositions organized into a spatiotemporal chain of events. In this context, film studies could seek inspiration in the renewed "neo-narratological" interest in narrative worlds and worldmaking that is trying to remedy the overemphasis on questions of temporal ordering in classical narratology.[18]

An environmental reappraisal of the diegesis obviously gestures in the direction of media ecology, which revolutionized our thinking about media by addressing them less as communicational tools than environments capable of changing the human condition.[19] This connects the environmental notion of the diegesis with the broad definition of media that we, for instance, find in the work of Walter Benjamin as the spatially extended environment, the milieu, the atmosphere, and the Umwelt in which perception occurs (Somaini 2016, 7). As John Durham Peters (2015) has recently reminded us, the communicational notion of media as message-bearing institutions is relatively recent in intellectual history (2).

It is thus important that the diegesis is conceptualized as relatively autonomous from the narrative chain of events, as Noël Burch (1979, 1982) pointed out early.[20] Gesturing toward a non-textual comprehension of the diegesis, Thomas Elsaesser (2004) has more recently argued that it is the question of diegesis more than questions about the digital versus analog that demands us to redefine the very "ground" of the moving image in its multiple sites (103). When the primacy of narrative is challenged many other modalities of constructing the diegesis become apparent. In this lies an implicit reconfiguration of the traditional relation between stylistic means of expression and narration that provides us with a way out of the theoretical deadlocks that film studies inherited from the classical narratological dichotomies of "narration versus narrated," "form versus content," or, indeed, "diegetic versus nondiegetic."

This book draws on a host of disciplines, methodologies, and theoretical and philosophical frameworks in its reconceptualization of the cinematic diegesis as environment, including the 4EA approaches within the cognitive sciences, affective neurosciences, ecological psychology, media-philosophy, filmology, (neo-) phenomenology, contemporary atmosphere research, as well as the relatively new discipline of (German) media-anthropology. All these share a common effort to overcome "intellectualism" and its separation not only of the mind and the body but also the body and its (techno-mediated) environment. Moreover, it challenges the intellectualist doctrine, identified by Gilbert Ryle (2009), dictating that the primary epistemological relation we have to the world is mediated by mental operations and steered toward the intellectual grasp of true propositions (16).

Both film semiotics and cognitive formalism frame their theories of narrative comprehension around the capacity to grasp the filmic narrative mentally in the form of propositional knowledge. Narrative comprehension is thus believed to differ from our affective and sensorial impressions (that can be flawed) and instead be contingent upon the ability to express our knowledge of this world in a verbal form that devaluates our practical and skillful navigation as embodied agents in (artificially crafted) environments (cf. Zerilli 2015, 261). The narrative we know has become the narrative we can *recount* or *verbalize* in the form of the literary plot summary. On this level, the narrative is reducible and transmedial.[21]

This book argues that the filmic narrative is not first and foremost to be conceived as a *representation* but an *enaction*; i.e., the narrative materializes in a diegesis that does not exist prior to the cinematic encounter but is brought forth by the embodied spectator in its interaction with the narrative, semiotic, aesthetic, affective, atmospheric, and technological arrangement of the film material. This claim, derived from the "enactive" branch of embodied cognition (e.g., Varela, Thompson, and Rosch 1992; Colombetti 2014; Gallagher 2017), rejects the assumption—not just prevalent in the cognitive sciences but also in narratology—that cognition is rehearsed on the basis of a representation of the world conceived as independent of the perceptual and cognitive capacities that perceive it and as performed by a cognitive system that itself exists independently of the material intensities of the world (Varela et al. 1992, xx).

In contrast to classical cognitivism, enactivism understands cognition to be a form of "embodied action." Cognition is thus embodied (it depends on the sensorimotor capacities of the organism) and embedded (these capacities are embedded in a more encompassing biological, psychological, and cultural context that points to the codetermination of animal and environment) (173). In conceptualizing cognition as action, enactivism emphasizes the inextricable relation between sensory (perception) and motor (action) processes. Following this Merleau-Ponty-inspired branch of cognitive philosophy, cognition is a product of the "structural coupling" or the history of interactions between an organism and its environment. Cognition is therefore not just embedded and embodied, but also enactive because the world is brought forth (i.e., enacted) in the encounter between the embodied organism and the environment (174). Cognition is thus also necessarily relational and affective (Colombetti 2014, 18).

This book aims to explore the important ramifications that the replacement of the common notion of filmic text (pregiven world) plus mental representation (pregiven mind) with the enactive and ecological principle of codetermination between organism and environment has for how we think of the diegesis: in particular, as this pertains to the necessity of integrating the embodied act of perception into the structure of the filmic environment (for a pioneering work on cinema and enactivism, see Tikka 2008).

In order to target the specific organism–environment relation of *mediated* environments, this book further draws on recent advancements made within a strain of German media philosophy that goes under the name of "media-anthropology" (*Medienanthropologie*). Not unlike enactivism, media-anthropology is concerned with couplings of media and embodied organisms. Yet, rather than taking as its outset the cognitive (neuro)sciences, media-anthropology aims to formulate an understanding of anthropogenesis that is both media-theoretically and media-philosophically informed (Engell and Siegert 2013, 5). Rather than inquiring into the universal and transcultural essence of human existence, media-anthropology shifts the perspective onto the procedures, operations, instruments, technologies, skillful activities, and spatiotemporal sites that define anthropogenesis. Both enactivism and media-anthropology thus allow us to capture the diegesis from the perspective of an "operative ontology" (Engell and Siegert 2017), which shifts perspective from "the given" onto a logic of producing, making, medializing, processing, transforming, etc. From such a perspective, the diegesis *is* nothing in itself; it has no essence that we can derive at through objective measurement, codification, or quantification, and no preexisting textual base. All we are left with are the processes of its becoming.

Although media-anthropology draws inspiration from post-human media and affect theory, it disputes its emphatic non-anthropocentrism (cf. Voss 2014a).[22] Instead of going beyond the human entirely, media-anthropology examines the material, aesthetic, dispositional, discursive, and technological affordances that contribute to anthropogenesis. Human experience, cognition, affectivity, and semiosis are conceived beyond their presumed essences or universalisms but as deeply dependent on "bodies" that are not just biological but also technological, artificial, material, aesthetic, and discursive.

As an object of experience, the diegesis is not just an *internal* reality that results from our cognitive mapping of the cinematic situation, its characters, events, etc. The diegesis is enacted, but the nature of this enaction is governed by the affordances of the medium. The notion of enactment thus needs to be complemented with a consideration of the specific "anthropomedial relation" underlining this enactment.[23] Of central importance thus becomes cinema's distribution of movement, where we are *moved* by the film but also *animate* it or breathe movement and life into it.

It is in this dual process that the feeling of being immersed in the film is produced. From this perspective, our ability to be caught up in the narrative space of *Dogville* despite its anti-mise-en-scène is not dependent on a suspension of disbelief. It is not necessary to look beyond the film's blatant, self-reflective mediation for us to become affectively and cognitively carried away by its narrative.

Dogville liberates the cinematic diegesis from mimetic realism, demonstrating instead, as Edgar Morin (2005) argued in 1956, that the magic of film is to be found in its symbiosis of the immersive and the self-reflective, the affective and the intellectual, the "real" and the mediated. If *Dogville* exemplifies cinema's ability to self-reflectively examine and play with the affordances of its diegesis construction, then media-anthropology reminds us that such forms of self-reflectivity can only be carried out *with* or *through* media.

To comprehend the anthropomedial relation of cinema, Christiane Voss has proposed the concept of *Leihkörper* (the "surrogate body"),[24] a media-anthropological reinterpretation of Vivian Sobchack's (2004) phenomenological notion of the "cinesthetic subject." Voss's intention is to shift the battleground from the *in abstracto*–defined spectator (cognitive or embodied) to the emergent *Leihkörper*, i.e., the anthropomedial relation. Drawing upon John Dewey's philosophy of aesthetics, Voss (2011, 2014b) argues that in the mental and sensorial-affective resonances of the spectator's body with the onscreen events, the film "loans" the spectator's body to produce a three-dimensional world. In this process, the spectator becomes a temporary *Leihkörper* for the film, and this body, in turn, becomes a constituent feature of the filmic architecture.

This anthropomedial conception of the spectator needs to be complemented with a corresponding environmental concept of the diegesis. Thus, just as the film material and its semantic-architectural design comes alive as a lived, atmospheric, or somatic space through its interactions with a felt body, the cinematic *Leihkörper* becomes the site of the *film's* affects, cognitions, kinetics, emotions, and movements. It thus becomes possible to carve out a stratified space that not only connects the *Leihkörper* to the diegesis but also ties together various levels of description ranging from the bodily autonomous (affective reflexes), techno-organic (motor resonances), environmental (atmospheres), and emotional (cognitively structured, object-centered, and intentional feeling states), to the cognitive-analytical, abstract, and self-reflective (associated with matters of representation, signification, plot composition, focalization, narrative structure, authorship, etc.). Media-anthropology thus poses a continuous flow between the organic and the technical; between affects, emotions, and cognitions; and between the pre-semiotic and the semiotic. Thus, "higher" cognitive performances (e.g., the ability to strain together dissociated images and sounds into a temporal gestalt experienced as an environment) are not isolated from basic affective operations, whose continuous rhythmicity defines the structural coupling of the embodied spectator and the cinematic material (cf. Voss 2014a, 64). Embodiment in cinema should thus be understood in terms of its enactive mediation rather than as simulations of our own, private bodily movements. Our capacity for immersion exceeds imitation. In drawing us into its world, while exposing at the same time its construction, *Dogville* demonstrates that immersion in the cinema requires no concealment of its mediation.[25] The diegesis is never "real" in the sense of unmediated; its reality (or mode of existence) pertains to its mediation.

Chapter 1, "The Diegesis as Environment: A New Theory of Film Worlds," examines the historical trajectory of the concept of the diegesis. Although the term originated with filmology, our current conceptualization of the diegesis owes more to its textual appropriation in film semiology, structuralist narratology, film musicology, and cognitive formalism. A broad designation of "the film world" in filmology, film semiology added a subtle reformulation of the diegesis as the discursive plane of the film that could be analytically isolated from questions of reception, psychology, experience, and affect. In response to the advanced criticisms that in recent years have been targeted at the diegesis as a flawed theoretical concept, this chapter offers a reconceptualization of the diegesis as environment rather than text. This chapter goes on to formulate the basic principles of the "diegesis-as-environment" and the material and affective semiotics upon which it is based.

Having accentuated the affective and material nature of the diegesis-as-environment, the second chapter, "The Atmospheric Worlds of Cinema," advocates for the primacy of the atmospheric in cinematic perception. This chapter provides an introduction to the contemporary interdisciplinary surge of "atmosphere research" and evidences the benefits of employing the advanced concept of atmosphere found in this work by contrasting it to recent cognitive-internalist models of "mood" in cinema. It will be shown that the concept of atmosphere accentuates the social, relational, embodied, affective, and environmental aspects of the filmic diegesis, whereas the notion of "cinematic moods" remains hermeneutically restrained as purely metaphorical since it is conceived from the perspective of an internalist and cognitive-subjective philosophy. Thus, whereas the concept of "mood" is understood as a "filter" onto a preexisting narrative world, an "atmosphere" is the actual, necessary ground out of which all filmic worlds emerge. Herein lies a new premise for understanding the narrative film: the atmospheric co-constitutes a film's textual, representational, and propositional dimension rather than being a surplus to it or superimposed upon it. The conclusive part of this chapter examines the atmospheric strategies employed by Alice Rohrwacher's *Happy as Lazzaro* (*Lazzaro felice*, 2018).

One of the most central and influential concepts of narratology is "representation." The third chapter of this book, "Narrative Experientiality and Affect," argues that the price of the narratological privileging of the representational is a neglect of its equally important experiential facets. A central component of a post-textual narratology thus becomes that of affect. Yet, this chapter offers a correction to affect theory by conceptualizing affect not in strict opposition to the representational, the linguistic, or the cognitive, but as the occasion to fundamentally reinterpret how these are understood when affect is introduced to the equation. It thus integrates into the very fabric of the representational narrative "text" the affective as an often neglected but necessary and essential component. Drawing upon Walter Ruttmann's *Berlin: Symphony of a Great City* (*Berlin: die Sinfonie der Großstadt*, 1927), this chapter argues that cinema's narrative capacities must be re-examined *through* the concept of affect and concludes that cinema as an art form feeds on resonances between "organic" and "technical" rhythms, and that the medium's most subversive, persuasive, exhilarating, attractive, disgusting, repulsive, appealing, and dangerous powers lie exactly in how filmmakers exploit these resonances.

Thus, the flow of movements between the embodied spectator and the techno-material film becomes essential for the emergence of the diegesis, and it is examined in the fourth chapter, "The Moving Camera and the Motor-Affective Arrangement of Films," via discussions of the moving camera and theories of cinematic motion perception. This chapter detects in the proto-cognitivist psychology of Hugo Münsterberg a trajectory between theories of internalization (we construct movement out of the film's still images; thus, the film exists in our minds) and externalization (the film is an externalization of human perceptual processes such as seeing, remembering, focusing, etc.) that has defined the history of film perception. In place of this internal/external schism, this chapter argues that the diegesis is a felt, moving, sensorial, ever-shifting world formed out of the rhythmic, dynamic, temporal, tactile, and kinetic sensations generated in the anthropomedial relation of the film. In reference to Mikhail Kalatozov's *The Cranes Are Flying* (*Летят журавли*, 1957), it is argued that the camera movement never stands outside the world it "represents" but actively defines the perceptual, cognitive, and affective arrangement of its affordances and thus its environmental qualities. This provides a correction of embodiment as necessarily shaped on ordinary *human* perceptual experience and aims to show how cinema facilitates an expanded notion of embodiment pertaining to the affordances of the medium and the modes of perception they enable.

This book's fifth and final chapter, "Narrative Spaces and Sonic Environments," examines how a novel sound aesthetics based on noises has reshaped the narrative affordances of cinema by altering the relation between the diegesis and the cinematic space. This sound aesthetics calls for the development of a narrative theoretical framework that once and for all eradicates the privileging of narrative time over narrative space; the comprehension of space as a passive container of characters, objects, and events; its visual bias; and its disembodied models of communication. Recent work in film sound scholarship has demonstrated that sound is today indispensable for cinema's kinetic and multisensorial qualities, and thus sound is a key player in outlining the cinematic diegesis as enacted in embodied perception and cognition. In order to understand the particularly mediated nature of film sound, this chapter argues that cinema operates on an isolation of sensory stimuli. Films arrange and design their visual and auditory "sensory isolates" to optimize the production of a multisensorial and affective experience of their diegeses. In *A Quiet Place* (directed by Krasinski 2018)—exemplary of the contemporary noise aesthetics of film sound—this is achieved through the creation of sonic envelopes.

The ultimate goal of this book is to deliver a reconceptualization of the cinematic diegesis as artificial, constructed, self-reflective, arranged, designed, and mediated, but also the subject of our immediate, affective, atmospheric, and somatic immersion that occurs when we transform the dissociated sounds and images of a film into an affective ecology, an Umwelt, or an environment. More basic to narrativity than the causal-linear sequencing of events is its implication of a world. How these worlds are not decoded, read, or inferred, but *enacted*, is the main topic to be explored in this book.

1

The Diegesis as Environment

A New Theory of Film Worlds

In the first lecture at the *Institute de filmologie* in the academic year 1950/1951, Étienne Souriau presented the basic vocabulary of the then recently initiated interdisciplinary field of *filmologie*. In this lecture, later published as "La structure de l'univers filmique et le vocabulaire de la filmologie," Souriau (1951) introduces to his audience a concept that has since become essential to film studies and narratology, namely, that of the diegesis/diegetic [*diégèse/diégétique*]. Heralded by Christian Metz (1980b) as a "little stroke of genius," the original conceptualization of the diegesis within filmology as "the world posed by a work of art" (A. Souriau 1990, 612) has also been criticized for being too sketchy and even tautological (Mitry 1997, 72; cf. Thanouli 2014). In either case, the diegesis— along with the derivative distinctions of "diegetic" (internal to the storyworld) and "nondiegetic" (external to the storyworld)—has become an established part of our film-theoretical vocabulary for addressing the "fictional world" or the "world of the story." Thus, despite its limitations, scholars have argued that it would be "futile not to use [the concept of the diegesis] in its accustomed sense" (Taylor 2007, 3). Or, as another proponent of the diegetic/nondiegetic terminology argues, there appears to be "little to be gained—and I would say definitely something to be lost—by substituting other terms for diegetic and nondiegetic in film sound and music studies" (Neumeyer 2009, 28).

Concurrently, the caveats of the concept of the diegesis, particularly the splitting of the term into the binary couple "diegetic/nondiegetic," are becoming increasingly evident.[1] Critics have argued that the diegesis is grounded in a representative conception of film language (Cecchi 2010, 2), that its theoretical commitments no longer resonate with the development of audiovisual media, and thus the concept is receding into the background as sensory experience becomes the primary organizing principle of audiovisual forms (Kassabian 2013, 102). Other critics have pointed out that theoretical reflections on the diegesis are biased toward the visual such that even in discussions of diegesis in relation to film sound the image remains dominant and the main point of reference (B. Carroll 2016, 50). While the debates have been spurred on by the inadequacies of the diegetic/nondiegetic distinction, the current "crisis of the diegesis" is rooted in disputes about what constitutes meaning and signification in cinema more

Enacting the Worlds of Cinema. Steffen Hven, Oxford University Press. © Oxford University Press 2022.
DOI: 10.1093/oso/9780197555101.003.0002

generally. In the current debates, the concept of diegesis is univocally being associated with the textual commitments of film semiology, structuralist narratology, and cognitive formalism that critics argue have excluded the embodied aspects of the film experience and failed to recognize the medium's material and affective mode of communication.[2]

Therefore, despite its evident usefulness, the diegesis—one of the most important terms of film theory—has been accused of forcing upon the analyst an inevitably textual and, by extension, disembodied understanding of films. Moreover, the textual diegesis is conceptually shaped upon the "unobtrusive" style of classical filmmaking that entertains the illusion of the diegesis as a world existing independently of its recipient. It has, however, been argued that the intensification of contemporary cinema and its increased attention to temporal dynamics, sensuality, physicality, and intense sensory experience have overridden the classical narrative principles that situated the cinematic spectator—epitomized by the wheelchair-bound Jeff (James Stewart) in *Rear Window* (directed by Hitchcock 1954)—as an unobserved observer.[3] The debates concerning the diegesis thus play into the context of a larger film-theoretical fissure between theories that emphasize matters of signification, narrative, and discourse versus those that highlight the sensorial, affective, and embodied aspects of contemporary audiovisual culture.

Given the central role of the diegesis to film studies, however, it would be naive to call for an abandoning of this term. Needed instead is a radical rethinking of the concept of the diegesis capable once and for all of dispensing with the disembodied semiotics that underlines its current textual form. However, this might be easier said than done, since it requires us to readdress the question of what constitutes signification in the cinema in the first place. As Alain Boillat (2009) has remarked,

> [a]s soon as one begins to examine the discussions in detail, one notes that the concept of "diegesis" and the questions raised by its definition number among the original concerns of the semiology of the cinema which filmology does indeed appear to have "prefigured," even if this relationship is sometimes rather underestimated by Metz's thurifers. (59–60, translation in Kirsten 2018, 131)

Rethinking the diegesis thus requires us to rethink what constitutes signification in the cinema. This chapter suggests doing so by framing the question of signification not in textual, discursive, linguistic, or formalist terms but in ecological, environmental, embodied, and situated terms instead. Consequently, I propose a reconceptualization of the diegesis as *environment* rather than *text*.

Given that the concept of the diegesis was popularized by Christian Metz within the framework of film semiology and later established as a key conceptual term within structural-linguistic narratology, cognitive film theory, and film music narratology,[4] the filmological origin of the term has often been obscured. In *The Complete Film Dictionary* by Ira Konigsberg (1987) we thus find the following entry for the diegesis:

> A term from semiotics applied to film criticism, especially by Christian Metz, that designates the denotative elements of a narrative—that is, all the elements of the narrative whether shown in the film or not. Diegetic elements include all actions and dialogue in their normal space and time, which rarely can be fully given in the film. (87)

This textual definition of the diegesis is contrasted in this chapter by what we shall refer to as the *diegesis-as-environment*. This concept has been designed to explore those qualities of the narrative film that have been systematically neglected by textual film analysis: the nonrepresentational, affective, atmospheric, material, kinesthetic, multisensorial, rhythmic, and sonic production of the diegesis. In recognizing narrative worlds as more than "texts," the diegesis-as-environment marks both a return to, and an elaboration of, the broad filmological definition of the diegesis as the world "posed by a work of art." Unlike the widespread conception of the *diegesis-as-text*, the diegesis-as-environment relies on resonances between the movements of the film and those of its embodied spectators for the transformation of the filmic material into a lived environment, habitus, atmosphere, milieu, or Umwelt. This neither marks a disposal of verbal, linguistic, or textual signification nor ignores the more complex organization of the narrative as studied by narratology. However, as we shall see, the shift from a textual to an environmental diegesis does resituate the textual modalities of signification as components within a larger material-affective semiotics of the cinema.

1.1. Toward the Diegesis-as-Environment

Like Rainer Maria Rilke's panther, the boxer is pacing in cramped circles in a ritual dance in the seemingly self-enclosed world of his cage, the ring. Framed from outside the ring in a low camera angle, the pace of his ritual shadowboxing is decelerated, his movements fast, yet unhurried, even delicate. The tone of the image is grainy and grim, and the audience is scarcely visible. The camera remains motionless as if fully absorbed in the movements of the boxer. The graceful tones of Pietro Mascagni's *Cavalleria Rusticana* (1889) are the only sounds to be heard. This is the world of Jake La Motta (Robert de Niro), the *Raging Bull* of Martin Scorsese's 1980 feature film. It is not a world of utterances and propositions; it is not a text. The film's diegesis is a felt, mediated environment that comes alive through its encounter with the spectator's embodied organism.

The opening scene of *Raging Bull* provides an example of how cinema can create affectively charged architectural spaces capable of adjusting our sentiments to those of its worlds and the characters inhabiting them. By modulating our embodied organisms according to the state of mind of Jake La Motta, the diegesis becomes a spatial extension of his emotional conflicts. Narrative comprehension is not a disembodied analytical activity that merely involves inferential elaboration or semiotic decoding. Understanding is not the mere recognition of something being there; meaning is not designation. Narrative comprehension is not isolated from bodily effects; it depends upon the organism exposing itself to the movements of the film, to its colors, editing rhythms, framings, camera movements, soundscapes, etc., that combine into its atmospheric design. However, in film theory's textual era—beginning in the 1960s and '70s with film semiology, structuralist linguistics, narratology, and cognitive formalism—the discursive nature of the cinematic medium became dominant, and it was believed that matters of signification, language, cognition, representation, and narration could be studied without recourse to the medium's kinesthetic foundation.

The diegesis-as-environment reinstates movement as essential to filmic signification and the notion of the diegesis. From this perspective, understanding a film's narrative world means partaking in its orchestrated flows, intensities, rhythms, cognitions, and affects. The diegesis-as-environment thus reframes the question of cinematic semiosis by modeling it not upon the arbitrary and disembodied linguistic sign but upon the flow of movements between spectator and film. The diegesis-as-environment thereby unites on the same conceptual plane two cinematic components that have long been polarized: the realm of material, affective, and kinesthetic sensations along with that of narrativity, signification, semantics, representation, and discursivity.

The diegesis-as-environment fluctuates between two states, where the first is the immediate filmic environment into which we are "immersed" and the latter pertaining to the more abstract notion of the film "world" as a totality, in the sense that Merleau-Ponty (1991b) has argued that "film is not the sum total of its images but a temporal gestalt" (54). Both the immediate, pre-reflective, bodily impression of the filmic environment and the more abstract modality of mapping it out are modes of ecological sensemaking that rely on the whole living organism in its affective, pragmatic, and skilled engagement with an environment of affordances.

With the diegesis-as-environment, however, we can no longer postulate a discursive or textual space that exists prior to or independently of the material affordances of the cinematic medium, the particular filmmaking techniques employed by the creators to communicate the filmic diegesis, and the embodied receptive act in which the diegesis is realized, animated, or enacted. Although such a shift from a textual to an environmental conception of the diegesis has a long series of ramifications for how we think about cinematic signification that will be explored throughout this book, it is worth highlighting three aspects here. First of all, the diegesis-as-environment brings elements to the center stage of narrative inquiry, whose narrative role has been marginalized by narratology such as affect, atmospheres, cinematic motion, and soundscapes. From a textual perspective, as we will explore later in this chapter, nonreferential elements and film stylistics were believed to be superimposed upon the film's text base, its propositional, denotative meanings.

This brings us to the second significant consequence in relation to an environmental conception of the diegesis, namely, that it postulates narrative comprehension to be anchored in material, affective, and embodied cognitive processes. Thereby we reject the disembodied notion of the spectator as a semiotic decoder or cognitive-analytical inference maker who transforms the textual material into a mental representation of the diegesis. The diegesis-as-environment constitutes a challenge not only to linguistic film theory, but also to cognitive film theories that rely on a basic linguistic assumption about cognitive functioning. Following this cognitive film-theoretical view, mental representation and conceptual thinking are organized in the same way as a language such that meaning is derived from the combination of individual representations and concepts. Thought is thus posited to share the same basic structure as language.[5]

In contrast to this linguistic model of cognitive functioning, the diegesis-as-environment argues that the embodied spectator transforms the prelinguistic but semiotically shaped film material, and its movements, rhythms, and intensities, into a place of valence, salience, meaning, and value, that is, into an environment (Umwelt) as conceived in the tradition from Uexküll to Gibson as implying both the surrounding world and the organism. The diegesis therefore relies on the embodied perceptual, affective, and cognitive modalities of ecological sensemaking. Put differently, the diegesis-as-environment is neither a text to be read nor a mental representation in the mind of the spectator; the diegesis is *enacted* in the technical sense given to the term in cognitive philosophy. The enaction of the diegesis further involves a media-anthropological process in which the film "loans" the bodily capacities of the spectators to come alive as a lived, felt space-time. Neither the spectator nor the film can thus rightly be said to exist independently from one another in the formation of the filmic diegesis.

Finally, in times when the embodied revolution of film studies sparks a "spatial turn,"[6] the diegesis-as-environment aids a radical rethinking of the narrative filmic space. Outlined is an inherently dynamic and temporal conception of space that breaks with the notion of space as the passive container of the narrative events of classical narratology. Instead, the narrative space actively defines, restricts, transforms, frames, molds, or otherwise determines the nature of the events that occur in it. The filmic space is not supplementary to the narrative; it is constitutive of it.

Rather than a neutral, objective, discursive, and textual space, the filmic space is readdressed as an architectural space designed for the atmospheric orchestration of cognitions and affects. We are thus no longer in the realm of the classical film-theoretical metaphor of the spectator looking through a window frame onto an independently existing world that unfolds in disregard of the voyeuristic gaze resting upon it. In its place a newly embodied model of filmic perception is manifested, where the perceiving organism enters into a copresence with the perceived. The narrative space—in fact, the narrative by and large—comes alive through a process of attunement between the rhythms and movements of the film and its audience. The temporal nature of the cinematic medium thus becomes important since the "tuning" of the spectator and film is always processual and durational. In the following section, we turn to filmology not only to examine the neglected historical roots of the concept of the diegesis, but also, more importantly, to excavate an organic model of the film experience that will help establish a link between the movements of the film and the movements of the felt body as constitutive of cinema's material-affective mode of communication.

1.2. Filmology: The Diegesis between World and Discourse

The diegesis, in the form we use it today, originates with the filmology movement, which marks the birth of modern film studies as a legitimate and serious subject of study and its commencement as an institutional practice.[7] Initiated in 1946 by the publication of Gilbert Cohen-Séat's filmological manifesto, "Essai sur les principes d'une philosophie du cinéma," and officially founded in 1950 at the Sorbonne, the "new science of film" would exist only until 1963. In mobilizing established academic fields such as sociology, philosophy, psychology, linguistics, aesthetics, and neurobiology to address cinema as an object worthy of scientific studies, filmology marked the beginning of modern film theory. In sharp contrast to André Bazin and the critics around the Cahiers du cinéma, filmology was driven by a desire for structure and methodology that stands in contrast to earlier and contemporaneous aesthetic discourses, and it thus marked the first significant attempt to delineate, structure, and institutionalize intellectual debates on the art and socio-psychological implications of the cinema.

This section zooms in on filmology, whose role in relation to modern film theory remains as undervalued as underexamined. It is the aim to draw out two trajectories of filmology: one leading to the advent of structuralism, narratology, linguistics, cognitive-formalism, and the diegesis-as-text. The other trajectory has only tentatively been explored. It leads from filmology to film phenomenology, embodied cognition, Deleuzian film philosophy, neurofilmology, and the diegesis-as-environment.

Founded immediately after the Nazi occupation of France, filmology recognized the potential power of the control audiovisual media (cinema and television) could execute as media of mass communication. Thus, filmology originated upon the conviction that the advent and increasing popularity of audiovisual media created a dire need of a systematic, scientific mode of inquiry designed to understand how these change the human condition. It has been argued that filmology was founded upon a tension between those researchers focusing upon questions concerning cinema's relation to signification and language and those who were occupied with studying the underlying psychological, physiological, and perceptual mechanisms that films draw upon (Lowry 1985b, 131). Despite unresolved tensions between its various disciplines, it is exactly its desire to tackle cinema from a plurality of positions that makes filmology attractive for contemporary film studies.

Filmology did not turn to disciplines such as philosophy, sociology, anthropology, and psychology to find already existing theories that could help explain the phenomenon of cinema; instead, their proposition was to turn to cinema and television to help understand how the "human condition" itself had changed after the advent of audiovisual medialization. Against the static conception of humanity found in positivism, filmology relied upon a dynamic (media-)anthropology.[8] Cinema transforms the natural environment and explodes the temporal and spatial limitations of lived experience by substituting chronological with affective time, thereby opening it up for a dynamic space that moves beyond Cartesian geometry. For these reasons, Henri Wallon argued that cinema not only relies on innate skills or previously learned capacities but also enriches the mind and opens up new psychophysiological dimensions that he believed were the task for filmology to explore.[9]

In order to aid the interdisciplinary empirical and theoretical study of a film, Souriau delivered a rigorous analysis of a film's seven levels of reality.[10] The basic filmological premise is that each film erects its own unique universe, with its own rules, systems of belief, characters, settings, and so on. The filmic existence consists of the "afilmic" (roughly corresponding to the external reality existing outside of the film), the "profilmic" (roughly meaning filmed objective reality as recorded by the camera), the "filmographic" (roughly meaning the film in its physical, material form), the "filmophanic" or "screenic" (roughly meaning the film as projected on the screen and through speakers), the diegesis/diegetic (roughly corresponding to the film's spatiotemporal storyworld), the "spectatorial" (related to the subjective experience of the audience), and the "creatorial" (related to the artistic, political, or moral intentions of the filmmakers).[11] The inscription of the diegesis into the binary constellation of diegetic/nondiegetic—probably its main use in film studies today—does not figure in the filmological vocabulary.

Some of the definitions provided by Souriau (1951) emphasize the representational aspect of the diegesis. The diegesis is thus "everything which concerns the film to the extent that it represents something" (237).[12] Other definitions highlight its status as an "autonomous reality," an independently existing reality, that coexists with the other filmic realities.[13] In this sense, the diegesis is "the kind of reality assumed by the film's signification" (237).[14] For instance, the character Forrest Gump and the actor Tom Hanks coexist on the screen, yet they pertain to different filmic realities (e.g., diegetic and profilmic). The diegesis further differs from the formalist narratological terms of "fabula" or "story," which refer less to the world of the story than to the sequencing of events into a narrative chain. As Gérard Genette (1988) observes, the diegesis is indeed "a *universe* rather than a train of events (a story); the *diégèse* is therefore not the story but the universe in which the story takes place" (17, author's emphasis).

Throughout his lecture Souriau refrains from formulations that firmly establish "where" the diegesis exists. Is the diegesis a product of the spectator's intellectual efforts and thus a mental representation belonging to the mind of the spectator (the position of cognitive film narratology in the tradition of Bordwell), or does it exist in the film as a text, whose signification derives from its place within a structure that preexists the act of its reading (the position of film semiology in the tradition of Metz)? In *L'univers filmique* (1953), Souriau defines the diegesis as all that belongs "in intelligibility (as defined by Mr. Cohen-Séat) to the story recounted, the world *supposed* or *proposed* by the film's fiction" (7, my emphases).[15] I believe Souriau's decision to hold both options open—supposed (in the mind) or proposed (in the text)—is intentional.[16] Although it is a principle he develops most vigorously in the context of his philosophy of "instauration" rather than in the few texts on the diegesis, Souriau ascribes to the worlds of artworks an "autonomous existence" that remains irreducible to both the text and its spectator and thus forces us to go beyond the subject–object dichotomy.

Alain Boillat has pointed out that Souriau's definition of the diegesis exceeds the discursive and textual interpretation ascribed to it by film semiology and narratology in the 1960s.[17] The diegesis is realized through a receptive act; it can only come into existence with the contribution of an intelligent being. Yet, the diegesis is still experienced as an external "reality"; it lays claim to an objective existence rather than being a proper subjective product of our minds. Fictional worlds, as Souriau observes in his 1943 philosophical opus magnum on *Les différents modes d'existence* (translated into English in 2015 as *The Different Modes of Existence*), can be studied "with the same objective spirit as that of natural history, history, or political economy" (152). Thus, when "Napoleon reread Richardson on Saint Helena, he carefully established Lovelace's annual budget; and Hugo, when he was preparing *Les Misérables*, tracked Jean Valjean's accounts for the ten years during which he did not appear in the novel" (152).

That the emergence of the diegesis depends on a cognitive act is underlined by Souriau's (1951) definition of the diegetic space as space reconstituted in the thoughts of the spectator (233).[18] In this respect, filmology anticipates the cognitive-formalist film narratology promoted by Kristin Thompson, David Bordwell, and Ed Branigan.[19] However, it is worth noticing that Souriau relies on a philosophical notion of "thought" and "thinking" that is distinct from the disembodied conception of thought as disconnected from bodily and emotional concerns that dominated first-generation cognitive film studies. In *The Different Modes of Existence*, Souriau argues that "thought has no other support than the very thing that it assembles and feels" (147).[20] If the diegetic world belongs to thought, we are far from the idea of a neo-Kantian cognitive subject that masters the narrative through inferences and hypothesis making. The spectator is not outside the diegesis, and thought belongs as much to the film as to the spectator.

Thus, for Souriau the world of imaginaries is not upheld by thought alone, and it cannot be reduced to a cognitive representation in the mind of the spectator. In fact, Souriau (2015) rejects a univocal identification of the storyworld with the imagination or the mind: "To consider [the worlds of imaginaries] to be simply supported by thought, is to regard thought as being capable of positing, arbitrarily and without being conditioned by anything other than its own decree, beings that depend upon it totally" (151). As Souriau (2015) argues, imaginaries, such as fictional worlds, "are not [. . .] limited to cases of the faculty of imagination. Their situation expands to embrace all that depends upon the feelings and emotions, as well. In fact, *the base phenomenon of imaginaries is often emotional*" (153, my emphasis). The worlds of films—and aesthetic beings more broadly—are not actualized through intellectual operations but come alive through our embodied investments into their material design. In relation to our present discussions, the diegesis thus cannot be ascribed to the intellect alone but depends on the whole embodied being of the spectators who "enact or bring forth a world of sense, namely, an Umwelt that has a special significance for the organism enacting it" (Colombetti 2014, 18).

Souriau thus shared the essentially phenomenological conviction that "man is not the creator of the world, but the consciousness by which the world is *realized*" (Lowry 1985b, 79, author's emphasis). The world of the diegesis is thus realized not *by* the sensitive-intelligent human organism but *through it*, i.e., through movements related to acts of perception, motor cognition, kinetic and affective resonances, as well as intellectual operations such as memorizing, assembling, inferring, categorizing, synthesizing, and hypothesizing. In this respect, Souriau develops the concept of "instauration"—a concept recently revitalized by Bruno Latour (2011) as Souriau's "most important innovation in philosophy" (8).[21] With the notion of instauration, Souriau refers to the feedback processes according to which an artwork takes form. Rather than the classical idea of an artist imposing a certain vision and form on a material, Souriau regards the instaurative process as a series of resonances between artist(s) and artwork. Consider how the cinematic editor, in order to reach the exact desired kinetic, energetic, and temporal patterning of a film, must go through a process of shaping the film material and then exposing herself in terms of her own how the patterning and rhythms of the edit resonate with her own bodily movements in order to evaluate if it "feels" right.[22] It is this ongoing conversation between artwork and artist that Souriau defines as the instaurative process. Following Lowry (1985b), this grants a new status to the material world of the film insofar as the instaurative process will "govern man by means of things, and things by means of man" (76). Thereby, the emergence of the diegesis in the instaurative act is based on what is a media-anthropological principle, namely, that neither our perceptions, feelings, and affects nor the formed material of the film preexists the instaurative act. In this sense, Souriau's concept of instauration is closely reminiscent of the cognitive philosophical notion of enaction. Once we consider the diegesis in relation to Souriau's philosophical aesthetics it becomes evident that the concept both evokes the biophysical, psychological, affective, and emotional feeling of *being there* and, at the same time, anticipates the structuralist turn toward filmic signification, meaning, language, and discourse as a more encompassing cognitive geography.

"Today," as Hanich and Ferencz-Flatz (2016) have recently stated, "a certain influence of phenomenology on the explorations of the French filmology movement during the late 1940s and 1950s is widely assumed as self-evident" (29). However, given the fact that we largely owe the resurrection of filmology to Metz, the conceptual heritage left by filmology is shaped more by structuralism than phenomenology. Nowhere has the connection between the rise of structural linguistics in France in the 1960s and filmology been studied as thoroughly as in Edward Lowry's monograph *The Filmology Movement and Film Studies in France* (1985b). Apart from Souriau, who Lowry regards as a "proto-structuralist" (6), the link between film semiology and filmology is most evident in the work of Cohen-Séat.

That cinema invites us into a space of discourses that should be studied systematically was a main thesis of Gilbert Cohen-Séat's *Essai*, the work that led to the formation of filmology. In this book, Cohen-Séat (1946) advocates for the strong connection between knowledge and systematization. To understand this first and foremost means to systematize (43). A systematic study of cinema was to be found in the equation of cinematic expression with language. Thus, in the inaugural issue of the filmological journal *Revue internationale de filmologie*, Mario Roques argued that the ability of films to communicate feelings and thoughts makes cinema a language [*langage*], albeit not a phonetic one.[23] This idea was followed up by two film-semiological articles in the *Revue*, now of little renown, by Roland Barthes (1960a, 1960b), exploring the "problems of signification in cinema."

Cohen-Séat (1946) had paved the way for a semiology of cinema by proposing a structural differentiation between the "cinematic" and the "filmic" fact (64–65). The cinematic fact targets the cinema broadly as an economic, anthropological, technological, cultural, and socio-historical institution, whereas the "filmic" fact refers to "all the elements of the film susceptible of being taken for its signification as a sort of absolute, from the point of view of intelligibility or the point of view of aesthetics" (Cohen-Séat in Lowry 1985b, 73).

In this fashion, the filmic fact comprises both aesthetic and linguistic concerns, however, as Metz (1974) would later specify, in a manner that allows for the isolation of the filmic discourse from broader sociological, psychological, biological, or economic concerns related to the cinema as institution. Thus, as Metz argues,

> The importance of this distinction between the cinematic and the filmic facts
> lies in the fact that it allows us to restrict the meaning of the term 'film' to a more
> manageable, specifiable signifying discourse in contrast with cinema, which
> [. . .] constitutes a larger complex. (12)

The notion of a "filmic fact" isolated not only from its historical, sociological, technological, and economic situation but also from the receptive act had, however, already been criticized in 1947 by Marc Soriano, who pointed out that the "filmic fact" necessarily implies the "cinematic fact" and thus cannot be isolated from it (cf. Lowry 1985b, 73). More recently, Laurent Jullier (2009) has criticized the narrow focus on the filmic fact and argued that a return to filmology should first of all be a return to a conception of film in the sense of what Marcel Mauss calls a "total social fact" rather than as mere "text" or "stimulus."

The separation of the filmic from the cinematic fact was, however, essential for the formulation of the film as text. Thus, Metz (1974) deemed it necessary to further restrict the filmic fact, which he found to be "too vast to attribute to it the principle of analytic distinctiveness suitable to a semiotics of the film" (14). Metz was keen to separate the sphere of semiotics from questions of psychology, reception, and the spectatorial and thus wanted the discursive realm to be distinct from matters of the "psychology of perception," of "cognitive psychology," and of the "psychology of emotions" (14). This isolation of the text from the receptive act is exactly what characterizes the diegesis-as-text. For Metz, "Semiotics, whether of the film or anything else, is the study of discourses and 'texts'" (13).

In cognitive film theory, the textual assumption is often connected to the conception of the narrative as a mental construct that ideally can be "embodied in a *verbal synopsis*, as general or detailed as circumstances require" (Bordwell 1985, 49, my emphasis).

Ultimately, the diegesis is considered to be a text that can be reduced to the literal or verbal significations of the film. Rather than the filmological diegesis it is this specific textual conception of the term that has caused the contemporary "crisis of the diegesis" due to its negligence of how the world of the film is experienced in an immediate, affective, and embodied manner. Thus, to properly readdress the question of the cinematic diegesis, we must begin with a reconsideration of its textual roots.

1.3. The Diegesis-as-Text

In a series of articles published between 1966 and 1972, Metz formulated the textual interpretation of the diegesis that dominates today. Yet he did so with a keen awareness of the problems that cinema posed to a sharp separation of its embodied appeal from its meaning-making structures. If, as Lowry (1985b) observes, there existed a tension between "perception" and "signification" within the filmology movement (131), film semiology resolved this tension by isolating a narrative layer that can be studied on linguistic grounds without recourse to the perceptive, affective, and material modalities of cinematic signification. Metz thus offered a conceptualization of the diegesis as independent of its recipient, whose role it became to *re*construct or "read" the film text, and it would be according to this interpretation that the diegesis surfaced as a key concept in film theory. Yet, Metz (1990) did more than just that; he equated the diegesis with the linguistic term of denotation, the literal or primary meaning of a word:

> [The diegesis] designates the film's represented instance [. . .] that is to say,
> the sum of a film's denotation: the narration itself, but also the fictional space
> and time dimensions implied in and by the narrative, and consequently the
> characters, the landscapes, the events, and other narrative elements, in so far as
> they are considered in their denoted aspect. (98)

Referring to Louis Hjelmslev's (1961) linguistic pairing of denotation/connotation as well as Mikel Dufrenne's (1973) differentiation between the expressed and the represented world,[24] Metz (1990) differentiates two planes of signification in cinema: the content plane (denotation) and the expression plane (connotation). Denotation is the basic plane of signification, and "it is represented by the literal (that is, perceptual) meaning of the spectacle reproduced in the image, or of the sounds duplicated by the sound-track" (96). Connotation, on the other hand, concerns

> the literary or cinematographic "style," "genre" (the epic, the western, etc.), "symbol" (philosophical, humanitarian, ideological, and so on), or "poetic atmosphere"—and its signifier is the whole denotated semiological material, whether signified or signifying. (97)

By equating the diegesis with denotation (and the represented world in Dufrenne's terms), Metz could extract a part of the film, its narrated world, from its artistic expressiveness and thereby make it susceptible to linguistic analysis.

For Metz (1990), the diegesis is as "important for the film semiologist as the idea of art" (97) because it enables him to address the film as "a signifying discourse (text)" (Metz 1974, 13). Or, as Metz (1990) phrases it elsewhere, it is "through its procedures of denotation, [that] the cinema is a specific language" (97). As Metz's mentor, Roland Barthes (1972), explicates, the goal of all structuralist activity "is to reconstruct an 'object' in such a way as to manifest thereby the rules of functioning (the 'functions') of this object," an intellectual operation that he accredits to a "certain immobilization of time" (214).

In *Elegy for Theory* (2014), D. N. Rodowick analyzes how the reduction of filmic signification to text and discourse was Metz's solution to the difficulties of mapping linguistic tools onto cinematic signification. In his early texts, as per Rodowick, Metz maps out the conflicted conceptual space of structuralism pertaining to the discourse of aesthetics versus that of signification, phenomenology versus semiology, and sign versus audiovisual imagery (153). Rodowick argues that Metz, to an even larger extent than Barthes, targeted the difficulties of refashioning structural linguistics to cope with nonlinguistic expressions (154). Faced with the multi-expressive medium of the cinema, Metz needed to isolate one aspect that could be susceptible to structuralist-linguistic analysis. In locating a system of signification, semiology was able to rediscover language in other realms and thus to embrace other forms of language. In order to establish a genuine theory of film, rather than a theory of cinema, Metz needed to perform a similar reduction centered on the isolation of only those components of the filmic fact that are discursive or textual (161).

Consequently, at the heart of the structuralist activity is the decomposition of the actual sensory material into its systematic functioning in a simulacrum (137). The structuralist activity is thus engaged with bringing something forth, which is not immediately apparent and as such cannot be grasped by the senses but only by the intellect. As Barthes (1972) declares, structuralism "makes something appear which remained invisible or, if one prefers, unintelligible in the natural object" such that structuralism "takes the real, decomposes, then recomposes it"

(215). We do, therefore, not perceive the filmic diegesis but "read" it as we do a text. However, as Rodowick (2014) concludes in his analysis, we can understand film as a discourse neither without considering the complex organization of its expression nor by isolating it from the psychological and cognitive mechanisms of perception (165).

It is exactly this exclusion of the experiential, phenomenal, psychological, and affective expressive modalities of film from the sphere of signification and the realm of the diegesis that makes the textual approach of structuralist-linguistic narratology, cognitive-psychological theories of film narration, and film music narratology driven by a disembodied semiotics.[25]

The disjunction of the film's expressive modalities from its narrative content thus presumes a degree of arbitrariness between specific artistic choices (e.g., camera movements, lightings, use of soundscapes, framings, etc.) as well as the corporeal-affective attunements to the content expressed (e.g., as when a dark space is *uplifting* due to its affective charge) and the literary, denotative content of the film. This has the analytical advantage of designating a basic layer of meaning, the diegesis, which remains self-identical regardless of the material affordances of the medium in which it is realized (e.g., the film, the book, the video game) as well as the embodied organism, whose experience it belongs to. It is thus not that the textual approach denies the existence of bodily and material meanings. Yet, these meanings are secondary and lie outside of the film's basic, discursive, literal, or denotative meanings as explicated in the formula that "the narrative is *reducible* without fundamental damage" (Barthes 1975, 269).

Consequently, we have the diegesis plus superimposed aesthetic, material, and affective meanings. This logic is widespread within textual narratology and guides the diegetic/nondiegetic distinction, where background music, for instance, is the superimposed meaning onto the diegetic, literal meaning of the film.[26] Our corporeal engagements with the stories play no part in the most basic narrative semiotics, and it is not until recently that the human body has begun to be accredited with a central role within narrative theory.[27]

Yet, even in its most verbal mode of expression, the dialogue, filmic signification cannot be isolated from its affective components. As Béla Balázs (2011) has argued, "what attracts our interest is less what a person says than the sound of his voice. In dialogue, too, what is decisive is not the content, but the acoustic, sensuous impression" (195). Moreover, the very idea of denotation as "the irreducible origin of all other, more extended meanings" (Andrew 1976, 185)—essential, as we have seen, to the diegesis-as-text—has been disputed, most significantly by Barthes, who introduced this distinction to structuralism in the first place.[28]

The diegesis-as-text thus relies on a method that reduces signification to an abstract discursive system decontextualized from other concerns. The crisis the concept is currently undergoing thus pertains to the friction that exists between object and method, i.e., between cinema's multifaceted modes of communication (e.g., camera movements, music, rhythmic editing, costuming, verbal language, etc.) and the restrictive linguistic semiotics that continues to frame our study of it.[29]

For a revised appreciation of the diegesis in film theory we need to integrate the strain of filmology dealing with questions of signification in cinema with its phenomenology-inspired psychological studies on movement and perception. As is becoming increasingly clear, the rise of discursive film theory in the 1960s involved a disconnect from a tradition of film theory (including filmological research) pivoting around questions of movement (both of the film and the embodied spectator). In this context, filmology marks a decisive moment in the history of the study of film. It points both to early precursors of an embodied film theory such as the critical reflections of filmmakers as Louis Delluc, Jean Epstein, and Sergei Eisenstein and toward modern approaches such as Deleuzian film philosophy, neurofilmology, and film phenomenology. All share a fundamental interest in the kinesthetic foundation of the medium whether as expressed through its stylistics (the rhythm of editing, the moving camera, its composition), its ability to move its audience, or the portrayal of the affective lives of its characters. In the grand semiotic "immobilization" of the film, however, the diegesis was bereft of movement, or, perhaps more precisely, movement became syntagmatic, structural, sentential, disembodied, and related to a static ordering of narrative events into a causal-linear storyline.

1.4. Embodied Perception and the Environmental Diegesis

In 1978, as an intervention to the semiotic, linguistic, Lacanian psycho-analytical, and Marxist-Althusserean textual film theory then at its peak, Dudley Andrew (1985) published an article on "The Neglected Tradition of Phenomenology in Film Theory." Given the omnipresence of film phenomenology in contemporary film theory,[30] it might be easy to forget the marginalization of phenomenology in the era of textual film studies. In 1963, when film theory was beginning to become established as an academic discipline, *La Revue internationale de filmologie*, "the one journal devoted to theory along quasi-phenomenological grounds" (627), as Andrew remarks, had ceased to exist. Along with the untimely deaths of early proponents of a phenomenological approach to the cinema including André Bazin, Amédée Ayfre, and Maurice Merleau-Ponty, this meant that at the birth of modern film studies there was "no one to challenge structuralism" (627). Ultimately, *this sustained lack* of an opposing tradition during its formative years has locked film studies "within a structuralist project and vocabulary" (627).

Consequently, much of the theoretical and conceptual heritage of film studies is rooted in a structuralist and textualist conception of the film—the diegesis being no exception. If the textual conception of the diegesis was outlined in the early film semiology of Metz, the phenomenological, embodied, and affective aspects of the term still need to be rediscovered—not least because the general direction of the field is turning from the text to embodied perception.[31] The concept of the diegesis is a key player in reconfiguring the question of signification in cinema and for the development of an embodied, post-textual film semiotics. As Andrew remarks in his classical essay, "We can speak of codes and textual systems which are the results of signifying processes, yet we seem unable to discuss that mode of experience we call signification" (627).

Although not a part of the filmology movement, it shall be argued that Merleau-Ponty's sole essay dedicated entirely to cinema, "The Film and the New Psychology," is useful for excavating the embodied and affective logics pertaining to the diegesis. We know that this essay, originally delivered as a lecture in 1945 at Institute des Hautes Etudes Cinématographiques, had an enormous influence on filmology, in particular on those studying the psychology and perception of cinema.[32] We could thus imagine a counterfactual historical trajectory in which the concept of the diegesis was developed and advanced in a dialogue with Merleau-Ponty's phenomenology of embodied perception. This essay not only presents us with a concise criticism of the atomistic modus operandi that guides the textual diegesis; it also helps us to articulate some important principles that will advance our understanding of the diegesis-as-environment. Accordingly, we shall argue that the diegesis is a temporal gestalt and thus the direct object of filmic perception as rooted in kinetic resonances flowing between the embodied spectator and the film.

One of the key insights that Merleau-Ponty derives from the "new psychology" (i.e., gestalt psychology) is the notion of the film as a temporal *gestalt*. By this Merleau-Ponty (1991b) means that the film is not assembled on the basis of an undifferentiated mosaic of atomistic sensations, whose sum amounts to our sensory impression of the film. The idea of gestalt replaces the principle of juxtaposition with a primordial organization of the whole (49). During the film experience our embodied organisms are directed toward the structures, rhythms, compositions, configurations, movements, and atmospheres of the film that have been designed to modulate our kinesthetic, perceptive, cognitive, affective, and emotional sensorium. What Merleau-Ponty suggests is that the film's temporal gestalt, its diegesis, rather than being the product of an internal simulation—a sort of cognitive-analytical map of character, events, and situations—is a dynamic and emergent entity that constantly transforms as the film unfolds. Therefore, a film takes on meaning not by referring to ideas that are already established and acquired but through a spatiotemporal arrangement of elements (58). Cinematic

THE DIEGESIS AS ENVIRONMENT   31

form is neither passive, static, and inert nor "owned" and "immobilized" by the faculty of intelligence (memories, schemas, inferences, judgments, etc.); it is a product of the rhythmic unison of the film and its embodied spectator. As Merleau-Ponty insists, "A movie is not thought; it is perceived" (58).[33]

Consider how we acquire knowledge about the other's "inner" states through their actions, behaviors, facial expressions, and gestures. Rather than being mediated by arbitrary cultural conventions, Merleau-Ponty (1991b) argues that there is no difference between "signs and their significance, between what is sensed and what is judged" (50–51). How can we separate the bleak sentiment incorporated into the dark highways and gas stations of a film noir like *Hitch-Hiker* (directed by Lupino 1953) from its narrative content, its literal text, without betraying their primordial unity in embodied perception? Similarly, what is gained from separating Nino Rota's famous "Godfather Waltz" from the diegesis of *The Godfather* (directed by Coppola 1972, 1974, and 1990) given that this melody immediately transports us into the world of the films? How are we to understand the advanced narrative use of color schemes from *All That Heaven Allows* (directed by Sirk 1955) to *Moonlight* (directed by Jenkins 2017) without accounting for the affective impressions of those colors on our embodied beings? When Erich von Stroheim in *Greed* (1924) employed the laborious Handschiegl color process to turn the whole world golden, its symbolism was not just to be interpreted but to be sensed, to be felt. By isolating the film's discourse from its embodied impact, textualism has turned the film from an *object of experience* into an *object of analysis*.

From this we can extract a displacement of meaning in the film from its basic text (the sum of its denotations, its syntax, and discourse) toward a pragmatic semiotics rooted in the behaviors displayed by performing techniques (body movements, attitudes, gestures, facial expressions, body language, intonations, makeup, costuming, etc.) and filmmaking techniques (camera movements, editing rhythms, framings, soundscapes, lighting, color grading, etc.) that communicate non-linguistically via a direct activation of our embodied senses. All these are techniques that connect to human feeling and thinking through movement; they thus rely on the principle of "dynamogenesis," i.e., the relation of movement to thinking and feeling.[34]

Consequently, Merleau-Ponty rejects an overtly "internalist" conception of emotions as pure "inner realities" to be discovered scientifically via external measuring of the (neuro)physiological state of the experiencer. Affect does not exist inside the perceiver's mind or soul. Just as the world is already impregnated with structure and form, it is already impregnated with affects and cognitions. The world is never neutral but always charged. Thus, Merleau-Ponty urges us to reject the idea that love, hate, and anger are "inner realities" only accessible to the person who feels them (52). Cinema is evidence that emotional states such as anger, shame, hate, and love are not hidden at the bottom of another's consciousness but materialize as types of behavior or styles of conduct visible to others. Emotions and affects thus exist *on* this face or *in* that gesture or bodily posture (52–53).

In cinema, our perception of characters, events, and situations needs no further reading or decoding to transform a facial expression into a *sign* of an emotional state. A facial expression is not a representation of an affective state; it enacts it. We immediately recognize the sadness on Joan of Arc's (Maria Falconetti's) face in the extreme close-ups of Carl Theodor Dreyer's *La passion de Jeanne d'Arc* (1928); we do not take it as a "sign" of sadness.

Similarly, the diegesis is experienced as our immediate, yet mediated, spatio-temporal environment. It is immediate in the sense of being manifest to us in its kinetic, material, affective, and semiotic presence. The diegesis pertains to the entirety of the audiovisual structure, and any attempt to disassemble its parts into strict categories—e.g., diegetic versus nondiegetic, story versus discourse, content versus style—betrays our initial, multisensorial experience of the diegesis as the environment of the film.

When reading "The Film and the New Psychology" today one might get the anachronistic feeling that Merleau-Ponty is criticizing the textual approach that would come to dominate the film-theoretical discourse from the 1960s until phenomenology would re-emerge in the 1990s. Merleau-Ponty's attack on "classical psychology" thus contains both a criticism of the semiotic position that would reduce the visual and auditory stimuli of a film to textual units and ignore their constitution in the embodied perceptual act and of "cognitivism" that would posit the mediation of inferential, analytical, or intellectual operations on the sensorial inputs for the diegesis to emerge in experience. To understand how Merleau-Ponty's seminal lecture diverts from the textual orientation, let us begin by briefly examining some recent efforts to reconcile Merleau-Ponty's embodied phenomenology with structuralism and cognitivism retrospectively.

Pierre Rodrigo (2005) has argued that Merleau-Ponty advances a structuralist model of cinematic meaning according to which the image is the atom of meaning, comparable to the linguistic unit that takes on meaning according to its role within a larger system, i.e., the totality of the film. If meaning solely arises from its place within a system, then meaning is not dependent on embodiment but, rather, generated arbitrarily as a result of systemic difference. However, even if Merleau-Ponty underlines the structural component of meaning, the point he is making in the essay is not structuralist but perceptual. Thus, he speaks of groups rather than juxtaposed elements as being principal and primary to our multisensorial, embodied perception (48).[35] This is why he argues that we do not think of the world in the act of perception; the world, rather, organizes itself in front of us (51). We do not cognitively organize the tones of a musical composition into a melody; rather, we perceive each tone according to the primary juxtaposition of the melody (49). The main point is that sensory experience cannot be reduced to the sensory input data of which it consists but, rather, appears immediately as a holistic structure or global expression (*Gesamteindruck*). This principle can be exemplified in reference to the extraordinary scene of Abel Gance's *La Roue* (1923) depicting the protagonist Elie's (Gabriel de Gravone's) mortal fall from a cliff. Just before the fall, the film uses a series of increasingly brief edits from Elie's life evoking the trope of life flashing by moments before death. At first the images are recognizable, but then they become almost single frames that form a new rhythmic, poetic, and highly kinetic portrayal of the fatal fall that is stripped bare of denotation, leaving us with a pure, affective *Gesamteindruck* of the situation.

Merleau-Ponty's criticism of classical psychology is, by extension, also a criticism of (first-generation, disembodied) cognitive film studies.[36] Nonetheless, in his recent reappraisal of Merleau-Ponty's film essay, Daniel Yacavone (2016) draws attention to its affinities with the cognitivist theories of Bordwell and Branigan. The agreement rests upon the assertion that "each viewer must seek to understand this version of reality on the basis of what, from the standpoint of each moment in time, is limited, incomplete information" (168). While this statement might be deemed uncontroversial as such, it does threaten to obscure the fundamental differences between cognitivism and Merleau-Ponty's embodied phenomenology with regard to *how* we go from perceptual stimuli to a "complete" perceptive impression.

It is true that both positions underline the activity of the perceiver in perception, yet the comparison conceals the explicit "anti-cognitivist" stance taken by Merleau-Ponty in the essay.[37] Whereas Bordwell and Branigan place cognitive operations (inferential elaboration, memory, judgment, hypothesis making, schemata application, etc.) as the primary vehicles behind the construction of a whole from the incomplete parts, Merleau-Ponty (1991b) maintains that our basic perception of the diegesis (understood as temporal gestalt) is not intellectual, abstract, or analytical but embodied, direct, pragmatic, and participatory. Perception is the placing of ourselves (imaginary or not) in the scene or the global organization of the field (51).

At the heart of Merleau-Ponty's criticism of classical psychology—and by extension of both the structural-linguistic and cognitivist-textual approaches—is that it has abandoned the actual sensorial and affective world we live in and replaced it with its placeholder created for the purposes of scientific inquiry (Merleau-Ponty 1991b, 54). Structuralism replaces actual perception and experience with the scientific simulacrum of the "text" (cf. Barthes 1972). By the same token, cognitivism, just as in classical psychology, turns perception into a deciphering of sense data by the intelligence, where the perceiver must dig out the meaning of certain signs. In both cases, "I am presented with a text which I must read or interpret" (Merleau-Ponty 1991b, 50). Thus, both cognitivists and structuralists conceive the diegesis as a set of mosaic data, which is "reconstructed," "read," "decoded," or otherwise intellectually deciphered for us to engage with.

Despite its self-proclaimed embodiment much film theory remains rooted in an intellectualist, textual, and disembodied conceptual heritage. In Maarten Coëgnarts' (2019) radiant application of Lakoff and Johnson's (e.g., 1999, 2002, 2003) embodied conceptual metaphor theory, we thus encounter the textual assumption that the core of filmic signification can be reduced to a literal conceptual skeleton, e.g., its text, which resembles its "bare plot structure." Here the diegesis is firmly dislodged from its material and embodied anchorage and reduced to the basic, literal text.

Daniel Yacavone's (2015) excellent study on "film worlds," which rightly criticizes cognitive film narratology for "losing sight of aspects of the concrete perceptual, affective, and experiential (or 'phenomenological') character of the film-viewing experience" (xvi), elaborates on the semiological (Metz) and phenomenological (Dufrenne) theoretical separation of the representational/discursive and aesthetic/expressive realms of the film. Thus, for Yacavone, "it is vital and necessary to distinguish between the more or less skillfully constructed fictional story-worlds present within narrative films and the larger, multidimensional, and aesthetically realized worlds of films as artworks" (4). Yacavone thus proposes the dual notion of the *world-in* (the world of the represented instance) and the *world-of* (the embodied-affective-expressive-cognitive aesthetic world). In this regard, Yacavone pleads for a "returning to Metz's particular version of the diegetic field of a film as largely a matter of 'denotation'" (26). The diegetic or fictional reality of the film, its "world-in," is "grasped and pieced together by viewers, however easy or challenging this may be in specific cases" (25). In what is ultimately a reappraisal of textual film analysis, Yacavone emphasizes the experiential co-presence of the aesthetic, affective, and representational, while wanting to preserve the denotative as what is , "largely 'given' by the camera in the form of the iconic and what [Metz] refers to as the 'analogical' character of film images, as highly recognizable pictures of things in the world" (26). Yet, this insistence on denotation might obscure the fact that our perception is always infused with affect.

As Merleau-Ponty (1991b) argues,

> It is impossible to understand perception as the imputation of a certain significance to certain sensible signs, since the most immediate sensible texture of these signs cannot be described without referring to the object they signify. (51)

If we consider the diegesis in environmental terms, there is no reason to postulate a denotative layer of the film. Cinematic perception does not come sliced up according to separate denotative and connotative input channels. Neither our ordinary, nonmediated "real-life" perception nor cinematic perception is segregated into neat categories of denotation/connotation, cognitive/affective, or diegetic/nondiegetic. Rather, the whole of the perceived combines into a new reality (or, to use Souriau's terminology, mode of existence), the gestalt or the diegesis, which we experience in an immediate manner as the temporary, (mediated) environment of our perception in its continuous transformations as it unfolds in time.

In *A Page of Madness* (*Kurutta ippeiji*,1926), Teinosuke Kinugasa's silent era masterpiece that was considered lost for half a century, the director conveys the story of a devoted husband, who has taken a job in the asylum of his wife, who is undergoing a nervous breakdown. Interesting is the film's abstinence of verbal expression (e.g., through the use of a *benshi* or intertitles). Instead, we are presented with fast rhythmic editing, mood-laden visual imagery, framings that distort habitual orientation (e.g., upside-down), oneiric inserts, animated graphics superimposed over the photographic image, and a lack of narrative exposition. The film is not constructed upon a linguistic and grammatic form of editing such as the "brick-by-brick" editing of Pudovkin (cf. Burch 1979, 129). Instead, it uses cinema's expressive means to enact an affective state that does not mirror or simulate the emotional conditions of its characters as much as it guides us into our gradual understanding of the trauma the couple endures. That the film is not comprehended on a purely intellectual level, and the fact that we cannot reduce its diegesis to clear denotations, does not make the film meaningless.[38] The essence of its diegesis is not revealed by reducing it to its propositions; it, rather, exemplifies Merleau-Ponty's idea that perception is not an elementary exercise of the intelligence and to genuinely understand others requires us to rediscover a shared bond between the world and the subject, whose roots run deeper than analytical intelligence (52).

We should not think of the diegesis as composed of literal, referential meanings but as a sensorial reality, of something that emerges due to the ability of the cinematic material to *move* us. In reinterpreting the diegesis as environment the singular elements of a film (e.g., a musical theme, a cut, a camera movement, a color scheme, a composition, etc.) conjoin with our embodied perceptual capacities to form a new structure or configuration that must be captured holistically rather than atomically. Consequently, our environmental reinterpretation of the diegesis must be complemented with a post-textual, affective semiotics.

1.5. The Post-Textual Semiotics of the Environmental Diegesis

Faced with the question raised by Barthes (1977a), "How does meaning get into the image? (32)," Metz (1990) answers that it is not on the individual level of the images but only through their syntagmatic structure within a narrative system that the images gain meaning. For Metz, the rule of the "story" is so powerful that the individual images disappear behind the plot it has woven so that the cinema "is only in theory the art of images" (45). Consequently, the "sequence does not string the individual shots; it suppresses them" (45). From this Metz derives his well-known formula: "Going from one image to two images, is to go from image to language" (46). The root of filmic signification lies not in the individual filmic images themselves but in the "grande syntagmatique" (1966) that defines their reassembling into larger narrative structures.

However, in going from the individual image to their meaning-generating functions within a larger semiotic system, Metz circumvents the role of the embodied act of perception as essential to the emergence of the narrative or diegesis. This structuralist semiotics advanced by Metz has most noticeably been rejected by the philosopher Gilles Deleuze in *Cinéma 1: L'image-mouvement* (1983) and *Cinéma 2: L'image-temps* (1985). First of all, Deleuze is critical of the idea that filmic signification "gets into the image" from the outside rather than belonging to it from the onset. For Deleuze (2005), narration is merely a consequence of the visible images themselves and their direct combinations and never a given (26). Instead, the diegesis emerges and continues to re-emerge as a property of the audiovisual material, their atmospheric qualities, and various filmic techniques (e.g., mise-en-scène, soundscapes, camera movements, montage, etc.), as these are coupled and resonate with the perceptual, affective, sensorimotor, and cognitive-epistemic operations of the spectator.

Rather than being the product of the encoding of the what and where of a narrative (denotation), the diegesis emerges out of the complex reciprocal processes in which the individual sound-images become meaningful in relation to the world they imply, a world that in turn is contingent on the sound-images in what amounts to a continuous feedback loop. The "singular" and the "whole" are thus continually and dynamically co-constituted by each other to the extent that "cinema does not just present images, it surrounds them with a world" (68).

For the same reasons, it makes little sense to single out the discourse or the story, the narration or the narrative, the *fabula* or the *syuzhet* as being primary in cinema. Jonathan Culler (2001) has observed that the relational pairing of story and discourse prevalent in narratology assumes either the former or the latter to be the determinant and the other to be the product. Yet, both choices miss some of the curious complexity related to narratives and thus fail to account for their impact (208). An alternative hinted at, yet never carefully elaborated, by Deleuze, is to argue that narratives emerge out of a continuation or modulation of real material intensities.[39] Such a materialist-affective narratology would not run into the structuralist-narratological cul-de-sac of determining the primacy of either story or discourse. Both story and discourse, if we wish to keep these terms, are emergent properties of the deeper-lying anthropomedial relation pertaining to the film experience. It is in this context that the principle of dynamogenesis (that connects thoughts to movements of the body) can be used to argue that prior to any apparent distinguishing of *content* from *form* there are resonances between the cinematic material and our corporeal, affective, sensorimotor, and neurological bodily experiences that constitute the basic form of filmic signification.

The "instauration" or "enactment" of the filmic narrative is thus based on what Deleuze (2005) calls a "signaletic material" (*matière signalétique*). This includes:

> all kinds of modulation features, sensory (visual and sound), kinetic, intensive, affective, rhythmic, tonal, and even verbal (oral and written). [. . .] But, even with its verbal elements, this is neither a language system nor a language. It is a plastic mass, an a-signifying and a-syntaxic material, a material not formed linguistically even though it is not amorphous, and is formed semiotically, aesthetically, and pragmatically. It is a condition, anterior by right to what it conditions. It is not an enunciation, and these are not utterances. It is an *utterable*. (29 author's emphasis)

The post-textual film semiotics developed in this book substitutes the linguistic sign with the "signaletic material" as the basic material out of which cinema signifies. This matter operates prior to all formalized expression and corresponds neither to Saussure's (1998, French original 1916) description of prelinguistic thought as a shapeless and indistinct mass nor to the amorphous film image in Metz's semiology upon which the language of narrative imposes meaning. Moreover, where Merleau-Ponty assigns value to the manner in which the embodied organism transforms the lifeworld of an organism into a meaningful environment or Umwelt, the signaletic material reminds us of the bidirectionality between the organism and its environment. Thus, it is not just the organism that changes its lifeworld (diegesis) in the act of perception; it is also the environment (the diegesis) that shapes the organism (the viewer) in the filmic experience.

The notion of the diegesis-as-environment is rooted in an embodied and pragmatic post-textual semiotics that implies an ecological model of the spectator. Within the framework of "neurofilmology," Adriano D'Aloia and Ruggero Eugeni (2014) have formulated the notion of the "viewer-as-organism." Inspired partly by filmological research on perception and the psychomotor roots of spectatorship and partly on modern research on mirror neurons, the authors develop a model of the viewer not yet dichotomized into the two major paradigms of modern film theory: the "viewer-as-mind" (e.g., semiology, structuralism, cognitivism, and analytical philosophy) and the "viewer-as-body" (e.g., phenomenology, Deleuzian film philosophy, and affect studies). The Archimedean point of the former is cognitive processes; the latter turns to the body to find autonomous and automatic bodily responses that guarantee an immediate and nonintellectual relation between spectator and screen.

Rather than seek a dialectical solution to overcome the dichotomy, D'Aloia and Eugeni suggest that the epistemologically more convincing model of the viewer-as-organism should be founded upon an elaboration of the viewer-as-body that is oriented both backward to filmology and forward to "4EA" (embodied, extended, enactive, embedded, and affective) perspectives within cognitive philosophy—which the authors suggest expanding into a "5EAR" model (adding "emergent" and "relational" to the list). The viewer-as-organism is itself produced in the cinematic situation and constitutes itself in the film experience in complex, dynamical, and provisional forms (19).

From this perspective, comprehension in cinema cannot be reduced to textual decoding (Metz) or inferential elaboration (Bordwell). Yet, rather than circumscribe cognitive processes altogether, the authors suggest implementing these into a larger set of processes such that the viewer-as-organism is involved in a host of different processes (sensory, perceptual, cognitive, emotional, motor, active, mnemonic) of coordination and synchronization (19–20). The temporal dynamics of the "interpretive" process of film viewing means that the perceptual input, along with already owned resources, becomes the starting point for new configurations, themselves potential resources for new processing (20). The viewer-as-organism—not unlike the notion of temporal gestalt in Merleau-Ponty—operates not with representations but "configurations." In this fashion, the immediate affective reaction (e.g., the affect caused by a low rumbling bass) can change the organism's configuration of the environment (e.g., the alley now becomes a threatening alley) and thereby reconfigure our experience (the alley is now experienced as threatening). The diegesis-as-environment and the viewer-as-organism thus stand in a reciprocal relationship to one another and codetermine each other. Ultimately, the cognitions, perceptions, and affects pertaining to the cinematic experience cannot be regarded as "internal" processes of the brain or mind of the spectator but should, rather, be seen as emergent out of the dynamic coupling of the viewer-as-organism and the diegesis-as-environment in the film experience.[40]

1.6. Conclusions

We are now able to summarize the main characteristics of the reappraisal of the diegesis as environment proposed in this chapter. Among the key principles derived from filmology is the notion of the diegesis as an "autonomous" reality that coexists with other modes of filmic existence such as the pro-filmic (the filmed reality) or the screenic (the play on shadow and lights on the screen and the sound waves, as these exist independently of any cognitive or affective investment made by an embodied spectator). In reference to Merleau-Ponty it has been argued that the diegesis can further be seen as a dynamic and temporally developing gestalt, a form of multisensorial total impression (*Gesamteindruck*) that is the object of our immediate perception rather than a retrospective operation of intellectual elaboration. The diegetic space therefore does not exist as a static container that events can either be inside or outside of. What is inside and outside shifts according to perspective and the temporal evolution of the gestalt. Instead of reducing the elements of an image or a shot to linguistic facts or the sum of a film's denotations, the diegesis comprises all of the audiovisual elements that combine into a total and atmospheric impression of the film world that precedes later cognitive-analytical distinctions (thus, the cinematic setting and the "audience effect" produced by it cannot *par tout* be excluded from the diegesis).[41] Consequently, the diegesis cannot exist in the film as text but must be produced in the film experience. The diegesis is thus not an object but an emergent and relational entity that can neither be ascribed to the film nor to its spectator. It exists solely as a product of their dynamic interrelation.

The cinematic diegesis comes into being on the basis of the medium's dynamogenic powers. Thus, rather than trying to understand cinematic signification in spite of the body, the diegesis-as-environment calls for a post-textual, affective semiotics that situates cinematic meaning in the resonances between the movements of the felt body and the arrangement of the film's audiovisual material. Just as this implies an affective conception of cinematic space, the diegesis is also unrestricted by a causal-linear ordering of events (associated with narratology) and thus capable of exploring several temporal modalities such as temporal coexistence, the past's intrusion into the present, the anticipation of the future in the present, or the traces of the past in the material world. The diegesis thus operates as "a system of complete ubiquity that allows the spectator to be transported to any point in time and space" (Morin 2005, 62).

In terms of experience, we cannot postulate different sensory or cognitive filters into which the audiovisual elements neatly self-organize into the distinct autonomous realms of diegetic and nondiegetic. Thus, we experience Bernard Herrmann's shrieking violins in the famous bathroom scene in Hitchcock's *Psycho* (1960) as a constitutive part of the total audiovisual *Gesamteindruck* of the diegesis before we can install an analytical operation capable of categorizing the sounds as "nondiegetic." In a similar vein, the diegesis cannot be reduced to the auditory and visual sensory channels stimulated by the film. The diegesis is thus not perceived as an audio plus visual but as a multisensorial, mediated, and atmospheric world. Finally, the diegesis is not a mental construct, and the spectator is not its disengaged master. Far more, the cinematic spectator must invest her own bodily self into the emergence of the diegesis.

2

The Atmospheric Worlds of Cinema

In *Traffic* (2000) Steven Soderbergh uses a combination of color, filtration, saturation, and contrast to provide each of the three geographical locations—Tijuana, San Diego, and the U.S. East Coast—its distinct mode of expression. These stylistic choices cohere into a conceptual and symbolic gesture that casts a different light on drug dealing, consumption, and political decision-making from their various perspectives. This symbolism is not articulated in the filmic *text* but embedded in the distinct mediated environments the film produces. The symbolism arises out of the resonances between the film material and the movements of our felt bodies to give each storyline a distinct "feel." Narrative comprehension is here tied to a pre-reflective recognition of the "atmospheres" that prefigure the representational-propositional narrative content. In the following, we will refer to this initial, pre-reflective apprehension of the affective charge of the cinematic diegesis as "atmospheric perception." This chapter argues that cinematic perception and narrative comprehension are deeply dependent upon our recognition of atmospheres. The aim is to evidence what can be gained from making atmosphere a central concept in film narratology.

Among the most attractive features of cinema is indisputably its ability to embed its audience in atmospheric worlds or affectively charged virtual environments. One of the most prominent philosophers of atmosphere, Gernot Böhme (2016), defines atmosphere as the mediating force between the objective factors of the environment and the aesthetic feelings of (human) beings such that the atmosphere is what defines the way we feel about ourselves in an environment (1). To conjure up the desired atmospheres, films carefully use ambient soundscapes, music, colorations and filters, camera movements, mise-en-scène, costuming, makeup, camera framings, rhythmical editing, and countless other expressive means.

Atmospheres are essential to the environmental concept of the diegesis proposed in the previous chapter because they define the meaningful encounter between the organism and the environment. Atmospheres are thus quasi-objective, as Böhme explains, they are simultaneously out there, we can be caught in an atmosphere, yet at the same time atmospheres are not things; their existence depends on a subject feeling them (2). The concept of atmosphere thus helps us move beyond a textual understanding of the diegesis in cinema. Nonetheless, the integration of the atmospheric in film narratology is complicated by two main

Enacting the Worlds of Cinema. Steffen Hven, Oxford University Press. © Oxford University Press 2022.
DOI: 10.1093/oso/9780197555101.003.0003

factors. First, the literature on film and atmosphere is still sparse, and a comprehensive theoretical framework for the specific, media-generated atmospheres pertaining to narrative filmic worlds is in need of careful elaboration.[1] Second, the growing interest in "moods" within film studies relies upon a cognitivist, internalist, atomist, and psychological interpretation of filmic moods that threatens to obscure the spatial, social, relational, processual, media-anthropological, and holistic core of the atmosphere concept.

This chapter first introduces what for many film scholars is probably the unfamiliar resurgent interdisciplinary field of contemporary "atmosphere research" and then proceeds by drawing out an initial concept of filmic atmospheres meant to complement the diegesis-as-environment. Through a sustained discussion of three of the most influential explorations of moods in film—Greg M. Smith's "mood-cue approach," Carl Plantinga's notion of "art moods," and Noël Carroll's idea of mood as "cognitive bias"—it shall become evident how the concept of atmosphere differs from the current dominant cognitivist-internalist comprehension of filmic moods and how it exactly therefore can contribute to the revised film narratology developed by this book. Finally, this chapter concludes with a study of two distinct narrative strategies for employing atmosphere in Alice Rohrwacher's magic (neo)realistic fable *Happy as Lazzaro* (*Lazzaro felice*, 2018): one "immanent" (pertaining to the "realist," material qualities of the filmic Umwelt) and the other "transcendent" (pertaining to a character's ability to transcend or stand outside of the environmental and physical laws of the inhabited world, which lends a magic, allegorical, or fabulous atmosphere to the film).

2.1. A Brief Introduction to the Study of Atmosphere

The concept of atmosphere has often been theorized as a conceptual plane, where the subject and the object, the cognitive and the affective, and the narrative and the nonnarrative coexist (cf. B. Anderson 2009, 81). In his early study on *Stimmung* (mood, attunement, or ambience), Friedrich Bollnow (1941) argues that it concerns "the individual in his still undivided unity with his surroundings" (217). *Stimmung*, ambience, aura, mood, and atmosphere are all concepts for describing space as affectively charged.[2] In its everyday use atmosphere describes the immediate, affective impression a space makes upon us, as when we, for instance, walk from the hectic street into the holy space of a church. We have, in a certain sense, entered a new world (Böhme 2013, 95).

In 1924, film theorist Béla Balázs argued that the production of atmosphere was the soul of every art. Once atmosphere is present, technological and aesthetic shortcomings become secondary (Balázs 2011, 22). Yet, although the concept of atmosphere is today an integrated part of the vocabulary used to describe films, no substantial research has been undertaken to (a) provide a precise definition of the term beyond its vague and imprecise use in everyday speech, (b) develop a consistent theoretical framework for the study of filmic atmospheres, or (c) to unfold the concept of atmosphere narratologically as a term for describing the world or universe of the story, i.e., the diegesis-as-environment.

Concurrently, the concept of atmosphere has become increasingly important within a growing, interdisciplinary body of research that has revitalized twentieth-century philosophies on mood, *Stimmungen*, aura, and atmosphere.[3] Conceived affectively rather than meteorologically, atmospheres are studied in such varied fields as aesthetics, architectural theory, urban sociology, religious studies, human geography, anthropology, environmental psychology, security studies, and mobility research.

The two most important figures of this contemporary body of atmosphere research are the German philosophers Hermann Schmitz and Gernot Böhme. In the scope of his new phenomenology (*neue Phänomenologie*) of the felt body (*Leib*), Schmitz's (1998, 2011, 2016a, 2016b) central concern is to demonstrate that human feelings are spatially extended and atmospheric. Following his mentor Schmitz, Böhme (1993), on the other hand, has defined atmosphere as a spatially extended quality of feeling (118) that opens up an intermediary space between objective conditions and subjective states (Böhme 2014a, 92). Unlike Schmitz, Böhme's key concern is the (aesthetic) production of atmosphere and how affective orchestrations increasingly permeate social space. Outlined in the following are the key principles of this growing body of research highly relevant to film studies and the film narratology proposed by this book.

Atmosphere, mood, and *Stimmungen* have often been used to designate a primordial unity of world and subject. Thus, we find already in the early work of Erwin Straus (1930) the idea of the atmospheric as involving a pre-reflective, precognitive, and sensorial exchange of communication between the felt body (*Leib*) and the environment (639). This resonates with positions within contemporary aesthetic philosophy, such as that of Tonino Griffero (2014a, 2014b, 2014c), who associates the atmospheric with affective modulations that operate before any meaningful separation of the subject from the environment can be installed. As Straus and Böhme before him, Griffero stresses the simultaneous spatial (emanating from an assemblage of things, landscapes, persons, architectures, and artifacts) and subjective (requiring to be corporally experienced or felt) nature of atmospheres. In much similar terms, philosopher Teresa Brennan (2004) defines atmospheres as being at once physiological, psychological, and social: "the transmission of affect, if only for an instant, alters the biochemistry and neurology of the subject. The 'atmosphere' or the environment literally gets into the individual" (1). Within architectural theory, Juhani Pallasmaa (2014) has argued that our capacity to grasp atmospheres without a detailed recording and evaluation of their parts and ingredients is our sixth and likely most important sense in terms of our existence, survival, and emotional lives (245). It is my contention that the concept of atmosphere has unique potential for advancing the notion of embodiment in film studies. However, this will only be possible if we acknowledge atmospheres as constituting the filmic diegesis rather than being an emotional filter onto the already constituted textual base of the film.

In order to analyze space as it is experienced rather than as analytically and objectively measured, Ludwig Binswanger (1933) coined the important notion of the "tuned space" (*gestimmter Raum*) in which the "I" and the "space" are unified (629). Whereas space in physics, geometry, and mathematics is conceived as measurable, quantifiable, and objective, atmosphere research conceives space in organic, vitalistic, and affective terms as lived space, where the affective exceeds the boundaries of the individual body and obtains a spatial dimension as atmosphere. Today, this position is expressed in Schmitz's anti-psychological theory of feelings (*Gefühle*) as atmospheres poured out spatially. Feelings are thus not inner, subjective emotional states but far more social and spatial phenomena. While this thesis could be criticized for detaching feelings too radically from an experiencing subject, the spatial extension of affect is a recurrent argument found in the literature on atmosphere.[4]

Later in this chapter we shall examine at length the alternative conceptualization of the atmospheric as a non-spatial and purely psychological phenomena currently *en vogue* in theories on filmic moods. In the literature inspired by cognitive psychology and neuroscience explored later in this chapter, the principal meaning of mood refers to the psychological state of "being in a mood." The secondary, spatial meaning (e.g., "the mood of a scene") is taken to be a purely metaphorical description, because "narrative films cannot have mental states accompanied by bodily perturbations" (Plantinga 2014, 143). Contrary to atmosphere research, theories on filmic moods thus tend to reduce filmic atmospheres to their psychological component as mood states. Atmosphere research, on the other hand, conceives mental and affective states as situated, embedded, spatially extended, and thus co-constituted by the environment with which they interact.[5]

Atmospheres are experienced and sensed; we can be gripped, assailed, or immersed by them; and we can distinguish the elements that contribute to an atmosphere. However, just like the air, the atmosphere itself cannot be the object of perception. This is the argument raised by the French sociologist and urban planner Jean-Paul Thibaud (2003, 2011) for whom an atmosphere (or ambiance) is not an object of perception but its condition. For Thibaud, the atmospheric is never a static being but, like the weather, a constantly changing process. This position has also been advocated by the anthropologist Tim Ingold (2007) for whom "the environment that we experience, know and move around in is not sliced up along the lines of the sensory pathways by which we enter into it" (10).

Atmospheres are thus not static beings, but indeterminate, ineffable, and constantly in the process of emerging and transforming (B. Anderson 2009, 79). Atmospheric space is constantly redefined by the flow of activities that occur in it (Thibaud 2014, p. 71).

Mikel Dufrenne (1973) captures the curious existence of atmosphere by reminding us that the forest obscures our perception of the tree just as the forest only can be seen through its atmosphere (68). Thus, conceptualizing atmosphere as the medium of perception reconnects the meteorological and affective conceptions of the term, whose dichotomization has been criticized for straddling the familiar divisions between nature and humanity, materiality and sensoriality, as well as the cosmic and the affective (Ingold 2015, 76). Atmosphere researchers have thus stressed the importance of rethinking "the materiality of atmosphere in terms that are simultaneously meteorological and affective" (McCormack 2008, 414). Recently, film-theoretical research has experienced an increasing interest in matters of ecology, climate, and weather condition as meteorological, but also necessarily aesthetic, atmospheric forces.[6] The world we inhabit is "a world of becoming, of fluxes and flows or, in short, a weather-world" (Ingold 2012, 81). Although the connection of atmosphere to meteorology is certainly a welcome one, we should not neglect that atmosphere is more than a meteorological precondition; it is something that can be and, indeed, is actively produced.

A growing branch of atmosphere research is therefore devoted to the study of the production of atmosphere in everything from public transportation, to security planning, to how we design our homes.[7] Of interest here is how atmosphere practitioners "intentionally shape the experience of, and emotional response to, a place through the material environment, seeking [. . .] to affect people's moods and guide their behaviour for aesthetic, artistic, utilitarian or commercial reasons" (Bille, Bjerregaard, and Sørensen 2015, 3). This intersects with insights from marketing research, where atmosphere long has been recognized as "more influential than the product itself in the purchase situation" (Kotler 1974, 48). In her examination of the powers of the affective orchestration of public life, Margaret Wetherell (2012) concludes that there is a dire need for the development of more practical, rather than abstract philosophical, theories of the circulation of affect.

The cinematic medium has no doubt been influential on other practices for orchestrating public space affectively (e.g., political campaigning, commercials, or fashion). In light of the increased aestheticization of social space made possible by new media forms (already thematized in relation to cinema in 1935 by Walter Benjamin with the concept of "aura"), Böhme (1993) argues that aesthetics should be less concerned with the representational status of an artwork and become more attentive to how it mobilizes sensorial, material, and affective components to produce *real* atmospheric spaces, with *real* social, ethical, and political consequences. Consider, as an example, D.W. Griffith's use of Richard Wagner's "Ride of the Valkyries" to accompany the ride of the Ku Klux Klan at the end of *The Birth of a Nation* (1915), thereby portraying the Klansmen as heroic defenders of the nation and consequently contributing to the evolution of the modern Klan (Simcovitch 1972, 52). Similarly, Soderbergh's use of "tobacco" filters in *Traffic* could be criticized for resorting to adverse cultural clichés as means for producing the atmosphere for its Tijuana segments.

Studying atmospheres, however, is not just relevant for aesthetic, political, ethical, or historical concerns, but also essential for film narratology. This is because the particular "quality of a story, whether read or heard, lies in the fact that it not only communicates to us that a certain atmosphere prevailed somewhere else but that it conjures up this atmosphere itself" (Böhme 1993, 124). The concept of atmosphere thus invites a mode of analysis interested in the "production of presence" (Gumbrecht 2003, 2012) that complements critical approaches to cinematic representation.

2.2. Atmospheres in Film Theory

Within classical film theory, the atmospheric quality of cinema was deemed to be of the utmost importance, as evident in Balázs' (1953) proclamation that atmosphere "is the air and the aroma that pervade every work of art, and that lend distinctiveness to a medium and a world" (22). Today, theoretical interest in atmosphere has been severely sidestepped by the structural linguistic and cognitivist presupposition of a layer of signification, the diegesis-as-text, isolated from our initial, atmospheric, and affective experience of the filmic material.[8] Given the narratological privileging of the propositional-representational dimension of the narrative (e.g., characters, goal-oriented actions, well-defined narrative scenarios, the plot, etc.), cinematic atmospheres have almost gone completely untheorized and unanalyzed.

Another contributor to the lack of scholarly attention to atmosphere is likely the vagueness of the term "atmosphere" and its interchangeable use with similar, yet nonidentical, terms such as air, ambience, environment, tone, genius loci, mood, *Stimmung*, aura, climate, or temperature. Etymologically "atmosphere" combines the Greek words *atmos* meaning "vaporous" or "gaseous" and *sphaira* meaning "ball" or "globe." The word "atmosphere" is thus an attempt to define a phenomenon, whose presence can be intersubjectively affirmed, yet whose precise character and nature is difficult to measure or to capture in analytical, categorical, discriminate, representational, and atomistic terms (cf. Rauh 2017). Added to this is the difficult ontological status of atmosphere as irreducible to the subject or the object, which makes it incompatible with the dominant strain of dualism at the heart of Western thinking (Böhme 1993; Schmitz 2016a).

Ultimately, cinematic atmospheres have suffered a similar destiny to that of descriptions in the novel. Begrudging the lack of scholarly attention devoted to descriptions, Monika Fludernik (2009) makes the following observation:

> Passages of description are often regarded as non-narrative (non-die-getic): nothing happens while the narrator describes a fair, a landscape or a character. Having said that, we also have to concede that description is actually central at the story level since the fictional world through which the actants move is only created through and by it. (117)

In line with the argument made in the previous chapter, the atmospheric might be of little interest for textual analysis, but it is hugely important for understanding the diegesis as more than the causal-linear chain of narrative events.[9]

An atmosphere presents not in itself a *narrative* situation, yet it might suggest or anticipate one. Nonetheless narrative situations always occur in atmospheres. Regardless of how pathos-laden and symbolically suggestive, cinematic spaces are de facto atmospheric spaces. Moreover, in the temporal unfolding of a film, atmosphere and narrative situation engage in constant feedback loops or continuous reciprocal causations, making their relation dynamic and complex. Consequently, we must resist the lure of regarding atmospheres as filters onto preexisting narrative worlds but instead see them as manifestations of how cinematic spaces are always already affectively and meaningfully charged.

A narrative situation can amplify (e.g., an imposing deadline of the protagonists), alter (e.g., when a character realizes that the joyfulness of a wedding merely serves to cover up a planned ambush), or relate ironically to (e.g., a romantic dinner gone wrong) an atmosphere. The feeling tone of an atmosphere can be perceived, although the perceiver is not herself caught up by the emotion transmitted. The atmosphere of a film scene might thus be perceived as tense, erotic, or spiritual without invoking in us a corresponding emotional or affective state, i.e., mood. Atmospheres can serve as expressions of the mood or existential state of a character, society, or a moment in history; they can be used allegorically, as an authorial comment; or they can perform all functions at once as in Lars von Trier's *Melancholia* (2011). Nonetheless, the nature of atmosphere is not representational or symbolic, but immediate, presentational, affective, evaluative, and synesthetic. In this fashion, the "immediate judgement of the character of space calls upon our entire embodied and existential sense, and it is perceived in a diffuse and peripheral manner, rather than through precise and conscious observation" (Pallasmaa 2014, 231). We recognize the universe of a Wes Anderson film before we are able to pinpoint the singular elements of recognition (e.g., vibrant costuming, theatrical and meticulous set design and symmetry in its camera work and world production, quirky characters, its child-hood nostalgia, as well as his "crate-digger"[10] soundtracks).

In his investigations into the phenomenon of atmospheres, Michael Hauskeller (1995) argues that perception is essentially atmospheric and affective. Atmospheres accompany us at all times and no non-atmospheric sensory modality exists. Our most basic manner of engaging with the world(s) we find ourselves in is thus atmospheric, regardless of whether we refer to natural or mediated ecologies (49). Existing between the environmental qualia and the embodied presence of the perceiving subject, atmospheres are not like typical objects or things (e.g., a table, a hammer, or a surfboard), but "quasi-things" [Halbdinge]. An atmospheres is experienced as quasi-objective, as something that does not belong to the recipient but something we happen upon or are assailed by and that we can communicate about intersubjectively, despite the fact that atmospheres depend on our being emotionally affected by them (Böhme 2014b, 43; cf. Schmitz 2007, 54–65).

Although atmospheres are *personally* felt, atmospheric practitioners can thus rely upon the intersubjective character of atmospheres. The fact that interior designers, supermarket decorators, cinematographers, or other atmospheric practitioners can produce atmospheres with a certain degree of reliability on their supposed effects comes down to a range of factors including cultivation and ha-bituation processes, ontogenetic factors, and our shared bioculturally embodied background (cf. Hauskeller 1995, 45–49). The fact that atmospheres are spatially extended and intersubjectively recognized makes them different in nature from corporeal stirrings such as hunger, pain, or sexual arousal that relate only to our present, personal corporeal state. In extension of this, films cannot take on these personal, bodily states. Films can be "slow" or "sedated" but not "tired"; a film can wake your appetite for food or sex, but it cannot itself be hungry or sexu-ally aroused. Films can be infused with atmospheres related to movement such as uplifting or depressing, but the film is not depressed or uplifted. Moreover, as atmospheres, qualities such as depressed, anxious, cheerful, melancholic, or romantic encompass both an affective state related to the organism as well as an affective quality pertaining to particular situations or environments (e.g., a cheerful afternoon).

Atmosphere also defines our basic social engagement, since atmospheres ra-diate not only from spaces and things but also people (Böhme 1993; Schmitz 2016b). In *Transmission of Affect* (2004), Teresa Brennan examines how atmospheres are capable of getting into the individual (1). This transmission of affect occurs between people sharing a space, and while it is social in origin, its effect is biological and physical (3). Atmospheric affects do therefore not ema-nate from within but impose themselves on the individual from the outside (e.g., "we were gripped by the atmosphere"; "the atmosphere was overwhelming"; or "there was a tense atmosphere in the room"). In atmospherically charged spaces, the affective energy of others enters the person, and the person's affects, in turn, are transmitted outward into the environment (8). In the cinematic theater, our reaction to the screen events can be amplified by the collective viewing experience; we laugh more when the room is filled with laughter. Yet, the social viewing situation might also bring a restraint to our involvement, as when the teenager suddenly finds himself watching an erotic scene together with his parents (cf. Hanich 2011). Atmospheric transmission contaminates the shared space between the members of the audience to create an "audience effect" (cf. Hanich 2018), but also the shared space between the audience and the characters.[11] The tension between Marianne (Liv Ullmann) and Johan (Erland Josephson) in Ingmar Bergman's *Scenes from a Marriage* (*Scener ur ett äktenskap*, 1973), for instance, is affectively transmitted such that it becomes a spatial quality that defines the space that not only the characters co-inhabit, but the audience, too. Nonetheless, the idea that affective states have a spatial and social dimension does not chime with the current cognitive definition of filmic moods.

2.3. Atmospheres, Moods, and Cognitive Film Theory

Film studies have experienced a modest, yet growing, interest in questions concerning cinematic "mood" or *Stimmung* (mood, attunement, or atmosphere).[12] Following the *Oxford English Dictionary* mood can both refer to a temporary state of mind or feeling and the atmosphere or pervading tone of something. Whereas the philosophical and aesthetic value of *Stimmung* to a large extent has been connected with its ability to encompass both personal feeling states and the "feel" of the environment (Wellbery 2010, 703–5), cognitive film scholars are disturbed by this use of mood to describe both subjective and environmental qualities.[13] Cognitive film scholars have argued that we should reserve the notion of mood exclusively to the corporeal-affective state of *being in a mood* and understand the use of mood to describe the "affective character" of a film as a metaphorical deviation of this primary meaning of the term.[14]

This is because cognitivism subscribes to what in the philosophy of mind is known as "internalism" or "individualism."[15] As Robert A. Wilson (2003) explains, internalism states that "what occurs inside the boundary of an individual *metaphysically* determines the nature of that individual's mental states" (257, author's emphasis). Internalism subscribes to the belief that affective states are to be understood on the basis of the body-brain in isolation from the environmental, historical, social, and cultural stimuli. From this perspective, the notion of the mood, atmosphere, or *Stimmung* of a film cannot be anything but a purely metaphorical description of the "potential elicitors of human moods" (Plantinga 2012, 461). In the following, I wish to evidence some of the shortcomings pertaining to the internalism of cognitive theories of moods, which I hold to be the chief obstacle for the introduction of atmosphere as an important film narratological concept. The aim is to replace the cognitive-internalist and subjectivist notion of filmic moods with the relational, situated, and media-anthropological concept of atmosphere in order to highlight the filmic experience as rooted in the dynamic coupling of spectator and film. Let us therefore begin with the strongest proponent of the internalist stance, namely, Greg M. Smith's mood-cue approach.

2.3.1. Greg Smith's Mood-Cue Approach

In *Film Structure and the Emotion System* (2003), Greg M. Smith draws upon insights derived from cognitive psychology and neuroscience to develop what he dubs the "mood-cue" approach. Following Smith, "the primary emotive effect of film is to create mood" (42). Smith defines moods as "orienting emotional states" and "predispositions that make it more likely that we will experience an emotion" (39). Moods are thus the organism's way of preparing for an emotional outburst, and filmmakers elicit moods to raise the spectator's emotional engagement with the film, its characters, and the narrative situation.

Smith's theory has grown out of an equal admiration of, and dissatisfaction with, the emotional theories of Noël Carroll (1990), Ed Tan (1996), and Torben Grodal (1999). The problem with these theories, according to Smith (1999), is that they inherit a series of cognitivist assumptions about emotions that correspond to the functions we normally associate with cognition. The functional model of cognitive philosophy defines the prototypical features of emotions as being action oriented (fear causes us to flee), object oriented (we fear something), and goal oriented (fear helps us to achieve the goal of survival). As Smith (1999) convincingly argues, the emphasis on action, objects, and goals allows cognitive film scholars to implement film's elicitation of emotions into already existing cognitive theories of narrative structure, which had already, at least in the dominant tradition of Hollywood narration, been characterized as constructed around the goals, objects, and actions of a character. "If one understands filmic emotions as object-, action-, and goal-oriented, then this privileges the portion of the film that most clearly fits these criteria" (105), as Smith (1999) concisely points out. For Carroll, Grodal, and Tan, "filmic emotions are inextricably character-emotions" (105), yet Smith wants to counter this cognitive film-theoretical tendency to elevate the characters (and our sympathy or allegiances with their goals) to the key structuring principle for the elicitation of emotion in cinema. Smith thus wants to bring renewed focus to the stylistic cues to which earlier cognitivist theories of emotion in cinema were able to grant merely a "subordinant role to the dominant schemas of motive, action, and goals" (65).

Nonetheless, just as Smith (2003) faults Carroll, Tan, and Grodal for choosing "concepts of emotion that are rooted in human agents, which prejudices them toward character-oriented explanations of filmic emotion" (81), I believe it is possible to argue that a similar subjectivist bias underlines the mood-cue approach. This bias is expressed in four interconnected ways concerning (a) its methodological outlook, (b) its reliance on the notion of "dual processing" of thought and feeling, (c) its suggested film-analytical procedure, and (d) its disembodied and rationalist view of filmic communication. Ensuing from my criticism of the mood-cue approach, I will demonstrate how the atmospheric might help us to overcome the subjectivist bias inherent to the mood-cue approach and thus open up for new ways of studying filmic moods.

First, Smith's internalist commitments cause his approach to be unnecessarily restrictive in its methodological outlook. This is especially evident in his conception of the "emotion system" as something that can be clarified and understood in isolation from environmental factors. According to Smith, "culture and socialization shape the individual but do not fundamentally rework the basic structures of the human" (10). In line with much affective neuroscience, Smith thus assumes that we can find the "core machinery" of moods and emotions by examining the brain. Smith thus inherits the tendency of neuroscience to overgeneralize or neglect the complex role of the environment. In this sense, the actual stimuli of the films, which Smith's theory is supposed to provide an understanding of, are evaluated solely according to how well they fit our neurobiological hardware: "Films are objects that are well constructed to elicit a real emotional response from our already existing emotion systems" (6).

We need deny neither the value of affective neuroscience nor that of cognitive psychology to advocate a theory of (filmic) moods that encompasses cultural values, norms, environmental factors, or social behaviors as regulating and modifying affective states rather than reducing the external world to relative straightforward "cues" (stimuli) that trigger a predetermined "mood-response." Smith's approach further risks losing sight of the specific mediated nature of emotions elicited by the cinematic medium. Indeed, cinema can invoke emotional states that are not one-to-one with their real-life counterparts. Even if an aggressive lion in a film and a real-life aggressive lion both induce an affective state we refer to as "fear," it would be wrong to equate these two emotional episodes due to their different environmental scaffolding (in one case the tiger can kill you; in the other it cannot). Additionally, a film can communicate a mood without arousing it (e.g., we are able to spur the erotic mood of The Night Porter [Il portiere di notte, Cavani 1974] without necessarily becoming sexually aroused by it). Therefore, although I agree with Smith that emotions in films are "real"; the distinct mediated variety of emotions that we experience in the cinema cannot be grasped with recourse to the emotion system exclusively. Ultimately, Smith's mood-cue approach reduces the relation of environment and moods to a simple stimulus–response link.

Second, the mood-cue approach is based on the notion of "parallel processing" of emotion and cognition (30–34). More precisely, Smith's film theory is formulated upon research first introduced by Paul MacLean (1949, 1952), which hypothesized a specific brain circuit for the emotional brain, the limbic system with its emotional core centered around the amygdala. Smith (2003) argues that the amygdala "'shades' the data with a particular emotional 'coloring'" (27). Moreover, the notion of an "emotional brain" is accompanied by the corollary idea that cognition resides elsewhere in the brain. For Smith (1999) the "[e]motional evaluation takes place in parallel to the conscious assessment of stimuli" (111). As Smith (2003) further explains, "Sensory data are sent to the cortex for conscious processing, while the same data are sent to the emotional center of the brain to gain feeling tone" (30). Smith's (1999) theory of how films arouse and express mood states is thus formulated upon the hypothesized anatomical division of the human brain into separate cognitive and emotional compartments that process the data dually. According to this model, the role of the "emotional" brain is to shade the raw environmental data with the proper emotional "coloring" and thus to prepare the organism for an action response to the situation (108).

In reference to this neurocognitive thesis about the architecture of the brain, Smith further assumes a separation of the filmic text (cognitive processing of the filmic data) from our affective-emotional evaluation of it (the shading of this data with emotional coloring). On this basis, Smith's mood-cue approach is in congruence with the Bordwellian separation of narrative comprehension (cognitive) from our emotional responses (the emotional shading). Following this logic, our affective, material, and emotional engagements with a narrative remain isolated from our cognitive processing of this world. Transferred onto cinema this means that moods are epiphenomenal to the cognitive comprehension of the narrative data, the establishment of the propositional, denotative textual base, which moods can only color in an affective tone. Thereby Smith has produced a cognitive theory of moods that has effectively situated the Saussuro-Hjelmslevian and cognitive narratological differentiation between the "what" (processing of narrative content) and the "how" (the particular stylistic means of expression and their affective impact) of a narrative inside the brain. In other words, the story/discourse distinction is now granted a neurological basis.

Before we proceed with the film-theoretical and narratological implications of this, let us briefly survey how this anatomical distinction has been disputed within contemporary affective neuroscience. Modern affective neuroscience has grown increasingly critical of whether the Western metaphysical dichotomy of passion and intellect is actually mirrored in the architecture of the brain (cf. Barrett and Bar 2009; Colombetti 2014; Pessoa 2013). Neuroscientist Luiz Pessoa (2013) has, for instance, examined research on the amygdala (the presumed seat of the so-called "emotional brain") and concludes that it is increasingly acknowledged that it performs important functions in cognitive, emotional, and social processes (38). Pessoa thus prefers to think of the brain as "cognitive-emotional," and his research evidences the integrative rather than interactive operationality of the brain.[16] When we consider the available neuroscientific data, he argues conclusively, attempts to characterize regions as either "emotional" or "cognitive" disintegrate (258). This does not mean that emotion and cognition are not useful categories for describing behavior or phenomenal experience. It means, rather, that these labels do not correspond to compartmentalized pieces of the brain (259).

In the article "See It with Feeling" (2009), affective neuroscientists Lisa Feldman Barrett and Moshe Bar argue that sensations from the body should be considered a dimension of knowledge or cognition because they aid us in identifying the nature of the objects we encounter, based, in part, on past reactions (1326). Visual perception then cannot be segregated from affective components, hence the title of their paper. The notion of "seeing with feeling" contradicts Smith's mood-cue approach because objects are no longer first perceived and then attributed an emotional salience, relevance, or value independently of cognitive assessment. Instead, visual stimuli and cognitive-affective impact coincide in perception. Seeing with feeling (what we refer to as "atmospheric perception" to underline the multisensory nature of perception), according to Barrett and Bar, entails that "affective response assists in seeing an object as what it is from the very moment that visual stimulation begins" (1327).

The third cognitive-internalist hindrance of the mood-cue approach concerns its film-analytical methodology. Smith's proposition of a "dual processing" of cognitive and emotional data causes him to obtain exactly the sort of cognitive bias of emphasizing narrative structure, action, objects, goals, and characters that he rightly points out characterizes earlier cognitive writings on film emotions. The problem is that Smith does not allow moods any constitutive role in the disclosing of the narrative world. Instead, moods are subordinated to the preconstituted narrative facts, which they provide an "emotional coloring" of. Smith therefore struggles to highlight the value of moods as anything but a communicational tool *about* the narrative or characters, or as a way for the film to express the proper generic framework for interpretation. Moreover, as Plantinga (2009b) points out, Smith often resorts to emotional (object-oriented) rather than mood (global-oriented) states to exemplify his approach. Smith's choice of analyzing *Stella Dallas* (directed by Vidor 1937)—a highly character-oriented film—is firmly rooted in the film's narrative "text," the manner in which it emotionally invites us to feel *for* Stella, and how it invites interpretation along the generic lines of the melodrama rather than the romantic film.

On similar grounds, Robert Sinnerbrink (2012) argues that Smith's approach winds up subordinating mood to the cognitive-oriented emotional states that are the result of character action, narrative situation, or generic convention (153). Smith fails to account for how complex affective states involve a host of stimuli that gain significance as part of a larger aesthetic or narrative context (154). The atomized "mood-cues" that form the basic building blocks of Smith's theory thus must themselves be situated in a broader, meaningful, and rewarding context. Mood-cues are not imbued with an inherent and universal meaning independent of the filmic context in which they appear but instead gain their value as part of a holistic, relational, and contextual total impression that precedes each atomistic cue and guides our apprehension of it. The relation of mood-cues and atmosphere is complex and reciprocal and not causal-linear as assumed by Smith. Consequently, mood-cues cannot be taken as the progenitor of moods.

Mood-cues in cinema are never atomistic, isolated, and discrete triggers of mood-responses, as Smith suggests, but are themselves embedded, situated, and codetermined by the more encompassing atmosphere or mood prevalent in the filmic diegesis or aesthetic presentation. The mood of a film must be more than a mere coloration of an already existing narrative, which is why Sinnerbrink conceptualizes it instead as the "baseline" form of attunement out of which the filmic world is unveiled (154).

Finally, let us address our fourth reservation about the mood-cue approach, namely, the disembodied theory of filmic communication that underlines it. Smith's notion of the dual processing of cognitive and emotional data causes him to postulate an overtly rational comprehension of how spectators engage with the mood-cues proffered by a film. Smith (2003) rightly points out that films do not "make" people feel and instead suggests that films extend "an invitation to feel in particular ways" and that individual members of the audience "can accept or reject the invitation" (12). Thus, one member of the audience can be swept in tears over a melodrama, while another might find this film's emotional tone too pathetic and banal. In this fashion, Smith retains a degree of subjective autonomy as part of our mood-responses to films. Yet, at the same time, Smith downplays the filmic capacity of overwhelming its spectators as an affective force coming from the outside. Smith instead presents a cognitive-rationalist account of moods as the organism's evaluation of the environment, where the moods "act as the emotion system's equivalent of attention, focusing us on certain stimuli and not others" (38).

Moreover, "to accept the invitation [of a film], one must be an 'educated viewer' who has the prerequisite skills required to read the emotion cues" (12). Yet, by using the term "reading" as the primary model for how we respond to the mood- or emotion-cues of films, Smith downplays the ability of cinema to overwhelm us affectively before we in any meaningful way have installed an acceptance or rejection of this invitation on a conscious level (this not only counts for "affective reflexes" such as the startle response but also for the generation of complex filmic moods that we might not be able to capture in linguistic or representational terms). Presupposed is a disembodied mode of filmic communication, where the film acts as "text" and the viewer as the "reader" of that text. According to this logic, filmic moods are reduced to "stylistic information" (76), "emotional messages" (85), and signifiers of "a particular feeling tone" (92). In this context, Plantinga (2009b) has criticized Smith's notion of the film as text and the spectator as a reader of that text for infusing film viewing with the patina of intellectual distance and downplaying the pre-rational elements of spectatorship (112). Contrary to Smith's over-intellectualization of mood-cues, Plantinga's approach "preserves room for unconscious and nonconscious spectator responses and for responses that, while not necessarily illogical or irrational, bypass the conscious inference-making that is mistakenly thought to underlie all cognitive film theory" (8). It is to this approach we now turn.

2.3.2. Plantinga and "Art Moods"

In expanding upon the work of Noël Carroll and Greg M. Smith, Carl Plantinga (cf. 2009a, 2009b, 2010, 2012, 2014; Plantinga and Smith 1999) has advanced a "cognitive-perceptual" theory of filmic moods. Recognizing the intricate, yet important difference between the moods of a film and the moods that a film might elicit in us, Plantinga proposes a differentiation between "human moods" and "art moods." As Plantinga (2014) observes, "We often think of moods as the atmosphere or tenor or tone of a film or film scene, and thus we associate moods with the 'feel' of a scene" (142). However, Plantinga suggests that we distinguish these two meanings of the term "mood":

> As audiovisual displays, narrative films cannot have mental states accompanied
> by bodily perturbations. When we use the word mood in relation to a narrative
> film, we either use the word metaphorically or we use it in some sense other
> than that we use to refer to human moods. I make this rather obvious point
> for the reason that we tend to run the two senses of "mood" together in our
> thinking, and it would clarify the issue to keep them separate. (143)

The challenge for cognitive theories of filmic moods is thus to determine this "other sense" of the term mood, which Plantinga—unnecessarily restrictive—identifies with "art moods." These "moods" are irreducible to and different from the affective, psychological state of *being in a mood*. Thus, in moving from "human" to "art" moods, we simultaneously move from the "real" to the "metaphorical." For Plantinga, to

> claim that a film has a mental or bodily state would be wrong because, obviously enough, a film has no mind or body. As an audiovisual display, it can be used to elicit actual moods in spectators, but literally speaking, it cannot have human moods itself. (461)

It is worth, however, noticing that Plantinga's argument hinges upon an internalist definition of moods, i.e., one that reduces moods to "mental states accompanied by bodily perturbations." Yet, moods can also be understood as resulting from the dynamic coupling of organism and environment as evidenced by the contemporary atmosphere research surveyed earlier in this chapter, as well as by the situated and scaffolded approaches to affect, mood, and emotion emerging from the cognitive sciences.[17] Thus, if mood is not already by definition reduced to the subject, Plantinga's differentiation of mood into those pertaining to the "artwork" and those to the "human organism" no longer applies. Mood instead becomes a way of describing the qualitative and affective relation between an organism and its immediate surroundings (or Umwelt). As Martin Heidegger (1962) argues, "mood [*Stimmung*] assails us. It comes neither from 'outside' nor from 'inside,' but arises out of being-in-the-world" (176).

Herein lies a major difference between the cognitive conception of mood and the theory of atmosphere that I advocate for in this chapter. Where cognitive theories understand moods as subjective feeling states (partly) mediated by conceptual thought, contemporary atmosphere research presupposes a dynamic coupling of organism and environment. If we reserve the term "mood" for the subjective, world-independent state of being in a mood, the atmospheric can be employed to understand the intersubjective, situated, embedded, enactive, context-dependent, and temporally anchored (both synchronically through skillful interactions with the environment and diachronically through the acquisition of emotional repertoires) nature of (human) affectivity. From this perspective, the (film) environment is to be regarded as a constituent part of the affective or emotional episode on par with the organism's bodily and cognitive capacities.

From this perspective, Plantinga's differentiation between "art" and "human" moods is problematic because it presupposes an independence of the organism's felt corporal state from its embeddedness in particular environments, mediated or not. Yet, we are not just embodied but also embedded beings that interact with the world and the animate and inanimate entities of it. Our moods therefore do not depend solely on the state of our organism, but also on our interactions with the world. The alternative to internalism is not the opposing pole of externalism but the overcoming of the internal–external dualism altogether. What is at stake is the formulation of an integrative, dynamic, and relational understanding of mood as complexly situated in the world, be it through cultural values and norms, the affective impact of material and environmental factors or entities, or the "incorporation" of environmental elements to the extent that these are experienced as belonging to the embodied self (e.g., a hearing aid).[18]

Contrarily, Plantinga's cognitivist-internalist approach draws and expands upon Smith's notion of mood as a coloration of the narrative content. According to Plantinga (2009b), a film cues the spectator into a mood that is congruent with the emotions and themes represented in the narrative. Thus, the metaphor of color becomes decisive for understanding the interrelation between the propositional text and the emotional and affective surplus value. Accordingly, "[e]motions and affects color the viewer's perception of a narrative, making it vibrant, enchanting, exciting, disgusting, suspenseful, fascinating, sad, happy, and so on" such that the "viewing of a narrative film is not merely an intellectual or cognitive exercise, but one colored by affect and emotion" (6). In this fashion, films represent characters and events but also "embody or prefigure ways of responding to them" (79), and consequently, we can think of narrative films "as representing narrative events presented in such a way that they are prefocused to provide a particular complex of affective experiences" (79).

Yet, in my contention, the characters and events of films do not exist outside of their atmospheric coloration in any meaningful way. The existence of characters in cinema is unveiled through their embeddedness in atmospheres, through them being part of a filmic diegesis. We do not first have characters and then an affective "coloration" of them. Our perception of the characters cannot be abstracted from our immediate affective, emotional, and cognitive apprehension of them. Consequently, our primary mode of engaging with cinematic characters is in the context of their atmospheric embeddedness. This indeed appears to be implied when Plantinga (2012) defines mood in cinema as something like "its 'character,' or at least those aspects of its character that are suffused with affect, that have an emotional tone or feel" (462). Regrettably, Plantinga's internalist definition of mood denies him the possibility of elaborating on the "affective charge" or "emotional tone" in a substantial way beyond its mere metaphorical status. Consequently, Plantinga, like Smith, must resort to the typical cognitivist-textual strategy of subsuming moods to the propositional, representational, and conceptually structured content of the film's narrative.

"What separates art moods from the mood of a day or a landscape," Plantinga (2014) asserts, "is that we take the art mood to express a perspective or point of view" (145). For Plantinga, a cinematic mood is thus a "tool used to communicate perspective" (145). Consequently, the mood of a scene or of an entire film can be presented as an expression of narrative point of view generally, or it may be developed as a character's perspective. Often, narrational and character point of view are united, as the film's narration will express an overarching mood to give us a sense of the protagonist's experience, as in Hitchcock's *Rebecca* (1940) (146). For Plantinga moods thus acquire meaning in relation to the narrative content. As such *Touch of Evil* (directed by Welles 1958) "*couples* narrative scenarios of corruption, betrayal, and death with low key lighting, night scenes, skewed and cluttered framing, and industrial settings littered with trash, oil wells, and rusting machinery" (Plantinga 2010, 86, my emphasis) and the musical *Oklahoma!* (directed by Zinnemann 1955) "uses high key lighting, balanced and symmetrical compositions, bright colors, bucolic natural settings, and plenty of sunshine to *accompany* its exuberant proclamations of the goodness of life" (86, my emphasis). Expressive stylistic devices and our affective responses merely accompany the narrative content.

By shifting the focus onto the narrative-communicational functions of moods, Plantinga shies away from discussing the ability of moods to embed us cognitively affectively in a world and to determine the quality and existence of that world in the first place. This is no coincidence since Plantinga's theory falls short when it comes to "art moods" that cannot be assigned representational or communicational functions (e.g., instrumental music, architecture, experimental cinema, or abstract painting) just as it cannot explain the moods of landscapes, social situations, or meteorological conditions as anything else than a metaphor.[19] Ultimately, Plantinga offers a rather restrictive theory of moods, where these contribute to emotional experience but by themselves cannot qualify as the basic orienting state that determines overall affective response (2009a, 142). Relying upon an opposition between mood (nonrepresentational) and narrative (representation), Plantinga instead concludes that narrative scenarios remain the most important cinematic structuring mechanisms (142). This argument, however, hinges on the independence of narrative scenarios from moods as well as the assumed autonomy of the textual core of the narrative from the coloration of mood.

Yet, Plantinga recurrently pushes the restrictive limits of his cognitivist-internalist assumptions that become a strait jacket for his theory of filmic moods. Thus, despite his plea to keep the subjective (human mood states) and the objective (filmic moods) apart, their co-presence is often implied. What else could underline Plantinga's reference to "orchestrated affects" (2009b) or "the affective character" (2012) of a scene or film? If, as Plantinga (2012) maintains, the suspenseful mood is a characteristic of the film text itself (470), is this definition of the filmic "text" not already reliant on the (potential) affective resonances between an embodied organism and the filmic material? And if so, does this not point toward a media-anthropological understanding of filmic moods that implies the coexistence of film and spectator in the genesis of the narrative world—one that, as Plantinga (2012) observes, prefigures "ways of seeing, ways of experiencing, ways of perceiving" (469)? In this sense, Plantinga's conception of mood already gestures toward a less restrictive understanding of mood, which is not univocally to be identified with "mental states accompanied by bodily perturbations." Understanding atmospheres requires more than an understanding of cognitive appraisals or affect programs; it requires an understanding of how our affective lives are environmentally scaffolded. In this context, Noël Carroll's conception of mood is interesting because it pushes the boundaries of the internalist stance of cognitivism even further.

2.3.3. Carroll on Moods: Cognitive Film Theory and the Limits of Internalism

In his article "Art and Mood" (2003a), Carroll addresses an important limitation of the cognitive theory of emotions, when it comes to understanding affective states that are not necessarily content based or object directed. Carroll thus stands as the cognitive scholar, who proves most willing to explore the boundaries of the internalist stance and thus the closest cognitive ally to contemporary atmosphere research and to advancing our understanding of the situated and scaffolded nature of (filmic) moods.

According to the standard cognitive interpretation of emotions, which Carroll argues is incapable of capturing moods, all emotions possess cognitive states directed at objects subsumable under general criteria that cognitive processing ensues in bodily or somatic changes (522). If we define emotions as object oriented and intentional, as the cognitivists do, then emotions are cognitively mediated. However, moods are exactly defined as global and not directed at any particular object, situation, or person ("It's not you, I'm just in a bad mood") (526). Thus, moods do not sit well with the standard cognitive definition of emotions.

If moods are nonintentional and nonrepresentational (i.e., not about something specific), while emotions are directed toward objects and have intentionality, then how can we be "sad" or "uplifted" by a movie? In order to approach this question, Carroll opens his essay on moods with the, for him, surprising claim that it is time for philosophers of art to look beyond cognitive theories of the emotions in order to broaden their appreciation of the affective life of art (523). Among the problems outlined by Carroll is the difficulty of providing a positive definition of what moods are in art. According to the general cognitive definition, mood "emanates from the self and engulfs everything it touches" (529); its direction is thus from self to world. However, moods in art, just like those pertaining to natural landscapes and weather conditions, are forces that regulate our mood states externally, i.e., from world to self.

In "On Being Moved by Nature" (2003b), Carroll examines how we appreciate nature by opening ourselves to its stimuli and exposing ourselves to it emotionally by attending to its aspects (369). In cinema, the direction of mood is not from self to world; we do not impose our moods onto the film; rather, the film modulates or regulates our mood states. Similarly, when we are struck by the grandeur of a waterfall, to use Carroll's example in the afore-mentioned article, with "our ears reverberating with the roar of falling water, we are overwhelmed and excited by its grandeur" (373). Carroll's example of being moved by nature bears some resemblance to the mood states induced by films. The waterfall, he writes, "moves us through its sound, and weight, and temperature, and force. The sense of mystery awakened by the winding path is linked to the process of moving through it" (374).

The description implies a dynamic coupling of organism and environment that appears incongruent with the cognitive-internalist conception of affective states. If moods depend "on the subject's bodily sense of her antecedent coping resources" (Carroll 2003a, 539), it is hard to see how cinema or the natural environment can elicit moods. Moreover, if moods are defined as objectless and global, how then can artworks (or nature for that sake) induce moods? As Carroll observes, to say that artworks induce moods is incongruent with the internalist notion that "the overall mood state is intimately connected to factors over which artists have virtually no control" (539), i.e., the physiological state of the body. If moods are ultimately down to the internal state of the brain-body, then neither nature nor art can rightfully be said to induce moods. Carroll holds this to be an unsatisfactory conclusion given our use of artworks to regulate our moods and their generic branding and marketing according to the mood they promise to put us in (think of horror, romance, or comedy in cinema) (538).

For Carroll, the ability of artworks to induce moods is undeniable. Consequently, the task becomes to resolve the apparent incongruity that results from the logical conclusion to the argument that if moods are linked causally to features that are internal to the subject, then they are out of the manipulative reach of the artist and thus art cannot induce moods (539). Carroll offers two answers to this apparent mystery. The first option is that artworks arouse moods indirectly through a "spillover" effect caused by the elicitation of emotional (content-based, object-oriented, and representational) feeling states. Although nothing stands in the way of this option, it does not solve Carroll's mystery given that most mood states with respect to art do not traffic in representation (545). We must therefore also account for how artworks elicit moods directly (i.e., not mediated by representational content) by arousing corporeal-visceral feeling states that are associated with the overall mood states of which they are components or constituents (539). This latter option brings Carroll out of his cognitive-representational comfort zone and brings him in the vicinity of the visceral and embodied form of communication of central importance to this book.

Carroll assumes that there is a direct stimuli response mechanism that can be accountable for this cognitive paradox. Accordingly, by triggering affective reflexes through a manipulation of variables such as speed, scale, lighting, and sound, the filmmaker has direct access to our nervous systems, bypassing the cerebral cortex and triggering automatic affective reflexes" (524). While this does not itself explain more complex mood states such as the serenity of a landscape or a film scene, it does hint at how films communicate by sculpting the movement of the film to impact our felt bodies, for example, through camera movements, the movement of props and characters, or editing techniques.[20] As is implied in the term *Stimmung*, music has a special role in accounting for the resonances between the material environment and our felt bodies. Music is highly suggestive of movement—it can be slow, fast, soaring, retreating, pausing, and so forth—producing a correlation of the impression of movement projected by the music and the affectively charged sensations in our bodies (548). These resonances, moreover, need not remain on a noncognitive level since the bodily sensations caused by the music (or other artworks) may not only prompt movement physiologically but also help enforce cognitive biases such as the tendency to imagine certain types of movement (550), i.e., dynamogenesis.

Carroll here no longer defends a strong internalist position, where moods are exclusively defined on the basis of internal bodily and mental processes, and he concludes that artworks can both arouse mood states and express these (553). Artists, moreover, use their medium to exaggerate the characteristics of a mood state, i.e., in film noir this is achieved by means of lighting techniques, rain-soaked streets, cheap bars, and hazy alleys (537). In this fashion, the "artists express mood states by clarifying them, notably by projecting their constitutive parts, especially their cognitive biases, componentially" (553).

Carroll thus opens up the idea that the environmental stimuli can themselves be expressive of moods. The artist is able to produce mood or atmosphere by arranging the artwork to express the cognitive biases that pertain to various mood states (one is more likely to focus on the uplifting elements in the environment when in a good mood). Artworks therefore do not just evoke internal, personal mood states; they can also *express* moods, where this expression does not necessarily involve arousing the expressed mood (553). Mood in art is thus more than a filter onto the cognitive-representational content of assembled narrative data; it preconfigures our corporeal-visceral relation to the worlds of artworks and erects cognitive biases that guide our evaluation of these. In his rejection of classic cognitivism to appreciate the affective nature of artworks, Carroll gestures toward a relational conception of moods that approximates recent developments in the cognitive sciences on affective and emotional scaffolding as well as current tendencies within atmosphere research.

2.4. Notes on a Filmic Theory of Atmospheres

The filmic theory of atmosphere outlined in this chapter differs from cognitive theories of mood in a series of fundamental ways. For a start it relies on a methodological pluralism, which means that it does not privilege affective neurosciences and cognitive psychology above other disciplines. Affective neuroscience and cognitive psychology certainly contribute to our understanding of (cinematic) atmospheres, but—as evidenced by the interdisciplinarity of atmosphere research—the same goes for a lot of other disciplines. The concept of atmosphere should thus lead us toward a more holistic mode of analyzing films, where the narrative meaning is not just a cognitive representation of the filmic text but pertains to our corporeal-affective investments into the rhythms, temporalities, movements and movement suggestions, and overall affective arrangement of the film as we enact its diegesis. This requires us to go beyond the affect–cognition dichotomy that, as we have seen, underlines the cognitivist separation of the narrative content (cognitive processing) from atmospheric filtering (affective processing). Filmic atmospheres therefore disclose or unveil the diegesis rather than color it with a particular emotion or mood as textual approaches assume. Finally, atmospheres are less to be understood on the basis of what is believed to be the already-specified narrative content; instead, the narrative content should itself be understood on the basis of its atmospheric qualities. As Robert Spadoni (2014a) observes, "if atmosphere cannot be separated from any other aspect of a 'film,' and if these aspects are not merely 'colored' by atmosphere but directly take part in its creation, then we need to rethink atmosphere's relation to the filmic whole" (154). Because atmospheres and moods catalyze affective states without matters of representation necessarily being involved (Gumbrecht 2012, 5), our grasp of them are pre-reflective, intuitive, and spontaneous and occur before the intervention of analytical dissection, before we identify its details or understand them intellectually (Pallasmaa 2014, 232).

The aim of this chapter has been to present the notion of atmosphere as an alternative, affective-environmental model of cinematic perception. When we enter an unfamiliar room, we immediately sense its affective charge. In a similar manner, cinematic perception involves an intuitive and immediate perception of the atmospheric charge; it simply relates to our bodily state in an environment.

Therefore, the primary objects of perception are not forms, shapes, edges, or (narrative, visual, or mood) cues that coalesce into a spatial whole (as Merleau-Ponty argued from the perspective of Gestalt theory). Even more immediate in perception are atmospheres that provide the background that make it possible for the intellect to even distinguish objects, forms, and colors in the first place (Böhme 1993, 125). Atmospheres precede the very notion of form let alone that of content.

Once moods are liberated both methodologically and epistemologically from its confinement to the human body-brain, new venues for exploring the regulation and modulation of affective states become available. One of the advantages of going beyond the cognitive-internalist understanding of moods is that it opens up a plurality of new ways of understanding our affective lives scientifically. Colombetti (2017b) has recently argued that "our environment inscribes its cultural norms into our moods, leading us to acquire culture-specific ways of feeling and behaving that can be regarded as part of our habitus, or set of incorporated social practices" (1443). Consequently, cinema is far from confined to the representation of already given moods; it is the producers of new moods, perceptions, and experiences. The concept of atmosphere is vital for understanding how our affective states depend on the nature of the environment with which we interact and how we orchestrate our environment to regulate, reproduce, or create new forms of affect.

In the era of textualism, we have been led to believe that we are outside the filmic world looking in upon it, when we are in fact the locus, or place, in which a "text" can be actualized through the movements of our mind-bodies, and thus the film shapes us as much as we shape it. The atmospheres and narrative scenarios of a film transform reciprocally because they are not truly ontologically distinct. The idea of atmosphere helps us conceptualize cinema's affective mode of communication through the imprints its discursive practices leave on our embodied beings. Atmospheres are so basic to cinema that they often recede into the background, giving us the illusion that they merely accompany the narrative events. In this context it becomes interesting to examine different narrative strategies for the employment of atmospheres. We thus conclude this chapter with a few remarks on the narrative role of atmosphere in Alice Rohrwacher's modern magical (neo)realist fable *Happy as Lazzaro* (*Lazzaro felice*, 2018).

2.5. Atmospheric Transcendence in *Happy as Lazzaro* (2018)

This chapter has been devoted to the primacy of the atmospheric in filmic perception and in the formation of the diegesis-as-environment. Among the main arguments raised is that atmospheres are not filters on top of prespecified narrative worlds (i.e., the diegesis-as-text); they emanate from the conditions of the narrative. Another central claim that we can take from the discussion of atmosphere in this chapter is that although we spur an atmosphere on our felt bodies, we are not one with it. Therefore, we are able to place ourselves above atmospheres by examining them analytically; reflect upon their constituent parts; raise a criticism of their aesthetic, political, or commercial use; judge them according to aesthetic categories (e.g., deem them cheesy, kitschy, or pastiche); and condemn their use on an ethical level (e.g., the atmospheres of superiority in which Adolf Hitler and Nazism are portrayed in Leni Riefenstahl's 1935 propaganda film, *Triumph des Willens* [*Triumph of the Will*]). Yet, we are never entirely outside of atmospheres; they form us as much as we form them.

From this it follows that atmospheres are both *immanent* and *transcendent*. In the following, I will focus on how the immanent and transcendent facets of the atmospheric can be employed to transform the rhetoric function of the diegesis-as-environment, thereby changing a realistic story into a phantasmagoric allegory. The atmospheres that pervade the diegesis-as-environment in *Happy as Lazzaro* emanate from the conditions a group of sharecroppers are living under in a deserted village in rural Italy called Inviolata ("Unspoiled"). The film opens with a medieval ritual that sets the feudal and pastoral atmosphere of the first half of the film. As dusk has fallen upon the village a young suitor accompanied by a choir of bagpipes is singing beneath the window of his chosen one. This ritualistic courting practice along with the women's headscarves, the workers' worn-out, one-size-fits-all clothing, the primitive and sparse living situation, where several families live under one roof, the sound of howling wolves, and the use of tools such as the sling bow all unify to conjure up the pastoral and prehistoric atmosphere of the film. Yet, the historical setting of the film is upset by a few modern utensils such as the single light bulb shared between the sharecroppers, a 1970s car, and 1990s Euro pop played on a Sony Walkman, all indicators that Inviolata exists in a temporal bubble, its own Umwelt, with little intrusion from the outside.

In collaboration with set designer Emita Frigato, Rohrwacher carefully ensures that the feudal clothing, the deserted mountainous location, the spartan and technology-deprived decoration of living spaces, as well as the small rituals around which everyday life in Inviolata are organized mark the seclusion of the place from modern, urban life. This atmospheric seclusion from modernity is accentuated by the Super 16 cinematography by Hélène Louvart with its rounded corners and grainy sepia undertones. The archival, nostalgic feel of this cinematography is thus inextricably linked to the feudal conditions that the sharecroppers are working under. Understanding life in Inviolata has as much to do with recognizing the atmospheres immanent in the materiality and practices through which this world is unveiled.

It is worth noticing that the environmental diegesis is not divided between those elements that emanate from the elements before the camera (e.g., acting performances, scenography, and the set, costume, and prop design) and those pertaining to recording (e.g., lighting and sound recording techniques, camera work, or the film stock on which the film was shot) or postproduction (e.g., color grading, editing, and background music). All elements, "diegetic" and "nondiegetic" in the textual terms, unify in the atmosphere of the film. There is no Inviolata existing beyond or before the atmosphere that radiates from it and the characters inhabiting this space.

Enter the twist: after the temporal envelope in which the villagers live is revealed to be the orchestration of Marchesa Alfonsina De Luna (Nicoletta Braschi)—the workers have been held in the belief that the long-abolished practice of sharecropping is still legal—the main character, Lazzaro (Adriano Tardiolo), a young, saucer-eyed boy of uncertain parentage, awakens (or resurrects?) decades after what must have been a deadly fall. Lazzaro (who's biblical namesake was restored to life by Jesus Christ) awakens to an entirely new setting. The people of Inviolata, having been freed after Marchesa's ploy was revealed, now live under no improved conditions in the urban wasteland. Lazzaro, on the other hand, completely transcends the environmental circumstances of the film. After Lazzaro reawakens he decides to walk to "the city" to reconnect with his Inviolata family. We see him walking as the seasons change, himself remaining completely unaffected by the environmental transformations. As Rohrwacher (2019) points out, Lazzaro never changes; the world changes around him.

Happy as Lazzaro produces its atmospheres to neither represent nor simulate the emotional states of its main character. Contrarily, the atmospheres are immanent to the world of the film. It is the non-transformation of Lazzaro to the environmental conditions that becomes the dramaturgical revolving point of the film. Through this non-change, the world of the film, its environmental diegesis, morphs from a realistic story into a magical, supernatural, and/or religious allegory. This has profound poetic effects, as in a scene when Lazzaro and his Inviolata family are drawn to a church by the majestic sounds of an organ. As the company is told to leave the holy place of the church, the music (i.e., the atmosphere) abandons its source (the organ, the church) and frees itself from time and space to accompany the villagers instead. The film's atmosphere thus transcends its material immanence. This marks the film's innovative narrative employment of atmosphere to convey its political theme, namely, that the conditions of the poorest remain *historically constant* even in the light of continuous proclaimed economic, political, and social progress. As Rohrwacher (2019) cynically remarks, "Nothing changes for the people at the bottom of the world, never." Thus, the filmic atmospheres do not represent, express, or simulate the emotional condition of Lazzaro; it is exactly in his magical-realist *indifference* to the changing environmental conditions that he emerges as a transcendent political allegory of the transhistorical oppression of the indigent. Lazzaro's constant, internal light-hearted mood despite changes in environmental factors, however, also demonstrates the limits of an anthropology that believes moods are internal, personal, or private belonging solely to the human organism with its "perpetual organs," bereft of the forces that come from without.

3

Narrative Experientiality and Affect

In Walter Ruttmann's experimental documentary, *Berlin, die Sinfonie der Großstadt* (*Berlin: Symphony of a Metropolis*, 1927), the hypnotizing rattling of a slow train approaching the city, the calm waves of the sea, empty street alleys, inanimate mannequins in window displays, machines of mass production, and crowds of workers ascending from the underground all unify into one visual rhythm. Although the film displays a series of events on a day in Berlin *anno* 1927, these events are neither forced into the schematics of a plot nor suggestive of a causal-linear propositional "text." Metz (1990) therefore describes the film as a purely thematic, non-story-telling film (206).

Yet, as a way of capturing urban industrialization, the film accentuates vital components that this chapter aims to reorient film narratology around, namely, experientiality, rhythmicity, and affect. Unfortunately, integrating the rhythmic-affective resonances of the embodied spectator and the film as essential for the emergence of the diegesis-as-environment proves a complicated affair. Part of the problem is that classical textual narratology freezes movement in order to study the narrative structures. Thus, both affective (as related to resonant movements of coupled bodies) and rhythmic (as related to patterned movement over time) movements remain outside of the core textual signification.

Another problem relates to the recent "turn to affect" in the humanities, where affect is theorized as autonomous and thus as operating independently of cognition, signification, and meaning. The separation of the intellect from the passion is entrenched in Western thinking and complicates the integration of affective experience into narrative film theory. Yet, cinema—having evolved as part "attraction," part "narration," to become the art form of the "narrative spectacle" par excellence—has always challenged such clear-cut divisions.

Berlin organizes its diegesis-as-environment through a visual rhythmicity that must be felt rather than grasped intellectually (Mitry 1997, 131); it becomes meaningful through our experience of its rhythms and affects rather than the temporal ordering of events. It thus mobilizes the cinematic medium to enact a *Lebensgefühl* (literally "feeling of life") connected to the affective flows and rhythms of urban living during the Weimar Republic.[1] Not exactly anti-narrative, the film organizes its world as an *environment* rather than a causal-linear sequence of interconnected events to study the urban individual as co-conditioned by the rhythms and affect modulations of the city visualized as a super-organism.

Enacting the Worlds of Cinema. Steffen Hven, Oxford University Press. © Oxford University Press 2022.
DOI: 10.1093/oso/9780197555101.003.0004

Rather than represent urban modern life, the film re-enacts it on the theatrical screen and thereby creates and defines it. An essential work within the "city symphony" genre, *Berlin* actively contributed to the creation, framing, specification, regulation, and determination of the *affective experience* of modern, metropolitan living *anno* 1927 and beyond.

Béla Balázs (1953) asserted that the visual music of the montage in *Berlin* plays out in a sphere that is parallel to its content (133). This chapter, however, argues that the film's affective elements, its rhythms and visual music, do not run parallel to its content but unavoidably shape and form this. It is the purpose here to overcome the presumed unbridgeable opposition between the narrative-representational and experiential-affective dimensions that Balázs, like so many others, readily ascribes to filmic works.

There is a tradition in narratology of separating the sphere of the affective from the pure cognitive layer of propositional content. However, the increased focus on issues of embodiment in the cognitive sciences; the interdisciplinary investigation into the philosophical, social, aesthetic, and ethical significance of atmospheres; and the rise of "affect theory" in the humanities are all signs that an affective intervention in narratology is long overdue.[2] As this chapter will evidence, such an intervention is, however, impeded by two challenges.

The first, narratological challenge, involves the structural-linguistic and cognitive-formalist frameworks according to which our cognitive and affective reception of the narrative are separated. The second, affect-theoretical challenge, concerns the conceptualization of affect as autonomous from matters of representation, cognition, signification, meaning, *and* narration. This chapter aims to overcome the dichotomy of narrative/cognition versus experience/affect and to underline their nonreductional unity in the diegesis-as-environment.

3.1. Narratology, Representation, Experientiality, Affect

The narratological distinction of cognition and affect relates to the double structuring of time that separates the "discursive present" from the "narrated past." This procedure isolates the narrated "contents" from the cognitive-epistemic, sensorial, rhythmic, and affective operations involved in narrative experience. Narratives thus rest upon a discrepancy between two temporal orders: the discursive present of narrative experience and the represented past of narrative signification. Seymour Chatman (1992) argues that this "double time structuring"—where the time sequence of plot events ("story-time") plays out in a different time from that of the presentation of those events ("discourse-time")—is a fundamental trait of narrative and that these two temporal orders are independent (122).

The events of *Berlin* neither are structured to "recount" a story nor invite for causal-linear reorganization, another defining trait of narrative representation. However, the film does *enact* its diegesis-as-environment, and this, I maintain, is a prerequisite of cinematic narration. It would thus be more precise to categorize the film as "proto-narrative" rather than "anti-narrative" or "counter-narrative."

The film therefore evidences another general trait of narrative worlds, namely, that they must be enacted by the embodied spectator to become actualized. For a film's narrative architecture to come "alive" as a narrated world it must be coupled with a cognitively *and* affectively equipped spectator. From the perspective of a film's actualization as world a second double temporal articulation can be formulated. Here the narrative architecture and its material-affective organization as well as the artistic instauration all occur prior to the filmic experience and thus belong to the past. The *enactment* of this architecture, where the predesigned filmic material morphs into an atmospheric and narrative world, occurs in the experiential present. It is the presence of this enactment that causes the feeling of "being there," a feeling that fades once the film is perceived from the retrospective position of analytical comprehension.

Cognitive film narratology's theoretical outset is in the retrospective analysis, where all the puzzles of the narrative can be accumulated and organized into a more or less coherent series of narrative events. Since this retrospective position is temporally removed from the experiential fact, it is assumed that affective and emotional responses are of no noteworthy theoretical import. Important instead becomes reassembling the cognitive path that led to narrative comprehension by tracing how the ideal spectator would have likely carried out a series of cognitive operations based on the "cues" (roughly meaning "stimuli") of the film text to organize the film's material into a coherent narrative. Although the spectator's cognitive engagement with the text may or may not trigger affective or emotional responses, this is not considered important since it is assumed that the basic establishment of the narrative text, of the film's literal, denotative meanings, occurs independently from or in "parallel" to the emotional reactions that our cognitive engagement with the narrative text might cause (cf. Chapter 2).

In *Poetics of Cinema* (2008), Bordwell advances such a cognitive-textual model of narrative comprehension, where instead of treating the narrative as a message to be decoded, he takes it to be a representation that offers the occasion for inferential elaboration (9). Since the primary work of establishing the narrative text is carried out by the spectator's cognitive faculty—categorizing, drawing on prior knowledge, making informal, provisional inferences, and hypothesizing about what will happen next (137)—Bordwell argues that setting the issue of filmic emotions aside, when explaining narrative comprehension, can be a useful methodological idealization. This is because, Bordwell asserts, we are able in principle to understand a film without discernibly having an emotional reaction to it (155). Anticipating potential criticisms of his methodological reductionism, Bordwell assures his readers that his model is in compliance with research on the intricate nature of cognition and emotion while acknowledging that our time-bound process of building the story is shot through with emotion (101).

It would be a mistake to reject Bordwell's cognitive poetics due to its lack of interest in the question of emotion and affect in film. Several cognitive scholars have evidenced that Bordwell's theory of film narration can complement work on emotions, character engagement, moods, and affect.[3] Two aspects of Bordwell's understanding of emotion, however, need to be addressed. First, Bordwell understands emotions in the tradition of "cognitive appraisal theory,"[4] according to which human emotions are the results of "a complex cognitive appraisal of the significance of events for one's well-being (Lazarus 1982, 1019). The important implication of this view is that the relation of emotion and cognition is posited in the causal-linear direction of cognition → emotion.

Consequently, emotions do not play a significant role for Bordwell because he assumes their relevance as having to do with how we react or respond to films, and although emotion is part of how we comprehend and understand films, it is not primary to establishing their most basic, literal components. The influence of cognitive appraisal theory is evidenced by Bordwell's brief account of the three functions of emotion in cinema. The first function is exactly that of appraisal such that "acts of appropriation are shot through with emotion" (51). The second relates to "affect programs," according to which nature has primed our species "to engage in encounters with others by making us sensitive to the slightest signs of their emotional states" (52). Finally, Bordwell refers to Greg M. Smith's idea of emotion as the affective coloration of the filmic content or plot. Here "emotion and comprehension mesh" (52), yet in such a way that we possess an "emotional intelligence" that functions as an extra vehicle for evaluating (appraising) the cognitive content. The assumption that runs through Bordwell's take on emotions is that there exists a basic layer of textual/narrative meaning that remains unaffected by corporeal affects and emotional appraisal and coloration.[5]

The problem here is thus not a lack of *interaction* between bodily arousal, emotion, and cognition but the very proposition of the actual existence of an anatomical segregation of affect, emotion, and cognition into various subsystems of the brain to ensure their segmented operations (cf. Colombetti 2007). This view has been challenged and contested in light of growing evidence of affective processes permeating appraisals. Yet, affect, emotion, and cognition are a lot more integrated on the level of neurobiology. It has been argued that in light of neuroscientific evidence, we need to shift from an *interactive* to an *integrative* framework given that "parceling the brain into cognitive and affective regions is inherently problematic, and ultimately untenable" (Pessoa 2008, 148). Such an integrative framework would need to incorporate affective processes as constituent rather than complementary to basic cognitive operations. And this, in turn, would force us to revise, redefine, or reject most standard definitions of cognitions. It is exactly this challenge that enactivism has taken upon itself in its redefinition of cognition, at its most fundamental level, as a form of sense-making enacted by the situated organism in its act of bringing forth a world of significance, valence, and meaning. Cognition then no longer resides within a system or organism; it emerges in time out of the many relations that make up the system. Giovanna Colombetti (2014) has examined how the enactive thesis can help overcome some of the issues with standard cognitive theories of appraisal as cognitively determined and suggested an alternative, enactive model of appraisal rooted in bodily aspects of emotion (83).

Despite these developments in the cognitive sciences, film narratology has relied on the interactive separation of cognition and affect to develop a science of stories that is indebted to a form of textual analysis exemplary of Ryle's "intellectualist doctrine." On the one hand, this has resulted in a series of ground-breaking cognitive explorations into emotions as steered by the representational and narrative textual base (ie., characters, situations, events, and plots). Despite the formidable analytical skills these authors exhibit, we are, at times, left with a noticeable domestication of emotions into the rational fold of the mind. What this means is that emotions are often subsumed within a cognitive framework and regarded as a structured complement to cognitive processes (G. M. Smith 1999, 103) or considered a part of the human system of reason (M. Smith 1995, 59). We are thus confronted with a new variant of the head–body dualism, where the smart, evaluative aspect of emotion is governed by the cognitive brain and affects are evolutionarily primed programs—blind excitations and reflexes—exercising no evaluative function (cf. Colombetti 2014, 98). Contrary to this cognitive domestication of emotion, I maintain that narrative "understanding" depends on the corporeal-affective spurring of atmospheres. If the filmic diegesis is reinterpreted as environment, we would no longer be able to bypass our emotional and affective sensibilities in the formation and comprehension of the diegesis. Narratives are thus no longer primarily defined according to their discursive textual base (i.e., plot) but according to how they are experienced.

In her groundbreaking "natural" narratology, Monika Fludernik (2010) contends that the experiential dimension, and not the plot, defines narrativity. Consequently, there can be "narratives without plot, but there cannot be any narratives without a human (anthropomorphic) experiencer of some sort at some narrative level" (9).[6] Although Fludernik addresses the experiencer *in* and not *of* a narrative, her research points to the insights to be gained from a heightened sensibility to narrative experientiality. Following the lead of Fludernik, yet unwilling to perceive experientiality as the only defining characteristic of narrative, David Herman (2009) offers a broad postclassical definition of narrative consisting of four "basic elements." Accordingly, narrative is (1) a mode of representation that (2) focuses on a structured time-course of events (3) to introduce some sort of disruption or disequilibrium into a storyworld (4) and to represent its events so as to also convey the experience of living in the story-world-in-flux. In brief, narratives are made up of situatedness, event sequencing, worldmaking/world disruption, and conveying the experience of how it is to live in its world (9).

Once experientiality is considered a defining—even if not *the* defining—trait of narrative, a reinterpretation of cinema's unique material-affective communicational modality must be carried out given that a central ingredient of narrative experience undeniably pertains to our corporeal-affective involvement. In most extant narrative theories, however, affect and emotion are assumed to enter the equation only "after the fact" (i.e., after the establishment of the core "text") as forms of reactions to stimuli that must be cognitively structured to become meaningful (cf. Colombetti 88). Affect—not yet captured into the rational fold of the cognitive mind—thus remains outside of meaning, representation, signification, and narration. This way of thinking about the relation of affect to cognition and emotion (as cognitively structured feeling states) paved the way for thinking about the "autonomy of affect" (Massumi 1995) as the unclaimed territory that cannot be colonized by the intellectualist doctrine. Affect thus emerges as a field of resistance.

Affect in the technical definition given to the term by contemporary "affect theory" thus ventures into the poststructuralist domain of the "unrepresentable" along with notions of the film's "third meaning" (Barthes 1977b) or "cinematic excess" (Thompson 1977). The following traces this line of thinking about the affective outside of cinematic signification or sociolinguistic fixation. Two reservations about this approach will be advanced. First, by opposing affect to linguistic-cognitive models of signification, affect theory actually ends up confirming these, if only to position itself as their antidote. Second, affect theory thus eliminates the opportunity to revise radically what cognition, representation, meaning, and signification entail. Ultimately, despite the increased attention given to affect in cinema studies, it has yet to present a viable challenge to the disembodied model of cinematic communication.

3.2. Affect Theory, Third Meaning, and Cinematic Excess

Bearing in mind that there is no single, generalizable theory of affect, the following refers to the vector of affect theory in the tradition of Brian Massumi's important essay "The Autonomy of Affect" (1995).[7] Emblematic of this essay, and the many subsequent theories of affect that followed it, is a concern for the nonrepresentational, non-propositional, noncognitive, nonconscious, transpersonal, and non-discursive operation of affect. It draws upon a philosophical tradition (including Spinoza, Nietzsche, Bergson, Whitehead, Simondon, Deleuze, and Guattari) that has constituted a challenge to the "intellectualist doctrine" of modern science. Shielded from any form of intellectualism, twenty-first century cultural studies have been preoccupied with the "irreducibly bodily and autonomic nature of affect" (Massumi 2002, 28). Affect is here conceived as a bodily force that circumvents the meaning-making processes and inferential elaboration of the conscious subject and thus prefigures it.

The notion of the "body" thus takes a central place in affect theory. However, it is neither the cognitivist nor the phenomenological body we deal with. Instead, it is a body that is first and foremost identified through its relations and couplings. The capacity of a body is thus not to be defined according to that body alone; it is always aided, abetted, and dovetailed in the field or context of its force relations (Gregg and Seigworth 2010a, 3). Affect theory, in this regard, supplements contemporary positions within the cognitive sciences regarding the "situated" and "embedded" nature of emotion and affect (e.g., Griffiths and Scarantino 2009; Colombetti 2017b). It also demonstrates shared viewpoints with a particular anti-Cartesian thread of affective neuroscience associated with the work of Antonio Damasio (1995, 1999, 2003), who equally draws inspirations from Spinoza's theory of affect.[8]

Unlike affective neuroscience, however, Gregg and Seigworth (2010a) clarify that affect theory is preoccupied with the *singular* rather than the abstract, pre-defined, or a priori body. Of interest is thus not the generic figuring of "the body" (understood as *any body*) that we find in the natural sciences but the individual, material body in its ongoing affectual configuration of a world (4). Consequently, affect theory operates with a broader conception of affect that is not restricted to the (human) organism. The body of affect theory is therefore also not the felt or lived body (*Leib*) of phenomenology. Affect is instead broadly construed to concern intensities that pass between bodies (human, non-human, part-body, etc.) that stick like glue to both persons and worlds. At its most anthropomorphic affect pertains to visceral forces that operate beneath, alongside, or aside from conscious knowing, insisting beyond cognitively structured emotions. Affect drives us toward movement, and by extension thought, but it can also suspend us (make us neutral) or even overwhelm us by the world's apparent intractability. Affect thus designates a body's ongoing immersion in the world's obstinacies and rhythms, its refusals, as well as its invitations (1).

The notion of affect that can be found in this literature is useful for drawing out the affective component related to the diegesis-as-environment as distributed between spectator and film. The sincere tone and sedated rhythmicity of *Vitalina Varela* (directed by Costa 2019), for instance, are grounded in the affective suspensions, obstinacies, and refusals (e.g., of narrative structuring, character identification, or entertainment) that pertain to this world. The film's distribution of affect thus creates a unique restrained bond between spectator and film. In this fashion, cinematic affects have less to do with the bodily perturbations that accompany mental states in cognition (cf. Plantinga 2014) than with the "baseline attunement" of spectator and film (cf. Sinnerbrink 2012). In this fashion, affect becomes an important concept for overcoming the internalism of the cognitive sciences. Just as cognition is no longer believed to be skull-bound but extends into or encompasses the environment (cf. Clark and Chalmers 1998; Sterelny 2010), affect is defined as the baseline attunement that attaches bodies to each other. There are thus possible lines of agreement between affect theory and the manner in which contemporary emotion researchers working within the domain of the cognitive sciences have argued that affect must be understood beyond the limits of the individual organism and taken to define instead the coupling of various bodies (Colombetti 2017a; Krueger and Szanto 2016). If we are to understand how cinema "transforms a two-dimensional wash of light into a three-dimensional world" (Branigan 1992, 33), then surely, we cannot limit our inquiries to a cognitive-conceptual comprehension of that world. Thus, whereas affect was systematically excluded by textual narratology, it becomes central for comprehending the atmospheric diegesis-as-environment. Yet, a genuine reflection of cinematic affect should not be found in how it stands in opposition to narrative, meaning, or cognition but how the genuine integration of affect forces us to rethink the basic semiotics of cinema.

In his pioneering study of affect, *Parables for the Virtual* (2002), Brian Massumi maintains that affect necessarily remains "outside expectation and adaptation, as disconnected from meaningful sequencing, from narration, as it is from vital function" (25). Consequently, Massumi not only favors a sharp differentiation between affect and narration; he also separates affect from emotion, arguing that they follow different "logics and pertain to different orders" (27). Each attempt to capture, describe, personalize, or narrativize affect is doomed to failure. The inability to capture affect as conceptual knowledge, a personal psychological state, or a linguistic description is what not only distinguishes the affective from the emotional, but also ontologically divides it from it:

An emotion is a subjective content, the sociolinguistic fixing of the quality of an experience which is from that point onward defined as personal. Emotion is qualified intensity, the conventional, consensual point of insertion of intensity into semantically and semiotically formed progressions, into narrativizable action-reaction circuits, into function and meaning. It is intensity owned and recognized. It is crucial to theorize the difference between affect and emotion. If some have the impression that affect has waned, it is because affect is unqualified. As such, it is not ownable or recognizable and is thus resistant to critique. (28)

Following Massumi, affect is attractive for a political philosophy because it defies the oppressive powers of sociolinguistic fixing and semiotic labeling. For him, affect constitutes an autonomous domain that modulates emotion and cognition, while remaining itself independent of the sociolinguistic demand for meaning. Affect is never actually present; it exists as a virtual field of potentialities that remains beyond analytical reach. In film studies, we find a similar desire to delineate affect as an autonomous domain that escapes any incorporation into the "intellectualist doctrine" of knowledge. In his influential study of the cinematic body, Steven Shaviro (1993) foregrounds "visceral, affective responses to film, *in sharp contrast* to most critics' exclusive concern with issues of form, meaning, and ideology" (vii, my emphasis).

Eugenie Brinkema (2014) has observed that affect theory in this fashion is continuing the legacy of 1970s semiotics interested in those aspects of the text that escape structural-linguistic signification, what Barthes, respectively, referred to as the "third meaning" (1977) and *punctum* (1981) and what neoformalism calls "cinematic excess" (Thompson 1977). As Brinkema rightly points out, all these share a common concern with the too-much dimensions of films that remain irreducible to coded narrative structures (42). To both contextualize and problematize the current "turn to affect," it is useful to trace out its kinship with poststructural and neoformalist precursors, who were equally interested in theorizing the outside of the text.

3.2.2. Third Meaning and Affect Theory

There is an affinity between contemporary affect theory and the "third meaning" observed by the late Barthes (1977) in the film image. Following Barthes, the third meaning is available to the critic via meticulous examination and, not unlike affect theory, exists as a byproduct of the material past of the mechanically produced cinematographic still photography. Barthes demonstrates that this third meaning falls outside of the semiotic model (whose validity is presupposed). The third meaning thus exists apart from the communication/information level (denotation) and the symbolic/signification level (connotation). It is thus neither "informative" nor "symbolic." Just as Barthes contrasts the third meaning to a Saussurean semiotics, Massumi (1995) opposes the autonomous affective register to "signification as a conventional system of distinctive difference" (85). Affect is thus "autonomous" from a conspicuously disembodied semiotics.

Just as Barthes (1977) detects a level in the image, where "meaning is frustrated" (57), Massumi envisions affect as an autonomous domain unbound by signification, meaning, and cognition. As a theoretical construct, the third meaning relies upon a sharp distinction between signifier and the signified, and form and content, yet more than anything else, it expresses the limitations of these heuristic distinctions. Similarly, Massumi carves out a subpersonal, nonconscious, and prelinguistic affective register that resists becoming textual.

Both Barthes and Massumi want to give expression to something that extends outside of culture, knowledge, and information, instead opening out into the infinity of language (Barthes 1977, 61) or, in Massumi's case, to an outside of the social and cultural order beyond sociolinguistic signification. For Massumi, affect is autonomous because it escapes confinement in the particular body, whose vitality or potential for action it is. The capture or closure of affect thus pertains to formed, qualified, situated perceptions, emotions, and cognitions (35).

Both Barthes and Massumi install an opposition between meaning, which is driven by cognition, linguistic fixation, and cultural significance, on the one hand, and, on the other hand, a domain of affect related to intense corporeal sensations that operate autonomously from meaning, because "the skin is faster than the word" (Massumi 2002, 25). In both cases, the thesis of dual processing discussed in the previous chapter in relation to Greg M. Smith's mood cue approach is tacitly assumed. In other words, both assume affect and cognition to operate autonomously or in parallel to each other. What Barthes argued about the third meaning could thus apply to Massumi's autonomous theory of affect as well, namely, that it acts as a "signifier without a signified" (Barthes 1977, 61).

Now, how are we to study affect or third meaning if it escapes sociolinguistic fixation? Barthes approaches this paradox by introducing a method of inquiry that isolates his object of study, the moving image, from its "natural habitat." According to this textual model—related to the classical scientific goal of "objectivism"—Barthes maintains that the third meaning "cannot be grasped in the film 'in situation,' 'in movement,' 'in its natural state,' but only in that major artefact, the still" (64). In creating a "laboratory" for the study of cinematic imagery, Barthes does not study *moving* images but film *stills*. Only in their frozen, photographic form can the third meaning of the images be captured. For Barthes, it is here at the epitome of a counter-narrative (63) that the genuinely "filmic" emerges (64). In complete accordance with the diegesis-as-text, matters of experientiality and affect must be frozen—deprived of their movements and rhythms—to gain meaning within the textual model of signification.

The third meaning can thus only be detected in the image once it has been removed from its actual *experiential* cinematic setting. This modus operandi resembles that of classical science in its search behind initial appearances (e.g., the film experience) for a hidden, more authentic reality (the third meaning/

affect) that exists in itself beyond discourse, sociolinguistic fixation, or cultural and subjective appropriation (cf. Morin 2007, 6).

Here the establishment of a nonrepresentational dimension is achieved in retrospect, or, in analytical detachment from the film's experiential modus. While the concept of the third meaning has heightened our sensitivity to cinematic aspects beyond their signification value, it has also contributed to the gap problematized by Vivian Sobchack (2004) existing between "our actual experience of the cinema and the theory that we academic film scholars construct to explain it—or perhaps, more aptly, to explain it away" (53).

In *Camera Lucida* (1981), Barthes advances the concept of the third meaning further by introducing the distinction between the *studium* and the *punctum* of a photograph. The studium corresponds to the obvious meaning of photographs as related to their symbolic meaning. Punctum, on the other hand, corresponds to the third meaning because it disturbs meaning. When describing the punctum, Barthes singles out its affective force, its ability to attract our interest and attention and to prolong perception. In a state of grief following the loss of his mother, Barthes develops the concept of punctum in an introspective study of the ability of the photographic image to arouse affective states such as love, grief, sadness, interest, and excitement that resist linguistic determination. The punctum thus "rises from the scene, shoots out of it like an arrow, and pierces me" (26).

The third meaning and the autonomous theory of affect both inevitably face the same paradox. This paradox, often spelled out in the literature on semiology, contends that if Barthes successfully convinces us of the presence of the punctum in otherwise insignificant details, then the details are no longer of the punctum but socially communicable signs, i.e., the studium (Allen 2003, 127; cf. Attridge 1997, 81–83). Does this paradox not apply to Massumi's notion of the autonomy of affect, too? To demonstrate the social implications and the instrumentalization of affect by right wing populism (Massumi's theory of affect is after all an ethical and political theory) and then to counter the ideological misuses of affect, a degree of sociolinguistic fixation of this concept is required and indeed carried out by Massumi. Barthes was aware of this paradox yet yields from its consequences. In his study of punctum in the "Winter Garden Photography," he writes,

> It exists only for me. For you, it would be nothing but an indifferent picture [...] it cannot in any way constitute the visible object of a science; it cannot establish an objectivity, in the positive sense of the term; at most it would interest your *studium*: period, clothes, photogeny; but in it for you, no wound. (73)

Massumi (2002) arrives at a similar impasse when arguing that affect remains "unqualified" and "resistant to critique." For him, affects are "bodily reactions occurring in the brain but outside consciousness" (29).

Yet, more pressing than this modernist problem of "representing the unrepresentable" is the postulation of affect and cognition as pertaining to different ontological registers (25). In accentuating the discontinuity of affect and meaning, poststructuralist semiotics and affect theory eventually reach the same cul-de-sac. Both perspectives carve out their outer limit in reference to linguistic theories of signification, yet neither problematizes the legitimacy of the disembodied assumptions that such a system of signification implies. Instead of evidencing the systematic exclusion of affect in the "intellectualist doctrine," both ultimately reinforce it. In neither case is the affective instance taken to be a demand for new modes of semiosis that would be able to integrate the affective into an account that challenges the cognitivist, disembodied, and dualistic nature of thought.

Instead, both appear to be satisfied with carving out a conceptual plane that cannot be captured within the framework of a disembodied semiotics. Thereby both poststructuralism and affect theory help sustain the disembodied model of signification, whose limitations they at the same time reveal. This is why affect theory has been accused of not even coming close to resolving the theoretical problems it claimed to confront (Brinkema 2014, xiv).[9] The notion of affect could thus suffer the same destiny as the "third meaning" in film theory, which was integrated into a neoformalist framework under the moniker of "cinematic excess." By examining the reintegration of the "third meaning" into a cognitive-formalist framework, it shall be argued that a concept of affect must be elaborated that not simply stands in opposition to the rules of the text but fundamentally change how the game is played.

3.2.3. Cinematic Excess and Affect

In her neoformalist film theory Kristin Thompson (1977) turns to Barthes's notion of the "third meaning" to capture those components of a film that cannot be inscribed into the meaningful organization of the film. For Thompson it is thus misleading to speak of a third *meaning* insofar as what is actually captured is an *elsewhere of meaning* (55). Exactly to underline the autonomy of "third meaning" from processes of signification, Thompson favors the term "excess" as elaborated in the work of Stephen Heath (1975). Consequently, Thompson (1977) understands cinematic excess as "those aspects of the work that are usually ignored because they don't fit into a tight analysis" (56). In basic neoformalist terms, cinematic signification arises from the combination of different structures into the formation of a coherent narrative. Outside of these meaningful structures lie those aspects of the work that are not contained by its unifying forces, i.e., its *excess* (54).

As Thompson explains, films create structures out of their images and sounds, yet they can never make all their physical elements part of their set of smooth perceptual cues (54). In film viewing practices, cinematic excess is often overlooked or ignored, and it becomes the task of the critic to "break up old perceptions of the work and to point to its little more difficult aspects" (57). Neoformalist analysis helps bring forth the work's ability to defamiliarize by attending to those aspects of a film that exist beyond or beneath narrative signification. Consequently, excess is not only counternarrative; it is also counter-unity (57).

Thompson's idea of a layer of material excess in film that resists incorporation into the narrative system of signification parallels Massumi's notion of affect as a residue of "irreducible excess" operating autonomously from the organism's meaning-making activities. Thompson's notion of excess, however, relies on the tacit identification of cinematic signification with narrative motivation. Thompson thus employs a restrictive use of what constitutes "meaning" to elements of narrative relevance or to self-referential artistic significance that exists for its own sake. Moreover, Thompson appears to equate "narrative" as such with "unifying narrative principles" (i.e., causal linearity, clear motivations, goal-oriented characters, coherency of events, etc.). However, despite the historical dominance of principles of unity in (classical) film narration, such principles are not essential to narration.

What concerns us here, however, is how Thompson fits the notion of cinematic excess into the textual distinction between "form" and "content." In her discussion of Sergej M. Eisenstein's Ivan the Terrible (Иван Грозный, 1944 (Part I) / 1958 (Part II)) from which Barthes also derives his examples of the "third meaning," Thompson argues, "Ivan must be an impressive character, but his impressiveness could be created in many ways. The actual choices are relatively arbitrary: a pointed head, a musical theme, close-ups with a crowd in deep focus, and so on" (58, my emphasis). All the singular affective components are deemed arbitrary to the production of the signified: Ivan's impressiveness. However, the film does not contain an abstract story level, where Ivan's character exists as "impressive" beneath or beyond stylistic features. His specific impressiveness is unveiled through these stylistic features. How we choose to characterize a thing has an effect on how we see the world, feel, speak, and act (Branigan 2006, 99).

For Thompson (1977) excess becomes detectable once we look beyond narrative (62), while narrative at the same time relies on the minimization of excess. Thompson thus believes that the rhythms created by hesitations or intensifications become foreign to the narrative if they persist longer than their motivations "allow for." By contrast this chapter wishes to demonstrate that the cinematic diegesis is not reducible to the film's propositional events; it arises out of the affective orchestration of rhythms of hesitation and intensification. For Thompson to determine what in a film "served its purpose," however, she resorts to a detached, analytical, and interpretative viewpoint that dismembers the *how* from the *what* of the narrative. This analytical detachment echoes Barthes's grounding of the third meaning in the cinematic still photography and Massumi's (2002) conception of affect as existing outside expectation and adaptation, as disconnected from meaningful sequencing, from narration, as it is from vital function (25).

Excess, third meaning, and affect, however, can only be said to escape narrative if the latter is conceived in an exclusively representational and analytically detached manner. From an experiential perspective, we must insist that excess, third meaning, and affect are regarded as vital components of narrative signification qua their experiential factor. Rather than attempting to capture excess and third meaning in the retrospective setting of textual analysis, these can be perceived as the experiential foundation without which the narrative cannot exist as a representational construct. Affect would then constitute our immediate, prereflective, atmospheric sensations out of which narrative meaning emerges and the ground for the unveiling of objects, things, or situations, determining but also determined by the particular rhetorical context (Branigan 2006, 272n.26).

Yet, instead of leading us out of the cul-de-sac faced by poststructuralists, who explored the limitations of a Saussurean semiotics, the postulation of the autonomy of affect transports us back to the last respirations of a disembodied theory of signification, reinstating it in order to repudiate it. By posing affect as radically separated from forms of meaning, consciousness, social meaning, narration, signification, and language, we deprive affect the possibility of fundamentally reworking how we think about these issues. Consequently, Ruth Leys (2011b) has argued that affect theory succumbs to "a false dichotomy between mind and body because they equate the mind with consciousness and therefore treat everything that can't be attributed to mental processes, defined in this way, to the behavior of the body" (801). Although this book owes a lot to affect theory, it refuses to designate affect as a domain that lies outside of narrative, meaning, and signification. Quite to the contrary, I will argue that we need to place affect at the very heart of cinematic signification.

3.3. Affect, Cognition, Signification

As a sphere of research sheltered from "signification" and "meaning," the "turn to affect" risks becoming entirely negative. Struggling with providing positive value to the concept of affect as other than the mere turning to a forgotten domain, the concept of affect has not become useless or meaningless, yet as Brinkema (2014) observes, "the effect of repeatedly intoning a polemic for force is the deforcing and deflating of that very concept" (xiii). Indeed, affect theory can be

criticized for having relied too heavily on "non-definitions" in their character-
ization of affect as *non*-narrative, *non*-meaning, *non*-cognition, *non*-represen-
tation, *non*-semiotic, *non*-signification, etc. Affect is often placed in opposition
to an impoverished notion of form as inert, passive, and inactive and posited as
the emblem of what is dynamic and unstable. It has meandered in the reprise
of descriptive terms such as speed, violence, agitation, pressures, forces, intensities, etc. (xiii). In a lucid play with Deleuze's *Difference and Repetition* (1968),
Brinkema bemoans how Deleuzian affect theorists offer more repetitions than
differences. She raises an important point, when she contends that affect cannot
lay claim to a place, where what is immediate, automatic, and resistant takes
place outside of language. Affect theory has not obliterated problems of form
and representation; it does not mark the moment where reading is no longer
needed (xiv).

According to Brinkema, divorcing affect from formalist "close readings" may
simply postpone the moment, where the turning toward affect becomes as no-
table for its critical revelations as for the novelty that was brought about its mere
turning toward (xiv). In extension of Brinkema's criticism, I contend that the notion of affect could benefit from a framework that insists on its nonrepresentational nature, without, however, disconnecting it entirely from formalist and
representational concerns. The potential of affect for the study of cinema lies not
in its blank opposition to narrative or representation, but in its capacity to re-
cast how they are presently understood. Therefore, instead of focusing on its autonomy, this chapter explores how "[a]ffect constitutes a nonlinear complexity
out of which the narration of conscious states such as emotion are subtracted"
(Clough 2007, 2). Rather than postulate a discontinuity of affect and cognition,
we need to account for their continuity in a nonreductive fashion.

3.3.1. Affect versus Cognition: The Media- Anthropological Intervention

A major thesis advanced by affect theory concerns the relation of embodied
beings and (media) technologies. Moreover, affect is not constrained to the
human body but theorized in relation to technologies that both enable new perceptual forms of "seeing" affect and new affective bodily capacities that go beyond the individual's organic-physiological embodied constraints (Clough 2007,
2). Affect theory has been vital in bringing to light our nonconscious and pre-
reflective couplings to media technologies, yet I argue that we need to replace
its *non-anthropological* with a *media-anthropological* notion of affect (Hansen
2004b; Voss 2010; Voss and Engell 2015a). We will elaborate more specifically on
the difference between the two later. In brief, whereas the former insists on the

non-subjective and non-personal force of affect, the latter understands mediated affects as products of human-embodied entanglements with media-technological bodies. From this it follows that narratives are affectively constituted—themselves situated between film and spectator—and thus cannot be meaningfully opposed to matters of affect.

Rather than being excessive to narrative, affect is actually the grain out of which narratives emerge. I ground this claim on two assumptions. First, against the autonomy of affect, I argue that affect is inextricably linked to emotion and cognition, yet that their interrelation is not causal-linear but nonlinear, complex, and dynamic. In addition, complex cognitive processes are the product of feedback processes, and while the exact role of affect can be difficult to specify, affect, emotion, and cognition are neither anatomically nor ontologically separated.[10] Second, because affect, cognition, and emotion are situated, embodied, and embedded, consciousness cannot be restricted to an a priori biological concept of the "anthropological." Instead, the "anthropological" itself emerges from an ongoing "technogenesis," i.e., the anthropological coevolution with technics (Stiegler 1998).[11]

Massumi's non-subjective and non-anthropological philosophy of affect is founded upon the work of Deleuze and Guattari. In *What Is Philosophy?* (1994), Deleuze and Guattari maintain that art transcends the individual subject and its personal affections, perceptions, and feelings:

> Percepts are no longer perceptions; they are independent of a state of those who experience them. Affects are no longer feelings or affections; they go beyond the strength of those who undergo them. Sensations, percepts, and affects are beings whose validity lies in themselves and exceeds any lived. They could be said to exist in the absence of man because man, as he is caught in stone, on the canvas, or by words, is himself a compound of percepts and affects. The work of art is a being of sensation and nothing else: it exists in itself. (164)

Art is thus a medium for creating "pure sensations" beyond mere human feelings; affect beyond personal affections, feelings, or emotions; and "pure percepts" beyond embodied perception. For Deleuze, the cinematic affection-image is affective not because it is located *in a body*, but because it abstracts bodily features such as facial expressions from their spatiotemporal coordinates (98). Thereby, the affection-image tears the image away from its spatiotemporal context to call forth instead the pure affect as the expressed (98).

Within the scope of his media-philosophy, Mark B. N. Hansen delivers a criticism of Deleuze's non-anthropological appropriation of affect. Like Deleuze, Hansen foregrounds affect, yet the main task of *New Philosophy for New Media*

(2004b) is a rehabilitation of Bergson's embodied conception of affection (133). Following Hansen, Deleuze reduces affection to a formal process of technical framing, which results in a disembodiment of affect that locates it outside the subject in the world of technically assembled images. In Deleuze's affect philosophy, which Hansen argues differs sharply from Bergson's philosophy of affect, the body becomes a passive site of technical inscription rather than an active source of framing, modulating, organizing, and shaping otherwise formless information into a world of significance (cf. Lenoir 2004, xx). Ultimately, Deleuze presents a disembodied version of Bergson's philosophy of affect, and in doing so he fails to acknowledge that concepts such as medium and mediation already imply the operation of a living organism, an embodied being (cf. Hansen 2006, 300).

3.3.2. Affect versus Cognition: The Embodied Intervention

A different, yet related, criticism of affect theory has been raised by the historian of science Ruth Leys (2011a, 2011b). Her criticism is primarily directed at the work of Massumi and the establishment of a liaison between affect theory and the work of affective psychologists Silvan S. Tomkins and Paul Ekman, who presented the thesis of "basic emotions."[12] The idea of basic, innate emotions, which do not involve cognitions or beliefs about the objects in our world, appears to represent exactly the type of biological reductionism against which the humanities in the heyday of deconstruction and poststructuralism were revolting. Within the "basic emotion paradigm" the body is treated as an autonomous and nonintentional system that shapes higher conscious processes yet itself remains biologically hardwired and automatic, and consequently resistant to cultural and cognitive stimuli.

According to Leys (2011a), the paradigm of basic emotions is attractive to affect theory because both posit a radical disjunction of affect from the "nonsignifying, nonconscious 'intensity' disconnected from the subjective, signifying, functional-meaning axis to which the more familiar categories of emotion belong" (441; Massumi 2002, 28). What Leys questions is not the endeavor to formulate a theory of affect as the continuous flow of "becoming"—of fluctuations, transformations, or modulations—that defies determination, form, or structure. Her criticism is directed at the formulation of this theory upon an allegiance to what she regards to be a reductionist biological paradigm. Generally, Leys agrees with affect theory in criticizing the computational, cognitivist, and disembodied picture of mind that long dominated the cognitive sciences. However, she warns against the strategy employed by affect theory of embracing "a highly abstract and disembodied picture of mind or reason in order to repudiate it" (459n.43).

Leys exemplifies this by showing how the concept of "representation" is employed in affect theory. In a first instance, representation is invoked to reject cognitivist-computational theories according to which the mind relates to the world via mental representations. Such a criticism of the computational-cognitive paradigm is now widespread and has been rehearsed frequently within "embodied cognition," which faults the mental representation theory for assuming a sharp separation between the cognizing, representing mind and the objects it cognizes (459n43). Leys detects a tendency in theories of affect, however, to deflate the technical notion of representation as mental representation found in the cognitive sciences, with the "nontechnical" use of the term referring loosely to everything that relates to signification, meaning, beliefs, ideas, etc. Because affect theory repeatedly conflates these two meanings of "representation," it oscillates between a legitimate criticism of the "representational theory of mind" and a more general, inherently problematic, refutation of signification, cognition, and belief altogether (458–59n43). Unlike the argument rehearsed by "embodied cognition"—that cognition is not "mind-stuff" but extends into the body and the environment (e.g., Gallagher 2005; Gallagher and Zahavi 2012; Varela, Thompson, and Rosch 1992)—affect theory relies upon the assumption that everything that is not meaning in the rationalist and cognitivist sense of the word belongs to the body proper (cf. Leys 2011a, 458).

Quite contrary to the ontological separation stipulated in affect theory between affect and cognition/emotion in reference to the disputed basic emotion paradigm, the ontological divide of affect and cognition is currently questioned by contemporary (affective and cognitive) neuroscience. In a "neurobiological analysis" that tellingly bears the title "Affect Is a Form of Cognition (2007)," Seth Duncan and Lisa Feldman Barrett argue that any thought or action is more or less affectively infused, meaning that no ontological distinction between affective and non-affective behaviors, or between "hot" and "cold" cognitions, can be postulated (1202).

It is worth noticing that similar arguments can be found within affect theory. Gregg and Seigworth (2010a), for instance, note that "affect and cognition are never fully separable —if for no other reason than thought is itself a body, embodied" (3). However, the challenge is not to say that the mind is embodied but to clarify how. We can only hope that affect theory will abandon the path of its poststructuralist precursors and join forces with advanced, non-reductive theories within the cognitive sciences that currently attempt to carve out the continuity of affect and cognition without collapsing their distinction.[13]

The strain of affect theory that challenges us to locate a domain within cinema, culture, the mind, or language outside of meaning must thus be abandoned and replaced by approaches that rethink language, meaning, signification, narrative, culture, intention, etc., on the basis of affect. There is a danger, as Lisa Blackman

(2012) has observed, that affect thereby will simply be psychologized and appropriated as a standard model of the mind. Needed therefore is the development of concepts and theories that "open up the psychological to post-psychological work that allows the complexity of brain–body–world couplings and entanglements to be analysed" (24). Both the concept of the diegesis-as-environment and the interpretation of cinematic perception as atmospheric perception attempt to open narrative theory up toward this line of work on affect.

In both cases the continuum between the nonrepresentational and the representational in cinema is fluid and continuous rather than separated by an ontological chasm. In his reply to Leys (2011a), "affect theorist" William E. Connolly (2011) argues that affect has gained such popularity in cultural and philosophical domains because it offers an alternative to the causal-linear logic typically invoked to explain our meaningful interaction with the world (792). Connolly's reply to Leys evidences the potential of affect theory to reinterpret cognitive and affective processes in complex and nonlinear terms. To describe the interrelation of cognition and affect, Connolly uses the image of stratification, where "each layer of the body/brain system enters into bumpy communications with others through a rapid series of crossings and feedback loops" (794). Thereby, Connolly reserves a differentiation between affect and cognition as pertaining to different functions and expressions, but in a manner that accentuates their continuity rather than discontinuity. Similarly, narrative experientiality is continuous with narrative's representational modalities. In other words, affect or excess in the cinema is not superfluous to representational concerns; rather, cinema's ability to represent is contingent on the affective capacities of the medium.

3.4. Affect, Representation, Events

When we think about narration in cinema, we often think about a series of well-defined events that can be organized into a coherent causal-linear story. In H. Porter Abbott's (2002) minimal definition, narrative is a representation of one or several events (12). In the following, my aim is not exactly to dispute this definition but to rethink its two main conceptual pillars—*representation* and *event*— once affect is brought into the equation.

Let us begin with the notion of the narrative event. One of the ways in which modern narrative theory has drawn inspiration from cognitivism is via the idea that the human "mind-machine" can be segregated into neat autonomous and modular parts. Following this model, perception represents internally the inputs from the external world. On the output side, action controls our responses and behaviors to these inputs. Operating between these two major executives are the organism's cognitive capabilities. According to this view, these three major systems (perception, cognition, action execution) work independently of each other like regional compartments in a global company. Following the cognitive philosopher Susan Hurley (2002, 2008), the executive separation and linear conception of perception, cognition, and action in cognitivism are known as the "classical sandwich model." This model, where perception and action are posed to be separate faculties belonging to distinct cerebral circuits, also guides the cognitive film-theoretical idea that we "pick up" the narrative event (perception input) and organize its place within the narrative context (cognition) that elicits emotional or affective responses (action output) (cf. Hven 2017a, 117–18, 121–28; Gallese and Guerra 2020, 12). Thus, in the major work of cognitive film narratology, Bordwell's *Narration in Fiction Film* (1985), the narrative event is construed as the product of the spectator's cognitive-inferential engagement with the cinematic text. Here the film presents cues, patterns, and gaps that shape the viewer's application of schemata and the testing of hypotheses (33). Matters of affect enter the equation only as a *response* or *reaction* to the cognitive establishment of the narrative "facts."

Yet rather than being purely rational and analytical constructs, story structures, as cognitive narratologist Patrick Colm Hogan (2012) has argued, are fundamentally shaped and oriented by our emotion systems (1). Consequently, the narrative event cannot be conceptualized as a non-emotional, cognitive "mental representation" intrinsic to the film in the form of "cues" picked up by spectators. Our isolation of something as an event and our attribution of a cause to that event are both crucially a function of emotional response, even if other systems are necessarily involved as well (16). Narratives might therefore not contain "events" in the manner presumed by cognitive film theory, which often operates with a mundane definition of events as "actions (acts) or happenings" or "changes of state" (cf. Chatman 1978, 44).

In a similar fashion, the way the notion of representation is used in narratology equally disregards affect. Bordwell (2008) writes, "Considered as a *thing*, a certain sort of representation, a story seems intuitively different from a syllogism, a database, and an fMRI scan" (2, emphasis in original). Considering the narrative as a "thing," however, implies its objective existence. This assumes that the narrative can be captured in what philosopher Daniel D. Hutto (2000) has termed the "object-based schema," which implies the existence of spatiotemporal locatable entities. Filmic narratives are not of this kind, because they are objects of experience, and "experience cannot be understood in terms of the object-based schema" (110). Experiences are not spatiotemporal objects or things existing independently of the perceptual act, but meaningful interactions between the subject and the environment. Is the narrative event a representation or an experience? So far, narratologists have almost univocally defined narrative in representational terms.[14] Yet, to understand narrative, it is not enough to pose a series of spatiotemporal objects, characters, or events that make up the narrative representation; we have to understand *how* these emanate in the narrative experience. The difficulty with narrative lies in its double nature as both representational and nonrepresentational. Narratives involve experiences *about* experiences.

However, if we agree that narratives, to some extent, involve representations, we must first qualify what we mean and do not mean with the word "representation." In their seminal work on enactivism, Varela et al. (1992) differentiate between a "weak" and a "strong" use of the term "representation," similar to the distinction Leys (2011a) criticizes theories of affect for failing to make. In the weak sense, a representation is that which can be said to "stand for" something else. Cinematic narratives are representational in this "pragmatic" sense of the word, where our organism's sensibility to light and sound make these physical properties "stand for" or "implicate" a much larger multisensorial world. This is the sense in which Souriau (1951) uses the word "representation," when introducing the concept of the diegesis. Yet, representation can also be used in a "stronger" form, as when "we generalize on the basis of the weaker idea to construct a full-fledged theory of how perception, language, or cognition in general must work" (135). A strong sense of representation is committed to the "representational theory of mind." According to Varela et al. (1992) this classical cognitive stance is committed to a two-fold ontological and epistemological premise. First, the world is assumed to be pregiven; i.e., it is assumed that the features of the world can be specified prior to the cognitive enterprise. In order to account for the relation between the world and the cognitive agent, cognitivism assumes the existence of internal mental representations in the mind or brain of the cognitive agent (e.g., in the form of images, symbols, or subsymbolic patterns distributed across networks). Ultimately, the representational theory of mind assumes the existence of a pregiven world that the cognitive agent learns about and acts in on the basis of a mental representation of its features (135).[15] Even if this description does not do justice to the complexity of cognitive representation, it serves to render visible a governing assumption of cognitivism, namely, that mental representation is essential a recovering or reconstruction of extrinsic, independent environmental features (136).

Transposed onto fictional worlds, this means that the theory of mental representation presupposes the existence of a pregiven world that the spectator must reconstruct, recover, and inferentially elaborate via a process of schema application, hypothesis testing, and inferential elaboration. The mental representation of the storyworld, which is assumed to be intrinsic to the film and recovered on the basis of "cues," thereby exists as a mental representation in the viewer's mind, and this representation in turn becomes the progenitor of our emotional and affective responses. That narratives are essentially cognitive constructs or mental representations is a widespread hypothesis in cognitive narratology. In her intro-duction to "narrative," Marie-Laure Ryan (2017) makes explicit the link between the textual approach and the theory of mental representation. She writes, "If a narrative is a text that brings a story to mind, a story, conversely, is a mental rep-resentation formed in response to the clues provided by a text" (518). Within the cognitive sciences, the computational model of mental representation (cf. Fodor 1983) has been widely disputed. However, certain researchers have advocated for a revised use of the notion of mental representation—crucial to the field—such that it is based in action rather than abstract symbol manipulation, thus making it compatible with the demands of dynamic, embodied, situated, and enactive paradigms of cognition (e.g., M. L. Anderson and Rosenberg 2008; Pezzulo 2011; Ellis and Tucker 2000). In film studies, Gallese and Guerra (2020) have presented an action-based approach to mental representations based upon the theory of "embodied simulation" (cf. Gallese 2005).

"Mental representations," in this body of works, are neither to be understood as abstract, syntactic, platform-neutral processes of symbol manipulation nor used to uphold a view of the mind as having epistemic access to the world only through its mental representation such that our most basic way of knowing about the world is indirect and inferential. Such a view is, however, widespread in narrative theories that hold the true seat of the story to be in the "mind of the recipient." From this perspective, "Narration only means something when it communicates with its public. It only truly exists in the mind of the viewer for it is in their mind that communication occurs" (Carmona 2017, 10).

In his enactive approach to literary narratives, Marco Caracciolo (2014a) formulates an experiential literary narratology that cannot be reduced to mental representations (10). Avoided is a narrow focus on stories as representational artifacts that prevents scholars from doing justice to narrative's experiential di-mension (31). Narrativity should be recognized both as a site of *representation* (of events, characters, etc.) and of *experience* (related to those undergone by both characters and recipients). Although the recipient's engagement involves representations at some level, the experience evoked thereby cannot be reduced to or equated with these representations. Additionally, a text or film cannot *rep-resent* the consciousness and experiences of its characters. What it maximally can represent is an *event* in which a person undergoes an experience (30). Experience therefore cannot be understood on a pure cognitive-analytical level but must involve an affective dimension that relates to our embodied-enactive engage-ment with the filmic environment that, combined with our "experiential back-ground," constitutes the ground out of which cognitive narrative representations emerge.[16] Consequently, even if narrative comprehension involves some sort of mental representation, narrative experience cannot be understood in represen-tational, object-based terms (49).

In cinema, neither the term "representation" nor "event" should be reduced to a cognitive construct. Rather, both are inextricably bound up in networks of meaning-making activities (related to the organization of the filmic material in terms of narrative, rhythm, atmosphere, or style, as these shape and are shaped by the spectator's sensorimotor, perceptive, affective, and cognitive operations) that constitute the filmic environment as determined by the organism's embodied capacities of sensemaking.

3.5. Narrative Affect, Embodiment, and Media-Anthropology

Thus far we have mainly approached the question of affect as related to the embodied human organism. To an unprecedented degree, however, the cognitive sciences are increasingly beginning to understand human thinking as coupled with or extended into the world of our technologies (e.g., Clark and Chalmers 1998; Clark 2000; Sterelny 2010; Menary 2010). Such work complements the long tradition in the philosophy of technology of examining the relation between man, the technical, and the "world." In the work of philosophers such as Ernst Kapp, Martin Heidegger, Gilbert Simondon, Hans Blumenberg, Helmuth Plessner, Bruno Latour, and Bernard Stiegler, we find a related strive to surmount the antithesis of the technical and the natural. Blumenberg has encapsulated the paradoxical dissymmetry between our self-conception and the technologically mediated environments we inhabit. He argues that if it is true that we today live in a world dominated by science and technology with mental capacities that are prescientific and pre-technological, then this is not least due to the fact that we have never stepped outside the antithesis of nature and technology [*Technik*] (Blumenberg in Scholz, 125).

An important contemporary media-theoretical task lies in the clarification of how processes of sensemaking not only extend *into* but also emerge *from* our techno-mediated environments. As Mark B. N. Hansen (2006) observes, media theory marks the unique chance to displace definitively the empirical-transcendental divide that has structured Western meditation on thinking, including the thinking of technics (298). In providing the infrastructure for thought, media have the ability to condition, prefigure, expand, restrict, augment, and modify both cognitive and affective experience (298).

The emergent discipline of German media-anthropology undertakes the examination of the anthropological as situated in and constituted by various media environments. Of central importance is no longer the decontextualized understanding of the "human" *in abstracto*, but to study how human forms of existence emerge from heterogenic modalities of (media-)environmental regulation (cf. Voss and Engell 2015b, 9). Affect thus becomes central for the media-anthropological conceptualization of man–media couplings. In opposition to the non-anthropological conception of affect in the tradition of Deleuze, media-anthropology understands affect as the glue that brings together the organic and the technical; the sensorimotor, emotional, and cognitive; and the atmospheric and the semiotic.

At its most basic, cinema is thus formed on affective operations that rhythmically continue to entangle the embodied spectator with the cinematic material (cf. Voss 2014a, 64). Thus, what makes the diegesis more than a mosaic of sounds and images exerting various viewpoints and leaping in space and time is the rhythmic flow of movements that not only ties the images together into a temporal gestalt but also weaves us into the world of the film, giving us the impression of "being there." However, such a theory requires an anti-dualistic theory of affect that does not dichotomize "rational cognitions" and "irreducible bodily affects." This is why it is important to stress that affect cannot be the mere placeholder of what escapes signification, language, and representation. Affect modulations are no longer exclusively to be conceived of as blind stimuli and autonomous bodily arousals. It is not reserved to what remains intangible, undetermined, or inarticulable. Mediated forms of affect evidence that these can be granted epistemic content and functions and thereby be considered part of thinking (cf. Voss 2014, 79).

Both the *Leihkörper* and the diegesis-as-environment are attempts to formulate a post-textual theory of film designed to explore cinematic narrativity in both experiential and affective terms. If the affective is to find a place in a narrative theory of cinema, we must stop opposing it to cognitive-analytical and textual-linguistic models of signification. Instead, we must invent new concepts that can replace, refine, or supplement textual models of cinematic signification—e.g., the diegesis-as-text, "mood-cues," or the diegetic/nondiegetic distinction—and theoretically address cinema's nonrepresentational, nonverbal, and affective modes of communication. Since the affective designates the ongoing rhythmic entanglement of the embodied being and its (mediated) environment, the nature of the rhythms that define our ecological beings becomes of central importance. With this in mind, let us consider the dual role of affect and rhythmicity in *Berlin* as constitutive of both the film's "anthropomedial relation" and its narrative representation of experientiality.

3.6. Affect, Experience, and Rhythm in *Berlin, die Sinfonie der Großstadt*

In *Berlin, die Sinfonie der Großstadt*, the pulsating rhythms of the montage, the music, and the diversely paced activities displayed on screen are not subordinated to an overarching plot but conjoin instead to convey an expression of life in the modern metropolis. Made in collaboration with the composer Edmund Meisel, *Berlin* is dramaturgically orchestrated as a symphony, whose montage, as Balázs (2011) has pointed out, is not causal but associative; events are linked not through logical sequencing but psychology (178).

For Balázs, the film does not provide a representation of an external reality, but an internal one. I will argue that it more precisely enacts a media environment: neither an objective nor a subjective reality. The film presents a mediated expression of the *experience* of a metropolis. Less a narratively organized presentation of events, the film is what Fludernik (2010) believes to be the quintessential definition of narrative, a representation of "experientiality." Regarded as an expressionist projection outward of the internal landscapes of the soul of the modern urbanite *anno* 1927, as Balázs does (178), *Berlin* is the cinematic kin to Georg Simmel's 1903 essay *Die Großstädte und das Geistesleben* (*The Metropolis and Mental Life*). Experiential in nature, its enactment of the psychological foundation upon which the metropolitan individual is erected (Simmel, 11) succeeds not by means of a plot but by affective rhythms, expressive camera angles and movements, and the musicality of the film, which amount to a "narrative," not of the journey of a heroic individual, but of the mass movements of urbanity.

While *Berlin* is almost bereft of emotional markers (i.e., cognitively "labeled" affects), it is a highly affective film. Although the affective quality of the film is expressed by a variety of modalities, the film's most prominent affective modality is rhythmicity. Rhythmicity here is not just related to musicality but to the way the film creates *affective resonances* between a multiplicity of bodies (between the movements of the masses and technical aggregates, between organic biological rhythms and musical rhythms, between the movement of transport vehicles and the camera, etc.). More than anything the film is a technological intervention into the patterned movements and affective rhythms that characterize modern, industrial city life (e.g., morning/evening; work time/leisure time, activity/rest) by means of the affordances of the cinematic medium. The result is a diegesis that is organized not around a train of events but as "optical music" (Balázs 1953) according to a five-act structure that follows the assorted tempos of the city during the respective phases of the day from sunrise to sunset. Irreducible to a narrative "text base," the film's diegesis expresses the experience of metropolitan life as conditioned by the rhythms of modern industrialization.

The film thus unites the biological, circadian rhythm—related to the affective changes in physical activity, metabolism, hormone production, cell activity, organ function, and body temperature and their rise and fall over, roughly, a 24-hour period—with the technical rhythms not only depicted in the images of city life but also expressed by the cinematic apparatus and its technical devices. One essay in particular, *Vom Wesen des Rhythmus* (*The Nature of Rhythm*, 1923) by

Ludwig Klages, has been particularly formative for how avant-garde filmmakers thought about rhythm and affect in the 1920s.[17] Inspired by the opposition between movement and time as proposed by Henri Bergson, and by the different rhythms of rural and urban living as described by Georg Simmel, Klages proposes a major opposition between "organic" and "machinic" rhythms (in his vocabulary *Rhythmus* and *Takt*). In brief, Klages associates *Rhythmus* with "organic" or "primal" rhythms (biological processes, tides, waves, etc.), whereas *Takt* is observed in the staccato measures of clocks and metronomes that impose upon the individual the rational, ordering, segmenting, and organizing activity of the intellect (Cowan 2007, 231). In Bergsonian terms, *Rhythmus* is to be associated with *durée*, while *Takt* represents the artificial division of time into discrete segments as associated with movement.

Modernity was intellectually preoccupied with providing the critical assessment and antagonization of these two archetypes of rhythm. Simultaneously, cinema—a medium for attaching, expanding, restricting, and otherwise structuring embodied perception via a technical apparatus—operates by cutting across this division (Bergson famously condemned cinema to movement, denying its ability to evoke *durée*). In the antithesis of the technical and anthropological posed by modernist thinking on rhythm, Fritz Lang's *Metropolis* (1927) presented "a forum for mediating between technological and organic rhythms" (Cowan 2007, 236). *Berlin*, on the other hand, "suggests a vision of filmic montage as a particularly apt medium for capturing an experience of modernity as the overcoming of natural rhythms" (227).

Michael Cowan thus perceives *Berlin* as a critical commentary (in the spirit of Klages and Simmel) on the negative influence the accelerated temporalities, rhythms, and affects have on modern urbanite individuals (and their mental health). In this fashion, the rhythmicity of *Berlin* "is gesturing toward a much broader perception of the disjuncture between organic and technological rhythms in the modern world" (230). In his monograph on Ruttmann, Cowan (2014) shifts attention to the filmmaker as a creator of what he, in an elaboration of Deleuze's image-taxonomy, terms "management images." Cowan is here less concerned with the "messages" conveyed in Ruttmann's films (e.g., as commentaries on debates concerning "organic" and "technical" rhythms) than with their actual, operational, epistemological, and ontologizing effects as management images.

This is important because it adds a new dimension to the inclusion of experientiality, rhythm, and affect as core constituents of cinematic semiosis. The management image is something other than a critical *commentary* on modern times and is itself a *practical* contribution to the affective-rhythmic regulation of the masses in the era of mass communication. We thus shift perspective from the representational-communicational to the media environmental.

As Cowan (2014) reminds us, Ruttmann, whose films were most often commissioned works, practiced experimental aesthetics "as an applicable art, one that could be used in product commercials, cultural publicity pictures, social and hygiene films, city advertisements, industrial films and wartime propaganda" (20). Although his films are nowadays mostly associated with a specific avant-garde aesthetic, Cowan aligns Ruttmann to a kind of filmmaking invested in regulating the masses of modern, industrial societies through rhythmic affects. The cinema of Ruttmann is, therefore, not just a *representation* of urban life; it is itself becomes "a tool for managing mass culture" and for regulating "perception, attention and audience reactions" (54). Consequently, as Cowan (2007) observes elsewhere, the "excitement about 'rhythm' in the 1920s cannot be explained by aesthetic concerns alone" (227). It is widely recognized that narrative cinema has ethical complications in regard to how, what, and who it *represents*; the ethical complications of its affective regulations, its atmosphere production, and rhythmicity remain in dire need of theoretical explication.

For Cowan (2014), perceiving Ruttmann as a creator of management images captures a continuity in the filmmaker's work in advertisements, avant-garde experiments, and fascist propaganda. Thus, if Ruttmann's films after 1933 are now widely understood as "fascist," the reason, Cowan suggests, is not that they applied experimental film to social and political tasks but because they used the medium of the cinema as an instrument of governance according to precepts that created management images for a fascist conception of the masses (174). Management images thus exploit the affective and persuasive powers of cinema not as an artistic medium but as a "tool" that is less concerned with narrative representation than environmental enaction. Since Ruttmann from the beginning had been fascinated with the regulation of perception and bodies in mass society (175), his is a political oeuvre par excellence. In bringing affect and rhythm to the forefront of cinema, Ruttmann explored how moving images could be *instrumentalized* whether for purposes of marketing, aesthetics, or political propaganda. *Berlin* renders explicit what is true of cinema more generally, namely, that it feeds on affective resonances between "organic" and "technical" rhythms, and that some of the medium's most subversive, persuasive, exhilarating, attractive, disgusting, repulsive, appealing, and dangerous powers lie exactly in how filmmakers exploit these resonances.

4

The Moving Camera and the Motor-Affective Arrangement of Films

In the celebrated "bear attack scene" of Alejandro González Iñárritu's *The Revenant* (2015), the director of photography, Emmanuel "Chivo" Lubezki, employs a long and complex camera movement that makes the camera almost dance around the action, at points moving so close to the bear that the damp of its warm breath is fogging the lens to create authenticity by exploiting our habituation to recording technologies. The camera follows the actions with minute precision, yet its movements suggest an element of surprise and of reacting to the events, which lends a sense of immediacy to the mediated environment. Accentuated by its dim naturalistic lighting, the film's narrative of survival in a hostile, natural environment is enacted on the basis of an embodied experience of moving through a continuous virtual space, where the moving camera creates the kinetic dynamics of the scene. Without concealing its mediation, the scene generates a feeling of directly perceiving the diegesis as if we were "looking through *a clean window*" (Lubezki 2016, my emphasis).

According to Iñárritu (2016), the camera movement serves to plunge the viewers into the world of the film: "Chivo and I rehearsed how we were going to film the scene over and over, with the idea that you're being submerged in this experience. You are there. You are being attacked" (25–26). Lubezki (2016) further adds that the goal was to achieve "a strong, visceral, immersive and naturalistic experience—not just to follow the journey of the central character, but to make it feel as if it was actually happening in front of their eyes."

The scene is but one example of how advanced camera movements have been employed to generate the feeling of entering the world of the film, of merging with it, and transforming it into our immediate felt environment (cf. Gunning 2020, 266). Despite, or possibly even because of this, camera movements have constituted one of the most fundamental challenges to the textual-narratological maxim that in order "to study movement one must interrupt it."[1] Discourse- and language-oriented theories of cinema have tended to marginalize the camera movement as constitutive of the cinematic diegesis in favor of montage, partly due to the latter's deceptive comparability to the linguistic lexicon of language, syntax, and grammar.[2] Daniel Morgan (2016) has argued that the camera movement has fallen victim to our tendency to think about the cinema in textual terms

Enacting the Worlds of Cinema. Steffen Hven, Oxford University Press. © Oxford University Press 2022.
DOI: 10.1093/oso/9780197555101.003.0005

as consisting of basic analyzable units corresponding to static shots, fixed frames, and still images (224). He identifies another problem as stemming from the paradoxical epistemological relation of the camera movement to the filmic diegesis, that is, to how the camera movement at once can be said to exist and not exist in the world of the film (223). On the one hand, the camera movement draws us into the diegesis by creating the illusion that it resides within a world that extends all around it, thereby providing the impression of experiencing the diegesis from within (225). At the same time, the camera *creates* the world it gives access to, or, to phrase it in enactive terms, it "lays down the path in walking."[3]

This makes it a great conceptual starting point for studying the dynamic, cinematic exchange of movements between the technical assemblages of sounds and images and the embodied perceptive motor resonances of the spectator that this book argues is essential for the emergence of the cinematic diegesis as a media-generated environment, milieu, or Umwelt.[4] This chapter emphasizes the distribution of movement in the filmic experience to unfold a notion of cinematic "embodiment" that avoids anthropomorphizing cinematic technologies (camera as eye) and techniques (camera movement as surrogate of our own movement) by modeling these upon aspects of human embodiment.

Rather than reduce technologies and techniques to their analog function in human embodiment, we ought to examine how they alter the embodied perceptive act. The "camera-eye" can thus be conceptualized as an anthropomedial relation (an entanglement of the organic and the technological) that, even when it *simulates* ordinary human perception, forms a specific perceptual modality that differs from ordinary embodied perceptual experience. Note in this context that the early alignment of the human eye and the camera centered around the recognition of the camera as affording a new, enhanced mode of vision capable of making us, in the words of László Moholy-Nagy (1967), "see the world with entirely different eyes" (29).[5]

Assuming a relational notion of perception as what brings an organism and an environment together, I hold it to be misleading to ascribe to the "film" or the camera an autonomous form of "perception." Cinema partakes in conditioning the perceptual attunement of its environment to our embodied organisms (e.g., through motor resonances, "movement suggestions,"[6] or kinesthetic empathy *but also* through symbolic and verbal expressive means). Therefore, the argument is not that cinema fundamentally alters the makeup of the organism's perceptual system; rather, it operates environmentally via its technological modifications, arrangements, or transformations of the nature of what there is to be perceived.[7] Our perception of the diegesis can neither be understood exclusively on the basis of our perceptual system nor solely on the affordances of the mediated environment. The handheld camera and the Steadicam, for instance, present two different techniques for modifying, expressing, and unveiling the filmic world. The handheld camera affords kinesthetic resonances related to instability, shakiness, disorientation, stress, urgency, etc., whereas the Steadicam moves in a more graceful, elegant, refined, and stable manner. In both cases, the camera movement points simultaneously to features of our perceptual system and to the cinematic environment.

Cinema depends on a sensing organism to come alive as an animated film, yet this does not restrict it to replicate or simulate anthropomorphic perception. In fact, a part of its attraction is exactly that it affords movements that are unrestricted from bodily restraints. The camera penetrates walls or floors, perceives microorganisms too small for the eye to detect, and can move in complete disregard of gravitation—levitating, descending, accelerating—through the diegesis. In *High Noon* (directed by Zinnemann 1952), for example, the camera elevates to expose the solitude of sheriff Will Kane (Gary Cooper), who has been abandoned by his citizens to protect the city alone. In *Inglourious Basterds* (directed by Tarantino 2009) the camera tracks down below the floors to reveal the Jewish family that desperately hides from the SS soldiers searching their house, and throughout almost the entirety of the 3D-film *Gravity* (Cuarón 2013) it is designed to create a cinematic environment devoid of gravity, whereas *Blue Velvet* (Lynch 1986) exploits the camera's microscopic vision in a camera track that searches below the surface of the small-town American idyl thereby revealing a deeper-lying decay hidden below the perfectly watered lawns of Lumberton, North Carolina.

By advancing an understanding of the cinematic diegesis as formed on kinesthetic resonances, it is argued that our feeling of being submerged into the diegesis requires no cognitive suspension of disbelief (the immersion is not epistemological; we recognize cinema's own mode of existence as distinct from unmediated "reality") but relies on the direct, affective, and sensorimotor nature of our involvement with the mediated environment and its technological affordances.

4.1. Internal and External Theories of Movement Perception

In a lecture given at the University of Chicago in 1948 entitled "The Significance of the Newtonian Synthesis," Alexandre Koyré (1965) presented the provocative thesis that modern science has split our world in two and substituted the world in which we live, love, and die with a world of quantity, of reified geometry, a world in which there is a place for everything but man. The world of science thus becomes utterly estranged from the world of life, which it remains unable to explain, not even to explain away by calling it "subjective" (15).

This dualism is institutionalized within the structure of our academic disciplines. The natural sciences deal with the material world while the social sciences have constructed a world of subjective agencies without recourse to the material world of things (Costall 1995, 468; Malafouris 2013). Modern psychology occupies a problematic position within this field, having to deal with the "subjective" domain with the tools of the natural sciences. Psychology was in a sense conceived in the split between an "inner subjective world" of sense perception, phenomena, and qualities and an "outer" material world of physical matter. And it was destined to explain how we overcome this gap.

Consequently, two themes dominate the history of the theory of cinematic movement perception, both of which are laid out in Hugo Münsterberg's pioneering work, *The Photoplay: A Psychological Study* (1916). Trained by Wilhelm Wundt and recruited to Harvard by William James, Münsterberg anticipates the field of cognitive film psychology by addressing how cinema activates basic "inner" psychological functions such as perception, attention, memory, and emotion (for an overview, see Tan 2018). Münsterberg (1916), the first to study the interface of the material world of the cinema and the mental realities produced by it, ascribed to the camera the ability to arouse complex cognitive, emotional, and affective states nonverbally. Cinema was bestowed with the unique capacity to express feelings and attitudes without the use of words by arousing them in the mind of the spectator through the subtle art of the camera (130).

The Photoplay is driven by Münsterberg's emphatic segregation of the world of the mechanical apparatuses from the purely artistic, inner world of the film (Langdale 2002, 11). Accordingly, Münsterberg holds cinematic techniques to be modulations replicating mental capacities, which give rise to unique inner experiences that bring our mind into peculiar complex states (56–57).

Two trajectories for thinking about cinematic perception followed from Münsterberg's pioneer study of cinematic movement perception. First, Münsterberg explains cinematic techniques by comparing them with mental operations (e.g., the close-up with attention). This "film/mind analogy"[8] contends that cinema *externalizes* "mental" processes. Thus, the film close-up is equivalent to the psychological process of attention to the extent it can be treated as an objectification or externalization of that process. The second idea has been particularly influential within cognitive psychological theories of film, and it concerns the *internalization* of the film as an "inner experience," "internal reality," or "mental construction."[9] As Münsterberg argues, we perceive the movement of a film but as something that does not have an independent character as an outer world process, because it is our minds that build it up from single pictures rapidly succeeding one another (135–36). In relation to cinematic motion perception, the idea is that since cinema contains no real movement but only a series of single images morphed into the unified film, the perceived motion is actually the product of our minds (Baranowski and Hecht 2017, 8). Münsterberg thus poses an *externalization of mental processes* as the structure upon which cinematic techniques have been developed and a *mental internalization* of these techniques in the construction of the film as an artwork that exists in our minds.

4.1.1. The Internalization of Cinematic Movement

Let us begin with the internalist trajectory found in Münsterberg, which is firmly rooted in classical psychology and the proto-cognitivist idea that our minds build movement out of a series of snapshots rapidly following one another. According to this "inferential theory of movement perception,"[10] vision is a series of snapshots that is rendered into a continuous perception by an internal cinematographic projector. For Bordwell (1989), the illusory sensation of self-movement in cinema is caused by the processing of visual cues. This self-movement can then be attached to a character, which might enhance the feeling of subjective movement. In F.W. Murnau's *The Last Man* (*Der letzte Mann*, 1924) the camera simulates the drunkenness of its main character by having the actor wheeled on the same platform as the camera, thereby creating the drunken effect of tilting from side to side, a movement readily associated with the drunkenness of the character. For Bordwell (1989), "Perception is not a passive recording of sensory stimulation; the sensory input is filtered, transformed, filled in, and compared with other inputs to build, inferentially, a consistent, stable world" (18). Important is thus how a film cues the spectator to execute a definable variety of cognitive operations (29), where the primary role of perception is the identification of a three-dimensional world on the basis of such cues (31). In this cognitive-inferential film theory, the film (the object) is modulated, determined, and completed by the spectator (the subject), whose mental capacities the film has been designed to match.

Bordwell's theory of how camera movements invite inferential elaboration is not only indebted to "New Look psychology"[11] but also the physiological optics of Hermann von Helmholtz. Following Helmholtz (2005), the brain bridges the gap between what is given to the visual system (the outer world) and what is actually experienced by the perceiver (the inner world). Thus, "the intent of vision is to see as distinctly as possible various objects or parts of an object in succession" (56). Since visual inputs in this "snapshot theory of vision" are ultimately flawed, a process of inferential elaboration is required. Helmholtz therefore envisioned the unconscious processes performed by the brain to be like inferences. We thus have direct access to the real events at the neuronal level only such that we sense the effect and never the external objects of the world (Helmholtz 1867, 430; for a discussion, see Gallagher and Bower 2014). Consequently, for Helmholtz (2005) perceivers have access to their environment only indirectly, i.e., by the construction of a mental representation of the world based on causal inferences. Our relation to objects, which might appear to possess the qualities of our sensations, belongs, however, only to our nervous system and does not extend at all into the space around us (377).

Today, the Helmholtzian thesis thrives particularly in the neurosciences, where most researchers are ready to endorse the idea that the neural processes underlying perception are inferential and representational (Gallagher and Bower 2014, 240). The cognitive film theory of Bordwell, given that it understands perception, cognition, narration, and camera movement on the basis of a series of audiovisual cues that the spectator construes via more or less conscious inferences, is essentially Helmholtzian. Since Bordwell (1977) installs the intellect—just as Merleau-Ponty (1991b) criticized classical Helmholtzian psychology of doing— as the mediator between world and subject, it follows that a camera movement is not to be felt or experienced but to be *read* perceptually (20). Since spectators are not aware of "reading" the movement, the "reading" must be construed at a preconscious level. Following the cognitive-inferential theory of cinema, sensory stimuli alone cannot determine a percept, which by itself is deemed incomplete and ambiguous. Rather, the organism *constructs* a perceptual judgment on the basis of nonconscious inferences (Bordwell 1985, 31).[12]

This view, however, assumes perception to consist in the synthesis of a series of incomplete "percepts" that are inferred and completed at each instant by the mind. Movement is thus quantified into a series of separate, analyzable entities. Against this comprehension of movement, Bergson (1991) argues that perception is always impregnated with memories (33), and thus always a continuum, never an instant. The film, as Merleau-Ponty (1991b) would claim in his Bergson-inspired lecture on the cinema, is a *temporal* gestalt.

From the perspective of psychology rather than philosophy, the "snapshot" view of vision has most vigorously been criticized by ecological psychologist James J. Gibson (2015), who asserts that we have been led to conceive a cinematic apparatus inside our heads, where pictures are sent from the eye up to the brain. Perception, Gibson maintains, is not a sequence of retinal snapshots joined by what is termed the "persistence of vision" (279–80). For Gibson, too, perception is not a series of static snapshots, but a temporal process.[13] A special sense impression, as Gibson observes, ceases when the sensory excitation ends, yet a perception does not. A perception does not *have* an end; perceiving is processual and ongoing (242). To understand how camera movements co-constitute the narrative it is not sufficient to recount how it invites cognitive-analytical or nonconscious inferential elaboration by stringing together a series of instantaneous cues. We need to account for how the camera movement is experienced, memorized, felt, and directly perceived as a temporal process that reverberates throughout the film and beyond. Thereby, however, we should avoid reducing the aesthetic function of the camera movement to embodied perception and instead understand its manifold roles in structuring and organizing the diegesis in its kinesthetic, affective, temporal, spatial, and cognitive modes of expression.

4.1.2. Cinematic Movement as Externalization of (Embodied) Perception

An alternative to the internalist position on movement perception has been to focus on how cinema externalizes not only the mental processes dealt with by Münsterberg but also subjective states like dreaming or more holistic embodied processes of perception.[14] In relation to the latter, Sobchack (1992) has argued that "in its modalities of having sense and making sense, the cinema quite concretely returns us, as viewers and theorists, to our senses" (13). In one of her early pieces, Sobchack (1982) declares camera movements to be echoes of the "essential motility of our own consciousness as it is embodied in the world" (317). The camera is thus an externalization of our embodied subjectivities, and its replication of the "directedness with which we actively, perspectively, and finitely inhabit the natural space of the world and meaningfully shape it into anthropological space necessarily entails *motion*" (317–18, author's emphasis). As Sobchack (1992) explains, "A film is given to us and taken up by us as perception turned literally inside out and toward us as expression" (12). Elaborating upon Sobchack's position, Jennifer Barker (2009) conceives "the camera movement to be the closest approximation of muscular movement of the human body" (110).

Similar claims can be found in approaches to cinema formulated in reference to cognitive psychology or neuroscience. For Bordwell (1977), we can hardly "resist reading the camera movement effect as a persuasive surrogate for our own movement through an objective world" (23). Drawing upon the thesis of "embodied simulation" (ES) derived from research on the mirror neuron system, to which this chapter returns, Gallese and Guerra (2020) experimentally investigate their claim that the Steadicam is perfecting "the spectator's feeling of being at the center of the story and facilitating the simulation of the interaction with the spatial element of the movie and with its character" (101).

The most influential, and also most radical, articulation of cinema's externalization of perception, however, remains Sobchack's (1992) thesis that the "mechanisms and technological instrumentation of the cinema can be understood as the film's body, functioning as its sensing and sensible being at and in the world" (205). Externalization in the film phenomenology of Sobchack turns perception "inside out" and makes perception itself perceptible. However, we might ask if it is necessary, or potentially misleading, to introduce the notion of the literal "film body" in order to articulate an embodied theory of cinematic spectatorship. Morgan (2016) has contended that the main problem with Sobchack's externalism is that it reduces the aesthetic function of the camera to the expression of *our* embodied mode of being in the world, when camera movements actually rarely function in analog to human motility and vision (230). Jordan Schonig (2017) has pursued a similar criticism of the camera as a surrogate embodied perceiver because it leads to an unnecessary reduction of the aesthetics of the camera movement to instances that approximate our familiar sense of being, moving, and perceiving the world and its movements (27). For all its good intentions of uniting the internal (the spectator's body) with the external (the film's body), granting the film a body of its own risks understanding the external world according to *our* embodied modes of being in the world. The technological mechanisms of the film thus become meaningful only when modeled upon the mechanisms of the embodied spectator.

What was lost in the splitting of the world into the material and the organic is a proper place from which to understand the technological, which neither belongs to the external, material world nor properly to the interior world of the body/mind. Technology cannot be reduced to the human; it is deeply inhuman, and the best-functioning technology has been created in opposition to the traditional image of what is human and living and only rarely as its extension or expansion (Zielinski 2006, 6). Technologies instead afford new modes of perceiving and experiencing. Cinema makes it possible to hear and see *by technical means* that alter the conditions of the human sensorium; there is no cinematic perception without a coupling with an organism's perceptual system. Although this book is undoubtedly indebted to Sobchack's embodied phenomenology, my focus is on the interrelation of the technical and the organic. My position is thus media anthropological and enactive rather than (merely) embodied and phenomenological.

In the first volume of his philosophical magnum opus, *Technics and Time* (1998), Bernard Stiegler argues that the technical object designates a third kind of being between the inorganic beings of the physical world and the organic beings of the biological world, namely, the "inorganic organized beings" of technical objects (17). What I attempt here is to conceive of cinematic embodiment in terms of the dynamic coupling of the biological spectator and the technical object of the cinema. The aim of the present chapter is to construe this coupling around the question of movement and motor resonances in relation to camera movement. It is argued that the flow of movements between the organic and the inorganic is what constitutes the transformation of the filmic material into a narrative environment, milieu, or Umwelt. The diegesis is thus animated through a "pursuit of life by means other than life" (17)—Stiegler's definition of technics.[15] From this we can derive at a narratological principle of motor resonances firmly rooted in the dynamic exchange of movements between the embodied spectator and the "inorganic organized being of the film."

4.2. The Cinematic Flow of Movements

That film is endowed with movement not only as a consequence of the cinematic apparatus but also through its coupling with the corporeal movements of its recipient was a thesis explored by filmology, most noticeably by the Belgian experimental psychologist Albert Michotte van den Berck and the social anthropologist and (later) documentarist Edgar Morin. Both studied the strong "impression of reality" aroused by the films and tied it to the medium's affective and kinesthetic form of communication responsible for causing the experience of "being there."

In an influential article published in 1948, "Le caractère de 'réalité' des projections cinématographiques," Michotte (1991a) provides a study of the "very vivid impression of the reality of the things and events perceived on the screen" (197). Inspired by Merleau-Ponty, Michotte (1991b) believed that thought, even abstract concepts such as causation, is rooted in the perception of movement. For Michotte, our basic empathetic involvement in a film, which occurs "when we observe what someone else is doing, and we ourselves live it, in some sense, rather than just understand it at an intellectual level, or classify it into some category or other" (209), has its roots in the embodied perception of movement. Building upon this notion of kinesthetic empathy, Michotte observes that "the emotions are intimately linked to our motor reactions" (210). In extreme cases of kinesthetic empathy, we can even be said to lose our subjectivity and "enter the skin" of the character (211). For Michotte it is the motor involvement in cinema that causes the actual world to recede "beyond the perceptual horizon" (217) as the diegetic world takes the status as our immediate environment. The filmologists studied the flow of filmic movements—e.g., motor resonances, motor empathy, and affective participation—from the perspective of the outreaching, world-orientated psychological mechanisms of the mind and perceptual organs.

These reciprocal dynamics (where the spectators invest their bodily movements in the film and breath life to it, but where the movements of the film also *move* the embodied spectator to arouse percepts, cognitions, emotions, and affects) have been elaborately unfolded in Morin's *Le cinéma ou l'homme imaginaire* (1956). Of central importance to Morin (2005) is the role of movement in cinema, which he maintains is the "decisive power of reality: it is in it, through it, that time and space are real" (118). In cinema, the material world has been bereft of its natural movement. Movement is, however, restored to cinema once the spectators induce their own movements onto the film material.

The vitality of the movement thus causes the feeling of life being animated, yet we do not perceive it as our movements. Instead, cinema gives rise to the vivid impression of perceiving "objective" reality. In cinema, movement gives body to forms (118–19). The filmic world is thus strung between "realities," traversing the supposed realms of the subjective and the objective such that movement has a "double face" as both a power of corporeal realism and an affective power of kinesthesia. Cinema is so bound to biological experience that it brings with it an inner feeling of life as well as an impression of external reality, neither feeling nor reality but the feeling of reality (130).

The film experience is thus a reciprocal exchange of movements that transforms the immobile and unaffected film material into a lived time-space, an Umwelt, or a diegetic environment. In reference to Souriau's (1953) studies on the affective rhythms of the filmic universe, Morin (2005) argues that film creates a symbiosis that forms a new modality of subjectivity that integrates the spectator into the flow of the film as well as the flow of the film into the psychic flow of the spectator (102).

Following Morin, cinema extends a "fluidity" to its universe and its objects by mobilizing the immobile stills and by breathing into them the dynamogenic powers that emit the impression of life (66). Morin aligns this dynamogenic state of the film with its "atmosphere" or "soul." We thus find here an analytical method for studying cinematic movement that differs substantially from the textual immobilization of the film but also from the tendency to reduce cinematic techniques to their ability to simulate quotidian embodied experience. It is the task of a post-textual narratology to capture the cinematic diegesis not just as a container of narrative events but as a spatiotemporal media-technological arrangement of "atmospheric affordances," that is, a "fluid universe," where time has acquired the movable nature of space, and space the transformative powers of time (63).

In this respect, Deleuze (2000) has identified a principle of *automatic movement* (or auto-movement) in cinema that differs from the notion of apparent movement, where the mind compensates for the lack of movement by imposing it on the immobile material. Unlike other arts, cinema not only puts movement in the image; it also puts movement in the mind (366). For Deleuze (2005), cinema is thus a cerebral art par excellence capable of producing a shock to thought, of communicating vibrations to the cortex, and of touching the nervous and cerebral system directly. Automatic movement thereby gives rise to what Deleuze calls a spiritual automaton that reacts, in turn, on automatic movement, creating a dynamic feedback loop between the embodied spectator and the technological apparatus (151). In his elaboration of the reciprocity of automatic movement and the spiritual automaton, Deleuze is heavily influenced by the early film critic Élie Faure, who in *Fonction du cinéma* writes,

It is in fact its material automatism which gives rise inside these images to this new universe which it gradually imposes on our intellectual automatism. Thus there appears, in a blinding light, the subordination of the human soul to the tool which it creates, and vice versa. It turns out there is a constant reversibility between technical and affective nature. (Faure in Deleuze 2005, 298)

It is possible to elaborate on these ideas of the flow of movements between embodied spectator and material film to argue that cinema operates on a principle of reciprocal movement in which the movements of the film reverberate with the felt body, only to be returned to the film in the form of "atmospheric affordances," "movement suggestions," and kinesthetic empathies. To do so we now turn to the ecological approach to perception.

4.3. The Ecological Approach to Perception

Within the scope of his ecological psychology, James J. Gibson has aimed to capture the motor resonances between perceiver and perceived by rejecting the internalism of psychology. Instead of studying the biological makeup of the organism, Gibson turns to the environment and its affordances to study perception. This reorientation of perceptual psychology toward the environment is what lies behind the term "ecological." In *The Ecological Approach to Visual Perception* (1979), his final and most influential work, Gibson proposes nothing short of a complete reorientation of psychology's internalism as he contends that the relation between the environment and organism is the true locus of perception as opposed to neurons, retinal images, isolated stimuli, and singular "percepts."

The position I will outline here differs from the first-generation film ecology that emphasized the "cognitive-evolutional" strain of ecological perception.[16] Although I cannot go into a detailed discussion here about these differences, they mostly concern the rigid schisms of culture versus evolution along with the overtly static conceptions of the environment and the brain/mind upon which the first-generation approach was formed. One example of this, taken from Joe Anderson's programmatic *The Reality of Illusion* (1998), must suffice here:

It may be difficult for film scholars steeped in the theories of the past couple of decades to accept the idea that basic perceptual processing goes on without conscious direction or intellectual effort and that the strategies employed by our perceptual systems are *not learned from our culture but are given to each of us by way of the genetic code we share as the member of a species.* And if the idea that basic perceptual capacities were shaped by the forces of evolution is difficult to accept, then it may be even more difficult to accept the idea that higher-level capacities, including language and various aspects of cognition, are also *built-in*. (36, my emphases)

Rather than on evolutionary hardwired perceptual mechanisms, my emphasis will be on Gibson's (2015) view of perception as being essentially a process of resonances and attunements between an organism and its environment. From this, Gibson derives the daunting thesis that perception resides neither *in* the organism nor *in* the environment. Perception is a direct, relational, durational, processual, and complementary capacity related to being-in-the-world. As Gibson explains, animal and environment form an inseparable pair; no animal could exist without an environment; and equally, though less self-evident, an environment presumes a living organism for which it is its environment. Thus, before life surveyed on earth there was a physical reality, a potential environment that we could refer to as a world, but not an environment (4). Ecology thus aims to overcome the dualisms constructed by modern science, most noticeably that between the organism and the world.

Two concepts become important for an ecological understanding of the cinematic diegesis, namely, *affordances*, a term coined by Gibson (1966) to refer to "what things furnish for good or ill" (285), which I have used in this book mainly to refer to the kind of experiences, sensations, motor actions, perceptions, cognitions, and affects that are enabled by the cinematic medium, its changing technologies, and its stylistics and techniques. The second term is that of *kinesthesia* or *proprioception*, which relates not to our perception of the environment per se, but to our own bodily movement and position in relation to it.

Let us begin with the concept of affordances. To see events, places, substances, and objects, such is Gibson's (2015) ecological credo, "is to perceive what they afford" (240). The concept of affordances is without doubt Gibson's most impactful concept (Mace 2015, xxvi); it also ranges as one of the most controversial and debated features of his ecological theory of perception (Heft 1989, 1; for a criticism, see Fodor and Pylyshyn 1981). Gibson (2015) defines affordances as what the environment offers the animal, yet in such a way that it implies the complementarity of animal and environment (119). An important feature of affordances is that they are in some sense objective, real, and physical. Yet, the truth of the matter is that an affordance is neither an objective nor a subjective property; it is both (121). It, in other words, cuts across the dichotomy of subjective–objective and helps us to understand its inadequacy. In this fashion, it is as much a fact of the environment as of behavior. It is both physical and psychical, yet neither. An affordance points both ways, to the environment and to the observer (121).[17]

Note that the concept of affordance is broadly construed to describe the organism/environment relation in the context of Gibson's general disregard of "stimulus–response" models of perception; his view of perception as active and direct "information pickup"; his anti-cognitivist notion of perception as "direct," non-inferential, and not mediated by retinal, neural, or mental pictures; and his general dismissal of conceiving perception in communicational terms.[18] Ultimately the concept of affordance offers a conceptual plane from which we can target the organism and the environment from the perspective of their entanglement.

The second concept is that of *proprioception* or (visual) kinesthesia, which refers to the part of perception oriented toward self-movement, i.e., the perception of the positions, movements, feelings, and sensations of the body. Taken together, the question that will concern us in the following is what kinds of proprioception or kinesthesia are afforded by the cinema and how this affects the emergence of the cinematic diegesis and our feeling of "being there." More specifically, it will be argued on the example of camera movement that cinema affords a mode of world-building that integrates the perceiver's self-movement into its diegesis, which by extension animates the cinematic environment and bestows this environment with the impression of being immediately manifested before us.

4.4. Proprioception and Kinesthesia: Learning to Fly with Gibson

In the 1940s a great number of young men were called into the U.S. Air Force to train to become pilots during World War II. Gibson was recruited by the Air Force, too, however, not to become a pilot but to conduct research on how best to train the novices. As Gibson explains, it seemed viable first to test whether the young men were able to identify what was necessary to land the plane before letting them experiment with real aviation. Among the things the student had to identify was the aiming point of a landing glide and the direction in which he was going. Gibson set up a test using a series of dolly shots toward a model runway (Gibson 1947). The subject then had to select the spot he was aiming for (A, B, C, or D as marked on the runway). In conducting this test, Gibson (2015) gradually grew skeptical of Helmholtzian optics and began to examine ways in which motion perspective was more than the "cue" of motion parallax (174).

Motion perception, Gibson found out, was not only directed toward the external world, but also toward the self, insofar as vision obtains information about both the environment and the self (175). This not only holds for vision but also is a general trait of perception that Gibson (1966) believed should not be understood according to separate input channels, but more complex perceptual systems, thereby pointing toward multisensorial, synesthetic, or multimodal forms of perception.[19] Gibson (2015) describes how information about the self and the environment are inseparable such that egoreception always accompanies exteroception and vice versa. Perception thus has a subjective and an objective pole specified by the information. Thus, perceiving the environment means coperceiving oneself (116).

When Gibson was training the young men into becoming pilots, he had noticed that to effectively land a plane, it was not enough to perceive the movements of the motion picture; it was essential that the trainee also had a sense of his own bodily movement through the illusory space. As Gibson (1947) notes in his research report, it is important to recognize that two different and distinct forms of movement perception can be induced by cinematic images: movements of objects and movements of the observer. It is particularly related to the latter that the pictorial screen obtains its three-dimensional qualities (10).

Cinematic spectators thus attune to the movements of the film in two distinct modalities: through a perceptual attunement to the movements of the film (affordances) and through an attunement of the perceiver's felt bodily movements to the movements of the film (proprioception/kinesthesia). According to Gibson, (visual) kinesthesis—the psychological mechanism that attunes movements of the world to those of the organism—is what allows us to cross the threshold and enter the fictive domain. Think of the Steadicam shot of *The Wolf of Wall Street* (directed by Scorsese 2016) that fluidly transports us around Jordan Belfort's (Leonardo DiCaprio's) office and plunges us into the corrupt and fraudulent world of a stockbroker. For Gibson (2015), the movements of a film (and its movement of us) are the cause of the very intense empathy that films can arouse in its viewer and for providing the vivid impression of being in the place and situation depicted (282).

However, the moving camera not only transports us into the diegesis. We tend to think about the diegesis as comprising only the movements of the film environment. Yet, to perceive the diegesis as a meaningful environment, we cannot envision it as an abstract, objective space. Thus, the diegesis comprises not only the movements of the film but also our proprioceptive and affective attunement to it. Gibson emphasizes that the cinematic diegesis is still "illusional" in the sense that its affordances (our ability of interaction with it as environment) are medially modified. Similarly, distinct camera movement techniques modify our proprioception of the diegesis. The Steadicam, for instance, activates a smooth and elegant transversal of a character's moving through space, whereas a body-mounted camera like the Snorricam—used extensively in *Requiem for a Dream* (directed by Aronofsky 2000)—fixates on the actor's face/body and holds it apparently motionless while the surroundings remain dynamic. This creates a dizzying effect that is often used to underline the lack of resonance between characters and their environmental surroundings. By contrast the Steadicam of

The Wolf of Wall Street transmits its smoothness, elegance, and refinement onto the character as perfectly in sync with the environment.

In an analysis of Gus Van Sant's *Gerry* (2002), Luis Rocha Antunes (2012) observes that the prolonged Steadicam movements of the film are used not to convey narrative information in the cause–effect manner suggested by traditional cognitive film theory, but instead to communicate the experience of "what it means to walk" (531). The cinematic walking of the film is elevated to a corporal gesture that conveys a direct, embodied comprehension of the two Gerrys (Matt Damon and Casey Affleck) of the film. Their personalities and growing fatigue are thus communicated by their style of walking and by how the moving camera conveys that walking. As Antunes observes, the moving camera mediates the relationship of the protagonists through a sustained motion that shifts from diagonal to lateral perspectives and from the back to the front (537). There is thus narrative "information" in the resonant movements that flow between the characters, the film, and its embodied spectators.[20]

Gibson (2015) believed our empathic involvement is best achieved with anthropomorphic camera movements, i.e., movements that *simulate* natural, human perception:

> The modes of camera movement that are analogous to the natural movements of the head-body system are, in this theory, a first-order guide to the composing of a film. The moving camera, not just the movement in the picture, is the reason for the empathy that grips us in the cinema. We are onlookers in the situation, to be sure, not participants, but we are in it, we are oriented to it, and we can adopt points of observation within its space. (285)

In *The Senses Considered as Perceptual Systems* (1966), Gibson examines the parallels between cinematic and ordinary perception. First of all, he grants the cinema great illusory capabilities for providing viewers with the approximation of "first-hand experience" and adds, "especially if the motion-picture camera takes the position of an actor in the scene" (317). This idea culminates in a normative cinematic aesthetics that favors an extreme use of subjective viewpoint such as *The Lady in the Lake* (directed by Montgomery 1947)—a film also mentioned by Sobchack—which Gibson (2015) argues is a form of filmmaking that "does not deserve the neglect in which it is now held by film producers" (285). Not unlike Sobchack, Gibson unnecessarily restricts the creative aesthetic potential of cinema's varied modes of proprioceptive engagement to movements that simulate or mimic rather than counter, resist, modulate, expand, or transform the laws of ordinary perception. This is, for instance, the case when Gibson evaluates the aesthetic practice of the jump cut as ill founded (286).

Although Gibson (1966) advocated intensively for a distributed theory of perception, where the perceptual act is in neither the environment nor the perceiver, he is wary of allowing the cinematic medium (and the filmmakers) too much control of the perceptual system:

> The perceiver is passive. He sits in a chair. He is not fully surrounded by the environment represented on the screen. He cannot alter what will happen in the virtual world. Even though he may be given the experience of walking, approaching, inspecting, and riding in vehicles, *it is not his experience for he did not get it for himself; most of it is imposed, not obtained.* (317, my emphasis)

However, is Gibson's description of having experiences or perceptions that do not univocally belong to the perceiver not one of the greatest insights on cinema that could be derived from his ecological approach? The earliest form of the moving image, Eadweard Muybridge's *The Horse in Motion* (1878), was after all created to settle scientifically—to make visible what remained imperceptible to the human sensorium—a dispute about whether or not the horse at any point has all of its legs off the ground in the trot or gallop. (It does.)[21] Cinematic perception is then paradoxically a direct, "unmediated," and embodied form of techno-mediated perception.[22] Cinema's illusory powers are thus rooted in proprioception rather than a cognitive suspension of disbelief. As Scott Richmond (2016) explicates in his Gibsonian proprioceptive aesthetic, the film provides a palpable kinesthesia that does not depend on epistemological deception. The cinematic illusion is thus not representational but occurs on the level of proprioception, which is phenomenologically prior to and distinct from representation (12).

For Richmond, our ability to inhabit the diegesis is thus a "result of the coupling of my perceiving and indeed proprioceptive body with the cinema as a technical system" (13), i.e., the anthropomedial relation constituted in the cinematic experience. A truly embodied film narratology cannot simply rely on foregrounding the spectator's felt body; it needs to capture the entanglement of the organic, the technological, and the material. The cinematic encounter is not that of an ancient, evolutionary hardwired perceptual mechanism that meets new technology, as was the conclusion of the first generation of Gibsonian film theorists. As Richmond (2016) argues, "cinema's ability to manifest a world unfolding before me is inseparable from its ability to modulate my sense of myself" (170). A contemporary theory that similarly understands our engagement with cinema in the form of embodied motor resonances has recently been formulated from the perspective of modern neuroscience.

4.5. Embodied Simulation: Intersubjective Affordances in the Brain

In 1988 a group of neuroscientists at the University of Parma—Giacomo Rizzolatti, Giuseppe Di Pellegrini, Luciano Fadiga, Leonardo Fogassi, and Vittorio Gallese—did an unusual discovery when doing research on "canonical neurons"[23] in the ventral premotor cortex of the macaque monkey. By accident, the researchers discovered a subset of neurons—mirror neurons—that fire not just when the monkey performs a motor action but also when it observes one being performed by another primate. In 1991, the team had conducted enough research to present their findings and submitted a paper to *Nature*, which, however, rejected it for its lack of general interest (Rizzolatti and Fabbri-Destro 2010, 223).

Confident of the scope of their discovery, the Parma researchers published their findings in *Experimental Brain Research* the subsequent year (Di Pellegrino et al. 1992), and in a 1996 article they gave the subset the name "mirror neurons" and defined them as a particular set of F5 neurons that discharged both during a monkey's active movements and when it observed the meaningful hand movements of the experimenter (Gallese et al. 1996, 596). The activities of mirror neurons are thus modulated both by the execution of an action and the observation of an action. Moreover, these neurons are sensitive to action specificity and thus display a degree of action recognition. Mirror neurons are thus distinguished from other "motor" or "sensory" neurons whose discharge is associated with either execution or observation but not both. They are also distinguished from other types of response to vision of objects or other non-action stimuli (Kilner and Lemon 2013, 1057).

As growing evidence was accumulated that a mirror neuron system similar to that of the monkey could be found in humans and that this system in addition to action understanding also plays a fundamental role in action imitation (Rizzolatti and Craighero 2004, 169), the potential explanatory powers of these neurons began to be recognized by the scientific community. Could mirror neurons explain the neural substrate of our ability to directly perceive the affordances of the environment?[24] Could it explain the relation between movement, emotion, and empathy in (aesthetic) experience?[25] Could it help explain language development?[26] Is the mirror neuron system responsible for intersubjective understanding and as such the neural seat of empathy?[27] In the midst of this euphoria, neuroscientist V.S. Ramachandran (2000) compared the discovery of the mirror neuron system with the discovery of the structure of DNA.

Research on mirror neurons, most often due to its inflated presentation in the popular media, spiraled into a veritable "neuromania" (cf. Legrenzi and Umiltà 2011; Tallis 2011)—designating a desire to explain everything about human life in terms of biological evolution and the brain—that caused an equally reductionist "neurophobia" resting upon a wholesale dismissal of the explanatory powers of neuroscience (Gallese and Guerra 2020, xviii). Where ecological psychology ventured out of the laboratory into the "wild" to discover the affordances of an environment as crucial to perception, modern neuroscience located the neurological substrate of our direct, embodied interaction with the world in a specific brain area and according to a particular kind of neuron. However, the identification of a neural mechanism that allows a direct mapping between the visual description of a motor act and its execution (Gallese and Wojciehowski 2011, 14) also provided new empirical evidence and a neural foundation for Gibson's postulation of a direct link between perception and action.

In 1998, one member of the Parma group, Vittorio Gallese, teamed up with the cognitive philosopher and simulation theorist of mind reading, Alvin Goldman, to formulate a more encompassing cognitive-neurological theory of intersubjective understanding: ES theory.[28] In the early 2010s, Gallese then began working with film scholar Michele Guerra on the application of ES to cinema. In *The Empathic Screen* (2020), originally published in 2015 in Italian as *Lo schermo empatico*, Gallese and Guerra present their groundbreaking study of the role of mirror neuron activation and embodied simulation in the cinematic experience. A central premise of the book is that mirror neurons are what allow us to *simulate* the affordances of objects and people. Thus, seeing an object means simulating a potential action. Objects are identified, differentiated, and categorized not just according to their physical appearance but also the effects of their interaction with a potential agent (25).

On a neurological level, perception and motor intention collide. The discovery of a direct bond between perception and (motor) action constitutes a major challenge to theories that understand this relation to be mediated either linguistically or by cognitive representations. To understand the purposes and motor intentions no meta-representation in linguistic form is necessary. When we are in another's presence while they undertake certain actions, we immediately comprehend most of their sensorimotor and emotional intentions without the need to explicitly represent them linguistically (4).

In this sense, both Gibson's ecology and ES demonstrate the primacy of movement and its forms of resonance in embodied relations (71). As Gallese and Guerra (2014) have argued elsewhere, ES is what enables our direct form of action understanding so that we can appreciate purpose without relying on explicit inference (108). One of the most fundamental ways of interpersonal understanding, according to ES, is thus the simulation of movements made, sensations felt, and emotions experienced by others (Smith 2020, viii). This is a far cry from the abstract, analytical, and inferential relation of agent and world of cognitivism. ES instead conceives our relation to the world as being embodied through our senses, emotions, feelings, as well as kinesthetic imitations.

Note that the move from research on the mirror neuron system to ES involves a transition from experimental research on a particular area in the brain to a more comprehensive theory of the direct, kinesthetic, sensorimotor, embodied, and empathic relation between perceiver and perceived.[29] We thus move from a relatively limited set of neurons to a full-fledged theory of (quasi-)embodied perception. As most theorizations work, we go from the empirically verifiable (mirror neuron activation and the mirror neuron system) to a more general theory of intersubjectivity, action recognition, perception, and empathy (embodied simulation theory). It is, to be sure, entirely unproblematic that new empirical findings spur new theories. The problems encountered by *The Empathic Screen*, as far as I can tell, concern the reverse movement that occurs when general traits of the cinema (our perception of the character's intended action, our feeling of empathy and of being there, our ability to simulate the emotional states of the characters, etc.) all need to be traced back to the activation of a particular kind of neuron.

Let me briefly stake out the territory. In applying a theory (ES) that highlights a particular form of environment/animal interaction (simulation), there is a risk that we reduce cinema's expressive-aesthetic potential to those aspects of it that most clearly involve mirror neuron activity and thus can be said to verify the theory on cinematic grounds. In other words, just as we argued in relation to Gibson, there is a risk that the specific and work-related aesthetic function of one element of the film (e.g., the jump cut) is decontextualized and evaluated solely on its suitability for the theory in question (e.g., the jump cut is discredited because it does not replicate the natural mode of ecological perception). If we put all our shares into one theory (ES), we risk losing sight of the overall, holistic, artistic, and aesthetic work of the film in order to validate the theory as universally applicable.

Relatedly, since ES is empirically justified by the discovery of mirror neurons and their activation in given situations, those cinematic means of expression that underline our embodied, kinesthetic, affective, but not necessarily *simulative* relation with the film might be devalued in favor of moments that highlight embodied simulation. For instance—although we should note that there are suggestions that mirror neuron activation also operates acoustically (Kohler et al. 2002)—the question of sound and music in cinema appears less suited for a theory of *simulation*. We do not necessarily simulate an environmental soundscape to feel immersed in it; it is enough that we simply hear it. Following from this, it is worth noticing that the highest quantity and most paradigmatic cases of mirror neuron activation are based on visual stimulation. Thus, we would expect a theory based on ES to emphasize the visual over the acoustic components of the film.

It is therefore not surprising that the moving camera becomes an essential component in the application of ES to the cinema. Gallese and Guerra maintain that the "presence of the camera and how it moves induces different responses from the embodied simulation mechanisms produced by the activation of the mirror neurons in the observer's brain" (106). Furthermore, for the camera to be the object of *simulation*, it must be ascribed a human agency:

> Our ability to share attitudes, sensations, and emotions with the actors, and also with the mechanical movements of a camera *simulating a human presence*, stems from embodied bases that can contribute to clarifying the corporeal representation of the filmic experience supported in the phenomenological field over recent decades, without seeking forms of dialogue with neuroscientific evidence or models. (68, my emphasis)

The general tenet is not new. As this chapter has shown, even before the discovery of mirror neurons the moving camera has been anthropomorphized to simulate, or act as a surrogate of, our own embodied being in the diegesis.

Gallese and Guerra, however, want to verify this empirically by studying a variety of camera movements—Steadicam, dolly, and the zoom—and hierarchize them according to their ability to activate the mirror neuron system and thus to induce embodied simulation. The authors present their findings as "solid neurophysiological evidence of the Steadicam's extraordinary ability to generate a sensation of immersion in the spatiotemporal dimension of film" (114). My interest is not to dispute the solidity of their findings (for a critical survey, see Turvey 2020), but instead to examine the subtle equation of mirror neuron activity with the cinematic capacity of generating a feeling of being immersed in the cinematic diegesis that Gallese and Guerra tacitly assume. Simulation might be a part of our immersion in the diegesis, yet the theoretical design of ES risks excluding factors that are not focalized by an anthropomorphic agent and thus not susceptible to simulation (e.g., colorations, montage, sound design, the overall atmospheric or narrative arrangement of the film, and indeed many forms of camera movements).

The moving camera is, after all, merely one component of a larger aesthetic and narrative arrangement that in combination provides the feeling of "being there." Yet, the authors employ an atomistic methodology to isolate singular components and study their role in ES activation. Thus, it is argued, "the involvement of the average spectator is directly proportional to the intensity of camera movements" (91). Kinesthetic involvement is, however, an effect of the whole arrangement of the film rather than irreducible to one of its components. Moreover, camera movements cannot be understood purely on the basis of their type of movement but need themselves to be contextualized as part of the narrative, aesthetic, or ethical design of the film.[30] Yet, just as language and discourse-oriented theories tend to display a predilection for montage due to its structural similarity with linguistic operations, Gallese and Guerra pitch the camera movement *against* other expressive means. Thus, "Many movie-goers would be ready to identify the filmmaker by his use of camera movements, but few would attempt this on the basis of the editing" (91). I believe this to be a highly disputable claim evocative of an unnecessary film-stylistic reductionism.

The problems spurred by the attempt to justify ES on the basis of an atomistic film-analytical methodology is further explicated by the authors' treatment of a brief, anthropomorphic camera movement in Hitchcock's *Notorious* (1946) toward a set of keys. In this scene, the main protagonist of the film, Alicia (Ingrid Bergman), intends to slip the key out of the key ring of her Nazi husband (Claude Rains). I am supportive of the idea that this camera movement contributes to the simulation of "grasping" such that we in a sense "embody" Alicia's motor intentions of reaching out for the keys without being detected (just as the monkeys simulate grasping). Yet, it is less evident why we should accept the claim that "the state of suspense in which we find ourselves at every viewing of *Notorious* has nothing whatsoever to do with the story" (54). Less evident is that the film more generally should be a testimony to Hitchcock's "almost complete indifference to the plot" (53). Do the authors suggest that the effect of embodied simulation single-handedly is enough to keep the viewers satisfied and entertained? If embodied simulation were so essential to the cinematic experience, could we not trigger it simply by a random selection of people (or monkeys) grasping for objects? And what in the nature of embodied simulation requires us to ignore or suspend the obvious narrative context in which this form of simulation occurs?

I am inclined to believe that what the authors wish to argue is that we simulate the camera movement and the act of grasping not *because of* the narrative context of the film. Simulation is direct and not triggered by cognitive mind reading. Yet, even if we accept this claim, it is simply not true that the movement is "indifferent to the plot" or that it has "nothing to do with the story." In fact, it is deeply entangled into the mechanisms of the story. First, the camera movement is motivated by events in the story: it directs our attention to a set of keys that are essential for the plot. It is of no surprise that Bordwell (2020) has been the first to point this out. Moreover, it is hard to bracket out the narrative context when addressing the creation of suspense in the scene. The motor resonances created by the camera movement are interwoven into the film's story about a woman fearing to be caught in the act of stealing the keys from her husband and the consequences that would follow from him realizing that she works as a spy. From the perspective I have developed in this book, Alicia's intention to steal the key is *enacted* by the very camera movement. The movement creates the diegesis in the very act by which it gives us access to it. Or better yet, the diegesis is constantly being re-enacted such that it always emerges from and implies its overall narrative and aesthetic context.

We must not forget that the *raison d'être* of embodied cognition is not to postulate the existence of bodily, pre-reflective, or innate mechanisms completely isolated from higher processes of cognition or content, but to rethink cognition as embedded in its many situational contexts. Embodiment is not the annihilation of so-called higher cognitive processes such as the engagement with a difficult plot. Direct experience should not be antagonized to more conceptual or scientific modalities of thought. ES presents an alternative to cognitivism, yet its warranted criticism of this position should not result in the opposite, nonsensical position that all there is, is direct, embodied, simulative experience. Yet, for Gallese and Guerra it is no longer feasible to talk of top-down segmentation of the events in a movie. Instead, we must think in terms of bottom-up mechanisms prompted by the physical elements that mark the transition between the shots and facilitate forms of embodied relations with the subject of the movie (51). From the perspective developed in this book, however, the problem is exactly this kind of division between processes of "top-down" (cognition) and bottom-up (autonomously bodily affects).[31]

This leads me to a final question. What kind of "embodiment" does ES promote? It appears to me that whereas Merleau-Ponty promoted a general theory of our embodied mode of being in the world, embodiment in ES is either contingent on a particular kind of neuronal activity or contingent on the broader activation of ES based on the mirror neuron system. Is all experience related to ES? If yes, why are mirror neurons ascribed a particular importance to embodied experience, simulation, and kinesthetic empathy, when these only underline a small aspect of experience? If no, is all experience that does not rely on ES disembodied and indirect? Moreover, is ES truly an "embodied" theory of our being-in-the-word or just a modernized version of Helmholtzian optics, where we experience not the world but an embodied simulation of it? Malcolm Turvey (2020) has suggested that ES is just standard neuroscience in embodied disguise. He points out that despite its reinterpretation of cognition in terms of embodiment and simulation, ES locates the viewer's purported experience of being transported into the diegesis in a brain area, namely, the activation of the motor cortex by camera movements. This mode of identifying an area of the brain (the motor cortex) that correlates with the activation of an observable form of human behavior (feeling that one is brought "into the scene"), Turvey points out, does not differ substantially from conventional cognitivist neuroscience. Ultimately, ES is not a theory about the body proper; it is, as the telling title of an article indicates, about "Finding the Body in the Brain" (Gallese 2016).

To be fair, it might be that the assumed distinction between the domain of the "body" and that of the "brain" is itself misguided and a reminiscence of their dichotomized past as divided into "corporeal vessel" and "soul." There is no brain that is not also body, no human brain without a body. The brain is embodied as much as the body is "embrained." Thus, despite the reservations I have just rehearsed, I believe the discovery of mirror neurons and the mirror neuron system to constitute important further evidence of a more basic, embodied, and kinesthetic relation between body and world. Mirror neurons provide evidence that from a functional viewpoint, action execution and observation are closely related processes, and indeed that our ability to interpret the actions of others requires the involvement of our own motor system (Kilner and Lemon 2013, 1057). Taking a more modest theoretical approach to what mirror neurons can and cannot help us explain about the film experience might prove liberating for future research. What I have been advocating in this chapter is a theory of the cinematic diegesis as reliant upon movement resonances between the embodied spectator and the material film. This perspective highlights the overall affective and narrative arrangement of a film rather than reducing embodiment to a single technique or modality of experience.

1917 (Mendes 2019) is a film comprised of one (apparent) camera movement and one of the most recent examples of filmmakers going to great lengths to invoke the feeling of "being there." If the filmmakers would follow the research of Gallese and Guerra (2020)—demonstrating the direct proportionality between the Steadicam and the spectator's involvement in the film—the Steadicam would be employed as much as possible. Yet, even if we agree that the Steadicam affords a feeling of being there, its use is always contextualized, and different situations require different camera movement techniques. Ultimately, Roger Deakins, who worked as the director of photography on *1917*, decided to shoot the film with the "Trinity camera rig," a relatively new technology that allows a single camera movement to combine a series of camera movement techniques and to calibrate its techniques on a moment-to-moment basis to match the kinesthetic dynamics of the affective and narrative arrangement of the film.[32] Rather than simply promote one technique (the Steadicam) or one modality of spectator involvement (simulation), we need to understand film as a complex arrangement of various techniques that combine into an overall (narrative and affective) design. Our embodied involvement with the film is not "given" prior to any technological intervention but *in it*. Simulation is but one modality of being-in-the-world, and it should be understood in the broader context of the technological, cultural, and social arrangement designed to elicit specified motor reactions and affects.[33]

4.6. Atmospheric Affordances: Attuning to the Affective Arrangement

Narrative film theory has traditionally sought to understand how a given film arranges its narrative material (characters, events, goals, motifs, etc.) into a more or less coherent narrative text. What this scholarship has failed to acknowledge is how the arrangement of the narrative is part of the larger affective arrangement of the film world. In order to elucidate this claim, Gibson's concept of affordances shall be expanded to include not only the potential actions that an environment affords but also its affective impressions on the embodied organism. We are thus aiming at a more fundamental relation of animal and organism than the visual motor and pragmatic one outlined by Gibson and Gallese.

In *Art as Experience* (1934), Dewey argues that the world is not value free or objective but directly perceived in all its emotional valence. Accordingly, the felt organism does not project its own emotions or feeling states into the experienced environment. Nature is itself hateful, bland, and morose, irritating and comforting before being mathematically qualified or divided into secondary qualities such as colors and shapes. Direct experience derives from the interaction of organism and environment, and it is in this interaction that human energy is gathered, dammed up, frustrated, and victorious. This interaction is full of rhythmic beats of want and fulfillment, pulses of doing and being withheld from doing (Dewey 1980, 16).

Similarly, this book argues that the filmic diegesis is impregnated with affects, atmospheres, movement impressions, pulses, and rhythms that are not projected onto it by the spectator but define their interrelation. Applied to the idea of affordances, this would direct it toward "whole situations" rather than individual properties or features of the environment (for a reading of affordances along these lines, see Chemero 2003). Affordances would thus point more broadly to the organism–environment relation not only in terms of motor intentionality but also affect. Tonino Griffero (2014b) has pointed to the existence of atmospheric affordances (44–47), where our immediate impression of our felt body and the perceived environment coincide. Griffero thereby aims to understand the atmospheric as a type of affordance, i.e., as something that is perceived immediately, directly, and pre-reflectively on the level of the felt body. Instead of just "affordances" or just "atmospheres," the concept of "atmospheric affordances" indicates the intimate connection between the pragmatic concept of affordances (concerning our potential to interact with an environment) and the affective concept of atmospheres (concerning our feeling states in a given environment). Both our pragmatic and affective relations to the environment are mediated by motor resonances, i.e., the flow of movements that attune the organism to its environment. Rather than pose this ongoing attunement solely in pragmatic terms (i.e., according to how the properties of an environment can be manipulated), as Gibson originally did, the notion of atmospheric affordances acknowledges that recognizing an object is more than knowing how to interact, manipulate, or do something with it; it is also to apprehend its affective valence and its overall value for the organism (e.g., "hateful, bland and morose, irritating and comforting") in its environmental context.

In cinema this ongoing attunement of audience and film is partly founded upon "affective arrangements." This concept refers to an assemblage of materials that form a local layout operating as a dynamic formation that comprises persons, things, artifacts, spaces, discourses, behaviors, expressions, etc., into a manufactured composition of dynamic relations (Slaby, Mühlhoff, and Wüschner 2017, 4). More than just texts, narrative worlds are affective arrangements designed to prompt, modulate, and produce particular kinds of affects in various sociocultural settings. Conceiving films as affective arrangements allows us to study their intentional organization of atmospheric affordances, as these are expressed either through cinematic techniques such as the camera movement but also through genres, narrative scenarios, the aesthetic fingerprint of their makers, the world-building of nonfictions forms, or the subversion of the diegesis altogether. In all instances, the affective arrangement is operationalized through the regulation of the flow of movements between perceiver and perceived.

4.7. Conclusions

In a celebrated scene in Mikhail Kalatozov's *The Cranes Are Flying* (*Летят журавли*, 1957), Veronika (Tatiana Samoilova) searches through a crowd of people for her beloved Boris (Aleksey Batalov), who against her expressed desire has volunteered to join the army during the newly erupted World War II. In a handheld tracking shot that moves through the masses, our perceptual perspective, not unlike Veronika's, is sometimes blocked by the many moving objects and persons that occupy the screen. The movements of the handheld camera along with the frenzied objects moving in and out of the screen *simulate* feelings of suffocation, restraint, convulsion, claustrophobia, and perceptual bewilderment that align the viewers with Veronika's desperate attempt to stop her loved one from going to war. All of a sudden, however, the camera frees itself from its alignment to Veronika's perceptual perspective and levitates above the crowd to reveal the hopelessness of the situation, revealing Veronika to be enmeshed in a convoy of military tanks.

The camera movement is neither an externalization of our embodied perception of the world nor a form of simulation. Instead, it enacts a new perspective on the scene as it fluidly (and, for many viewers, undetectably) detaches itself from its anthropomorphic alignment to Veronika. It changes the atmospheric affordances of the scene to no longer serve the simulation of Veronika's perceptual task, instead painfully laying bare her desolation. The elevated camera movement thus relies on motor resonances with its spectator, yet it neither simulates natural perception nor suggests to us through its movement to take it as a surrogate of *our* movement through the diegesis. It is a fluid and dynamic change of viewpoint that enacts the diegesis anew. As we move with the camera, the world transforms proprioceptively and perceptively before us. Thus, the levitation of the camera evidences that perception is not the apprehension of objects and their predicates, not a pure functional relation, but a palpable feeling, a quality of sensation (Richmond 2010, 284).

We *move* with the film in many other ways than what can be captured by simulation, mimicry, or imitation of natural perception such as when we are caught up in the "movement suggestions" or atmospheres of a film, or when we tune into its soundscapes. Attempts to model cinematic techniques (regardless of their aesthetic and narrative context) on the "internal" mechanisms of embodied perception fail to account for not only the creative potential of cinema's non-human traits, but also how embodiment relates not to the human body *as such* but to its historical interaction with (mediated) environments. The true potential of embodiment is not to be found in the alignment of world and body but in the challenges it poses to a priori determinations of the "human" and the way it gestures toward "human technogenesis," the coevolution of the human with technics. Ultimately, embodiment must lead to new ways of understanding the human through media technologies.

It is crucial that embodiment does not repeat philosophy's traditional repression of technics as an object of thought and its designation of it as the unthought (Stiegler 1998, 1: ix). Embodiment is not separate from technics; it never was. More than audiovisual cues for inferential elaboration, an externalization of our embodied mechanisms, a mimicking of ecological perception, or the activation of our motor cortex or mirror neuron system, cinematic motion perception is a particularly illuminating case of the media–man entanglement at the heart of the filmic experience without which there would be no narrative, no diegesis.

The diegesis is thus not a series of propositions but a felt, moving, sensorial ever-shifting world. The film is formed out of audiovisual material that in its resonances with the embodied spectator generates rhythmic, dynamic, temporal, tactile, semantic, and kinetic sensations. These sensations are furthermore modulated upon the technological affordances of the medium, and as each technical revolution brings a sensory surge to cinema it revitalizes the sensations of matter, speed, movement, and space (Chion 1994, 152). This book endeavors to take embodiment beyond the mere alignment of the embodied spectator and the film's perceptual or bodily capacities. In this chapter, this was done on the basis of motor resonances—the flow of movements between the spectator and the film—that it has been the aim to evidence are essential for understanding both the emergence of, and our immersion into, the filmic diegesis. Motor resonances allow us to capture the film's strong impression of "being there" on the basis of kinesthetic or proprioceptive movements that belong both to the spectator and the film. We are thus not split between believing and not believing in the cinematic world. Rather, cinema's technological modulation of perception allows us to have *direct* experiences of *mediated* worlds, a testimony to the brain's extreme adaptability when exposed to new environmental conditions. Arguably, one of the most significant technological modifications of our ongoing embodied attunement with the cinematic world has been afforded by the introduction and continuous advancements in sound technology. Spurred by technological advancements, it is within the study of film sound that the textual diegesis and its exclusion of the sensory and affective domain have reached their most apparent limitations.

5
Narratives Spaces and Sonic Environments

The sound of a church bell ringing over establishing shots of an almost empty Paris, the rhythmic clattering of a construction worker interweaving with the recurring snoring of a homeless person, then the sound of a broom, then a carpet beater, before a host of other noises conjoin to form the first musical piece of Rouben Mamoulian's musical *Love Me Tonight* (1932). The film's sonic unification of the displaced ritual activities into a musical ode to the living pulse of Parisian street life reigns as one of the earliest cinematic explorations of how our experience of place is anchored acoustically. After years of visual domination, film scholarship has begun to address the auditory on equal footing with the visuals. However, it is not enough that we begin to take notice of the importance of sound in the cinema; we should also take seriously the challenges sound poses to our theorization of cinema as founded upon the visual image. This is especially true when it comes to our perception of the narrative space and the diegesis.

Among the most pressing challenges facing the textual conception of the diegesis is that which pertains to the increased prominence of noise on the cinematic soundtrack. The term "noise" here refers less to the disturbances caused by unwanted sounds than to the aggregate of "insignificant" sounds that relate to a particular place at a particular time. Noises thus produce the affective and material qualities of the cinematic environment without, however, conveying narrative "information" about this place in a traditional sense.

Enhanced by advances in sound technologies (e.g., noise reduction and multichannel audio), modern cinematic sound aesthetics have increasingly explored the use of noise, ambience, musique concrète,[1] and musical sound effects to create complex acoustic architectures. Ambient noises are gradually being employed to orient the audience in the diegesis to the extent that the visual no longer operates as the only, or most important, referent for our immersion in the diegesis. Filmmakers increasingly use ambient sound effects to create a cognitive ecology on the basis of how buildings or landscapes create echoes, reflections, and reverberations that allow for the formation of space beyond visual anchoring.[2]

Though the auditory was long treated as accompaniment to the visual, pioneering film sound scholar Michel Chion (1994) pointed early to the existence of an acoustic "superfield," i.e., a spatial continuum or tableau that alters not only our perception of space but also how a scene can be produced. The superfield is more than the mere creation of cinematic space acoustically by a variety of sound

Enacting the Worlds of Cinema. Steffen Hven, Oxford University Press. © Oxford University Press 2022.
DOI: 10.1093/oso/9780197555101.003.0006

elements (e.g., natural sounds, city noises, music, rustling and bumbling, or whatever sounds define a sonic environment) that issue from outside the boundaries of the screened space; it is a radical reconfiguration of that space. In dramaturgical terms, the unframed space created by the superfield is able to perform the function of an establishing shot, yet in a more fluid, dynamic, and detailed fashion. However, the nature of sound is not *representation*; for sound to depict an environment, it must produce it. Contrary to the affordances of the visual frame, cinematic acoustics is neither onscreen nor offscreen; it is there or not there. A cinematic soundscape is not first and foremost a representation of some other place; it is the acoustic production of a cinematic space that may or may not refer to an elsewhere and whose aesthetic and narrative value is no longer a mere vehicle of the plot.

This constitutes a break with earlier sound aesthetics, where the role of the cinematic sound design was subordinated to the linear progression of the plot and where each sound needed to be visually justified. Contrarily, contemporary film sound aesthetics use more ambient sounds and musical sound effects to create an acoustic space that blurs the lines between the subjective and the objective (cf. d'Escriván 2009). Cinematic acoustics might remain largely "vococentric," i.e., privileging the voice, yet it has become increasingly important for filmmakers and sound practitioners to conjure up complex acoustic environments that do not just frame but express the narrative events. The increased focus on cinematic sound has put into question the once-taken-for-granted notion of the diegesis as a text consisting of a series of narrative propositions organized and inferred into a mental representation by the cognitive spectator.

In light of recent developments in both aesthetics and technology, film sound scholars have called for new theoretical approaches capable of capturing the increasingly intertwined elements of silence, noise, speech, sound effects, and music as an integrated whole (Greene and Kulezic-Wilson 2016, 2). No longer satisfied with trying to accommodate sound into dominant theories of film, film sound scholarship has made it evident that we need to break with the understanding of narrative as rooted exclusively in signification, representation, and textualism.[3] Given its reconceptualization of the nonverbal, nonreferential, and nonrepresentational as integral to the film's narrative world, the diegesis-as-environment should be a welcome tool for research in film sound scholarship trying to come to terms with the plethora of ways sounds contribute to the narrative in cinema.

The diligent acoustic work that is being put into the creation of the cinematic diegesis has reshaped the medium's narrative affordances. Where the diegetic/nondiegetic distinction is rooted in a textual comprehension of the medium, the notion of "soundscape" will help us redirect scholarship toward the affective and material production of the diegesis as a mediated dynamic and atmospheric environment. Far from being an academic niche term, the notion of "sound-scape"—a term popularized by R. Murray Schafer (1977) in the context of his World Soundscape project to refer to the complex of sounds that make up an acoustic environment—is now a staple in the music industry, sound art, and academia, and for promoting new sound technologies to the extent that the term has come to refer broadly to almost any acoustic experience regardless of context. Therefore, even if the term were originally associated with an acoustic ecology dedicated to the preservation of the sounds of natural environments, this chapter employs the term to address the affective media ecologies of cinematic soundscapes.

The main thesis of this chapter is that the development of a theoretical framework for the narrative study of film sound requires a prior re-examination of the filmic diegesis. The problems encountered by research on film sounds in relation to most extant narrative theories of film theory include a privileging of narrative time over narrative space founded upon an abstract and disembodied comprehension of space as a passive container of characters, objects, and events. It also relates to the visual bias of film studies expressed either through the tacit claim that the meaning of sound should be found in its relation to the visual (e.g., onscreen versus offscreen or diegetic versus nondiegetic) or through a reduction of the sonic-to-verbal communication. The argument made in this chapter is thus not exclusive to cinematic sound but sparked by how cineacoustics demands a more general rethinking of the cinematic diegesis. Let us therefore begin by considering the role of space in narratology.

5.1. From Spatial Containers to Affective Ecologies

In the magnificent opening scene of *The Ornithologist* (*O Ornitólogo*, directed by Rodrigues 2016), Fernando (Paul Hamy), the ornithologist, studies with painstaking devotion the natural wildlife of the remote river-bank in Northern Portugal to which he has traveled to study its plethora of bird species. The ornithologist's immersion in the animal wildlife makes him oblivious to the ruthless flowing of the river that causes his kayak to capsize. Despite its realism, the soundscape of the film is not "real," nor does it "represent" the soundscape of an actual Portuguese riverbank. The collage of recorded sounds that make up the film's captivating soundscape is a mosaic of individual sounds that have been taken out of their original environmental context and recombined into the entirely mediated acoustic environment of the film, an environment that includes brief interludes of musical noise composed by Séverine Ballon. The sounds are not *in* the diegesis; they constitute it.

One of the main arguments of this chapter is that recent developments in cinematic acoustics and sound technologies have installed a demand for a new conceptualization of narrative space. Cineacoustics thus forces us to reject what is perhaps the most enduring belief concerning narrative space, namely, that it is a container or vessel of the objects, characters, events, etc., of the story. This notion of space is firmly rooted in Western thinking and can be traced back to Aristotle's *Physics*, where it is argued that the topos (place) is to be conceived as a vessel, i.e., as a movable place that is not a part of the thing it contains. For Aristotle, since place is separable from the object, it is not form; and since it is a container, it is different from matter (Aristotle 2008, 209b27–33).

Similarly, we think of the events of a narrative as taking place, yet the events remain distinct from the narrative space that hosts them.[4] Even though our understanding of space naturally has advanced in the course of the more than 2,000 years since Aristotle wrote *Physics*, the notion of the container remains a powerful metaphor for how we continue to think of space and place. George Lakoff and Mark Johnson (2003) have argued that the "container metaphor for space" ranges as one of the most powerful metaphors "we live by." As physical beings we are set off from the world through the surface of our skins, and we experience the world as outside of us. Everything from rooms, buildings, houses, the natural environment, and other individuals is attributed with the orientation of inside and outside (29).

The space-as-container metaphor has also been pivotal for understanding narrative space whether as setting (the immediate space *in which* actual events occur), "story place" (the place *containing* the plot), or diegesis (the universe that *encapsulates* the story). This has led not only to an understanding of space as a passive vessel for the narrative content but also to a more general marginalization of space in favor of the temporal organization of the text within narrative theory.[5] Thus, Paul Ricœur (1980), to take but one example, holds "temporality to be that structure of existence that reaches language in narrativity and narrativity to be the language structure that has temporality as its ultimate reference" (169).[6] With their respective focus on the causal-chronological and sequential logic of the *fabula* and the indirect and direct presentation of time in the movement-image and the time-image, Bordwell and Deleuze, although from widely different theoretical perspectives, evidence the strong emphasis on temporality in film theory.

According to Susan S. Friedman (2005), a key figure in bringing renewed focus to narrative space in literary narratology,[7] mainstream narratology has tended to model the time–space axis of narrative on a "figure–ground binary." Thus, the "figure" we pay attention to is what happens to the characters, whereas the space in which these events occur is the ground we can willfully ignore. Friedman has eloquently demonstrated that narrative is thus regarded as the function of temporal sequence and causation that occurs in a spatial vacuum or against the static background of a spatial setting. In reference to Michel de Certeau's (1988, 115–30) analysis of narrative as "a practice of everyday life" that affords particular actions and spatial trajectories, as well as Franco Moretti's (1998) notion of narrative space as determining of narrative action, Friedman has challenged the dominant conception of narrative space as a container of objects, characters, and events. The space of a narrative, she insists, is more than a mere background to the temporal unfolding of events. Narrative space is not incidental to the narrative but generative of it.

The foregrounding of temporal concerns is thus not problematic as such; the real issue is the degradation of space in narratology. Narrative theory is thus guilty of what Michel Foucault (1980) analyzed to be a more general devaluation of space that has prevailed at least since Bergson. Time was treated as richness, fecundity, life, and dialectic, while space, on the other hand, was conceived as the dead, the fixed, the undialectical, and the immobile. For all those who confuse history with the old schemas of evolution, living continuity, organic development, the progress of consciousness, or the project of existence, as Foucault writes, the use of spatial terms has the air of an anti-history (70).

Despite Foucault's (1986) famous declaration that our epoch is above all the "epoch of space" and the increased focus on issues of spatiality this sparked in cultural studies, philosophy, and human geography,[8] narratology has only recently begun to generate more sophisticated questions about space, setting, and storyworld and to give them the attention they deserve. Indeed, in defining narratives primarily as sequences of events that unfold in *time*, narrative theory has often tacitly resorted to the problematic assumption of space as an inactive, static, immobile background or void that contains the places, things, and individuals that form the stuff of the narrative.

This is exemplified by the narratological distinction between narrative (forward progression of the plot) and description (the halting of the plot to explore the environment). In his exploration of description in cinema, Seymour Chatman (1984) argues, "Unlike narrative, whose textual principle is the sequence and sequencing of events in time from beginning to middle to end, that of description is [. . .] an arraying or delineation of the properties and circumstances of objects in their spatial or conceptual field" (4). This reduces narrativity to one of its temporal modalities, namely, that of the forward progression of plot events.[9]

A "slow" film like *The Ornithologist* revolves around another principle of narration that is not concerned first and foremost with plot progression but with the careful (acoustic) construction of a narrative space that gradually progresses to become increasingly mystic, eerie, and profane. The acoustic space of *The Ornithologist* thus simultaneously carves out the environment (description) and drives the events of the film (narration). Description is here *intrinsic* to narrative, yet narratology has always posed it as an antidote to the relentless temporal, forward progression of the plot.[10] This comes down to narratology's historical obsessions with binaries, in this case that of "time/narrative" versus "space/description."

The Ornithologist instead transforms description into a category of diegesis construction that operates with a topological rather than temporal-sequential organizational principle. In this context, Maria Poulaki (2011) has argued that description constructs a diegetic space that is not formed through the linking of elements into a causal-linear chain but, rather, as a networked system of links (149). Soundscapes form such topologies that link the elements of the film together as a network of material affects rather than according to the temporal-sequential chain of events that is often mistakenly identified with narration more generally.

If narrative space is dynamic, in flux, and constant in transition, then its nature cannot be spatial alone. The notion of narrative space is necessarily a configuration of both time *and* space. Therefore, more than creating a narrative space, cinematic soundscapes create what Bakhtin (1981) referred to as "chronotopes." These describe the intrinsic connectedness of temporal and spatial relationships as artistically expressed in literature (or film). Time becomes the fourth dimension of space. In the literary chronotope, Bakhtin argues, spatial and temporal indicators fuse into one carefully thought-out whole. Time thickens, takes on flesh, and becomes artistically visible. At the same time space becomes charged and responsive to the movements of time, plot, and history. The chronotope emerges in this intersection of axes and fusion of spatiotemporal indicators (84).

The chronotope thus vexes the notion of the temporal and spatial dimensions of narrative as inextricably linked. In film studies, Vivian Sobchack (1998) has pushed the notion of chronotope in a similar direction, arguing that chronotopes "provide the literal and concrete ground from which narrative and character emerge as the temporalization of human action, significant in its diacritical marking of both cultural and narrative space" (151). Recently, Pepita Hesselberth (2014) has advanced the notion of the audiovisual chronotope as a performative and embodied model for capturing the

> time/space/subjectivity configurations that the cinematic gives rise to, as well as the mobile, fleeting, embedded, embodied selves that the cinematic, para-cinematic, and post-cinematic leave us with, selves that are necessarily entrapped in (mediated) space-times, indeed can be said to exist of it. (10)

Following this lead, Francesco Sticchi (2018a, 2018b, 2018c, 2019) has carved out the notion of the chronotope as an operational, relational, embedded, and embodied spatiotemporality that arises in the dynamic coupling of spectator and film. Thus, "a filmic story-world is not a closed system but an organic reality that transforms, combines, and holds together a proliferation of discourses and dialogical concepts that are impossible to reduce to unitary and stable categories" (Sticchi 2018c, 69). Sticchi (2018a) discovers in Bakhtin's vocabulary, epitomized by the notion of the chronotope, a willingness to conceive narrative comprehension "as a constructive and dynamic process, impossible to be reduced to abstract, disembodied operations" (59). The chronotope is thus no abstract space-time but an affective media ecology. More than a mere semiotic construct, it is a narrative mediation of space and time whose emergence relies on the motor resonances that pertain to both the embodied (situated in a physical organism) and embedded (situated in a techno-mediated environment) nature of the cinematic experience. Filmic soundscapes are thus not the *background* of the narrative, but the spatiotemporal, affective grounding out of which the narrative emerges.

5.2. Soundscapes and Film Sound Analysis

Schafer's (1977) popularization of the term "soundscape" to understand sounds not as individual sound-signs but as part of a plethora of sounds that conjointly express an acoustic environment has proven instrumental to film studies. Today, the notion of the soundscape is a staple in the study of sound in cinema whether it is being used to study the acoustics of a historical period (e.g., Altman 2017; Birdsall 2012), of a singular work (e.g., Nardelli 2010), of more broad developments in cinematic sound culture (e.g., Ward 2019), or as an interdisciplinary conceptual plane capable of establishing a common ground for the dialogue between practitioners, academics, and artists on the art of film sound (Sider 2004). Since the notion of the soundscape was originally coined to raise awareness of the dangers of noise pollution according to a romanticized opposition between the purity of pastoral living and the sonic contamination of industrial urbanization, it paradoxically has come to highlight the aesthetic potential of "noises" in audio(visual) cultures.[11] The contemporary understanding of soundscape within sound studies thus differs radically from Schafer's original popularization of the term that is ripe with nostalgic yearnings for a pre-electronic and preindustrial soundscape (Toop 1995, 253). Such is a far cry from the conglomeration of recorded electronic sounds, environmental noises and ambiences, orchestral and popular music, dialogues, and sound effects that populate the soundscapes of cinema. Regardless of its past use, the strength of the concept of the soundscape lies in its expression of the convolution of sound, place, and time that invites holistic analysis of the total impression of the acoustic dimension of a transitory space. The term is thus not anti-semiotic but grounds acoustic semiotics in affective and material qualities that direct attention to the atmosphere or environment created by or with sound, thereby evoking the environment as an emotive environment or affective ecology.

Our interest in the term "soundscape" lies in the challenge it constitutes to the notion of the narrative space as a vessel containing the characters, objects, and events of the film. In its textual conceptualization, the diegesis is organized around the notion of a territorialized, framed space ontologically distinct from the nondiegetic elements of the film such as inserts, music without a source in the narrative, or end credits. Such demarcations are essential to our comprehension of narratives, and filmmakers often exploit our instinctive tendency to territorialize space. Yet, this is a modality that is rooted in our visual perception of the world. Thus, when we look at a territory our field of vision is defined by the boundaries of the territory, i.e., by what is visually accessible from the agent's particular situational perspective. Our definition of territories as bordered spaces is thus an act of quantification that is anchored in the visual perceptual system (Lakoff and Johnson 2003, 30).

When we consider our acoustic perception of environments, however, we will notice that it is decisively less framed, less territorialized, and less discriminated into categories of inside and outside. Auditory space has no favored focus. It determines a sphere liberated from fixed boundaries; it is a space made by the thing itself rather than the container of the thing. Rather than being boxed in and framed, it is dynamic and always in flux, as it creates and recreates its own dimensions on a moment-to-moment basis (Carpenter 1973, 35).[12]

Given that the textual diegesis as a container of the narrative is modeled upon the territorialization of the visual frame (e.g., diegetic/nondiegetic, onscreen/offscreen, voice-over), the application of this model onto film sound has proven difficult. One of the reasons for this is that the inside/outside paradigm of the diegetic/nondiegetic distinction disregards the fundamental nature of sonic objects as invasive, ubiquitous, and capable of penetrating through walls, bending around corners, and intruding into private spaces.[13] Addressing cinematic soundscapes necessarily moves us beyond the concept of space as the container of social activities. Sound never travels through empty space; the space itself is neither passive nor inactive. In fact, the material textures of space make sound possible, and thus (acoustic) space must be studied according to its own configurations, propensities, and material affective reverberations. The notion of soundscape thus poses a challenge to the prolonged visual bias of film theory.[14]

The main assumption driving this bias is the idea that if sound phenomena are to be meaningfully examined, they need to be conceived from the perspective of representation and a disembodied model of signification.[15] Yet, the reinvigoration of cineacoustic research has revealed the limitations of the language and vocabulary of film studies when it comes to addressing film sound and music studies. Overcoming the visual bias of film studies requires more than a turn to sound; it necessitates a rethinking of what in our conceptual and theoretical frameworks led to the visual bias in the first place. As such we must dispute the tendency to reduce signification to language and representation; the failure of textual semiotics to include the affective and material into the domain of signification; and the cognitive naturalization of theoretical, epistemological, or cultures biases.

In contrast to the diegetic/nondiegetic distinction, which is deeply entrenched in the visual bias of film studies, the notion of the soundscape captures the totality of the sonic design of a film as partaking in the production of the filmic diegesis. Instead of asking whether a sound belongs inside or outside of the diegesis, the notion of soundscape redirects our attention toward the acoustic production of the diegesis itself. The notion of the soundscape therefore does not study individual sound elements from the perspective of the already visually constituted diegesis but inquires into the role of sound elements in the establishing of the narrative space, the production of atmosphere, its contributions to the film's rhythms, how it ensures a temporal unity between images assembled by montage, and how it communicates the narrative. This contrasts with the label of "nondiegetic," which either assumes a realist conception of the diegesis according to which the narrative world exists irrespective of its presentation or threatens to ignore the narrational role of music, ambient noises, nonidentifiable sound effects, and other sound elements that are not visually sourced in the diegesis. In either case, the label of "nondiegetic" to a particular kind of film sound appears to hamper our understanding of how this sound shapes our understanding and experience of the filmic world. Alternatively, by giving analytical priority to the overall sonic design of the film, the notion of soundscape accommodates the plethora of roles of sound in the formation of the narrative environment, even if we intuit these (retrospective or not) to exist "outside" the portrayed world of the film. If the cinematic diegesis is partly defined by its acoustic environment (assuming there is one), it can no longer be claimed in any substantial way that a musical score exists inside or outside of it. This way of framing the narrative space disregards the distinct borderless construction of acoustic space and reduces it to the more analytically fixed territorialized space of the visual sensory modality.

Effectively, the diegetic/nondiegetic distinction is less an emblem of a renewed interest in film sound within film studies than it is the reinforcement of the field's continued visual bias. David Neumeyer's (2015, 63) five binaries for the function of film music exemplify how contemporary theories continue to comprehend the role of sound exclusively on the basis of its relation to the visual representation of the narrative: clarity versus fidelity, foreground versus background, diegetic versus nondiegetic, synchronization versus counterpoint, and empathy versus anempathy. According to this model, all that film music can do is to *relate to* or *accompany* the always-already visually depicted storyworld. The unquestioned assumption is that the visual image is solely responsible for the narrative that is believed to be hermeneutically secluded from the so-called nondiegetic sounds. What occupies the analyst, according to this model, is the many ways in which music and narrative interrelate in films. What is tellingly left out of this model is how music configures our overall impression of the diegesis. However, cinema does not give us audio plus vision but audiovision, and the overall impression of the diegesis alters as a function of this configuration as a cross-modal perception along the lines of the "McGurk effect."[16] In film music narratology, as pioneered by Claudia Gorbman (1987), however, the narrative is ontologically anchored in the visuals and the dialogues. Here what is deemed nondiegetic does not *denote* anything in the represented space; it figures merely "in the expression of mood, pace, and feeling *in relation to* the represented space" (32, my emphasis).

It could be argued that cognitive film musicology has salvaged the die-getic/nondiegetic distinction from its presumed ontological primacy. Edward Branigan (1986) has, for instance, presented a critical evaluation of the textual assumption of the diegesis and accused it of blurring the boundaries of narra-tion and narrative, as well as for its reduction of filmic signification to linguistic categories such as denotation and connotation. According to the cognitivist nar-ratological position advanced by Branigan, narration is the "overall regulation and distribution of a knowledge in a text" (38), and as such the diegetic and the nondiegetic are not *objective* cinematic facts inherent in the film text but the re-sult of interpretations that are contingent on the individual spectator's retrospec-tive establishment of the text's propositions. Branigan thus salvages the diegetic/nondiegetic construction by turning the diegesis into a retrospective cognitive construct that has lost its contact with our immediate material and affective ex-perience of the diegesis as a lived environment. If the diegesis is reinterpreted as a mediated environment, however, it becomes possible to address its direct expe-riential nature in holistic terms in a manner that is flexible enough to allow for corrections based on added or new information.

The notion of the filmic soundscape operates prior to the distinction of die-getic and nondiegetic—the distinction can be useful according to context, but it has neither ontological nor analytical priority—to highlight the overall sonic architecture of the filmic world. The focus is instead directed at the sonic design of the material and affective media environment. Barbara Flückiger (2009) has observed that sounds do not in fact give away their particular source (referential meaning) as much as their material components (material expression). Wood, metal, water, stone, and paper all have recognizable sonic signatures. And we are able to detect not only the acoustic material but also even its current material condition of sound objects, as for example, water as steam, rain, or ice (153).

Sound's material expressions further encompass an affective component that cannot be captured by the textual comprehension of the diegesis. The sound of rain on asphalt, windows, or grass each produces a slightly different variation of the organization of affect.[17] Important, however, is not the fidelity of the recorded sounds to a presumed reality but the impression a sound makes and its affective nuances. Important is thus less the sound as a referent of water hitting a surface, and more how it conjures up affective residues, whether of clothes being soaked, the refreshed feeling of water hitting your bare skin on a hot summer day, or the comfort of listening to the rain hitting the outside of your tent.

In these examples the material and affective components of the sonic elements are connected to *natural* sounds that—regardless of how insignificant and irrelevant they might be from a textual perspective—could be counted as "diegetic." In her study on sound design, Flückiger identifies a central yet overlooked component of cinematic sound designs, the so-called unidentified sound objects (USOs).[18] These sounds have no "meaning," and they reveal no connection or linkage to an identifiable source in the diegesis. An example could be Hans Zimmer's use of horns to create a rumbling "braaam" sound in (the trailer for) *Inception* (directed by Nolan 2000). If traditional scores are easily codified as background accompaniment to the story, USOs are ambient noises that define our perception of the narrative environment. It is thus not possible to ascribe them to the textual dichotomy of diegetic/nondiegetic, because their operational plane is the constitution of the diegesis itself. In being ambient sounds, USOs neither imitate a realist or natural non-mediated soundscape nor refer their listener to a material source. A USO is neither visible on screen nor to be inferred from the situational context. Rather than invoking a "fantastical gap" (cf. Stilwell 2007; Yacavone 2012) between the diegetic and the nondiegetic, USOs define the ambience of the narrative space. USOs are not to be resolved; they roam freely without apparent recognition of the boundaries of the textual diegesis.

In making apparent the rich use of USOs in contemporary mainstream cinema, Flückiger challenges the assumption that popular cinema has been streamlined to exclude (sonic) elements failing to make an immediate meaningful contribution to the film. USOs, by contrast, work in a direct, nonverbal manner to exploit our basic, precognitive apprehension of the affective qualities of an environment (e.g., a low rumble anticipates nearby danger). Sounds without an identifiable object thus contribute to the film's affective arrangement, for instance, by building up emotional tension or triggering instinctive affective reflexes such as the startle response. USOs are often employed to exploit the fact that threatening noises habitually are those that cannot be attributed to a known source within a reasonable time frame for the organism to establish a defensive response.

Flückiger's work on USOs is characteristic of a contemporary trend that gives voice to sounds that have traditionally been deemed *insignificant* due to their lack of discursive communicational value. It thus plays into a contemporary sound aesthetics increasingly populated by "noises," i.e., ambient sounds that do not communicate verbally or propositionally and thus cannot be ascribed to the textual system of the film. These noises come in two overall varieties. First, there are referential noises (sounds pertaining to objects, animals, human activities, weather conditions, etc.) that neither direct our attention to objects nor advance the temporal-sequential progression of the plot (e.g., the sound of wind in the trees). While these "noises" can be organized into the textual system of the film, they are deemed outside of the textual core of the film's signification. Second, there are ambient and environmental sounds bereft of an identifiable source (e.g., USOs, room tone, or the mass of indistinguishable noises that make up a soundscape such as an urban or natural one).

Both these types of noises have become increasingly prominent within a new paradigm of cinematic sound. This "noise aesthetics" has somewhat paradoxically been spurred by technological advancements in noise reduction. As Flückiger (2009) explicates this curious coincidence, "Vagueness and indeterminacy can function as stylistic devices only when they are not understood as errors. Thus, a technical prerequisite for such use of sound is high resolution with precise tonal definition" (157). By contrast, classical sound aesthetics needed to rely upon the easy recognizability and clear codification of both source and location of its sonic components to accommodate a theatrical environment that was burdened with the unwanted noises of the cinematic machinery (cf. Altman 2017).

The crisis of the diegesis has thus not only been spurred by recent academic developments (e.g., the increased attention to the embodied, affective, spatial, and sonic dimension of films) but also by a shift in sound aesthetics (partly spurred by technological advancements). The increasingly complex soundscapes that blast through the cinematic auditoriums—whether in the multiplexes or art houses—indicate the establishment of a sound aesthetics that has reconfigured the relation of sound and diegesis.

5.3. Soundscapes and the Aesthetics of Noise

Beginning with Luigi Russolo's 1913 futurist manifesto, passing over musique concrète to Jacques Attali's political-economic analysis of music, we find a modern fascination with the aesthetics of noise. For Russolo (1986), noise is the product of modern industrial life: "Noise was really not born before the 19th century, with the advent of machinery. Today noise reigns supremely over human sensibility" (3). Attali (2009) famously argued that it is not in silent representations but in noise that we are to find life:

> Our science has always desired to monitor, measure, abstract, and castrate meaning, forgetting that life is full of noise and that death alone is silent: work noise, noise of man, and noise of beast. Noise bought, sold, or prohibited. Nothing essential happens in the absence of noise. (3)

Armed with portable microphones, the directors of the nouvelle vague left the studios to record "in the wild" and to capture the abundances of noises that embodied modern life. In *Red Desert* (*Il deserto rosso*, 1964), Michelangelo Antonioni aligned industrial noises with the film's main protagonist Giuliana's (Monica Vitti's) growing feeling of disconnect, anxiety, and isolation. In this period, filmmakers were experimenting with new sound practices in direct contrast to the reliance on sound archives that characterized studio films from 1930 to 1965. Partly inspired by modernist experimentations, the New Hollywood filmmakers re-explored these sound archives, yet in a more playful and liberated manner to rediscover an unused potential of archival sounds.[19]

From the advent of a cineacoustic aesthetics of noise it is possible to derive a series of principles that demonstrate the changing relation of sound and the diegesis. First, the elements of the filmic soundtrack increasingly overlap such that sound effects are used to explore (musical) rhythms. This is combined with a more detailed, complex, and multilayered design of the acoustic environments that are most of all defined by the growing willingness of filmmakers to communicate their stories through the senses. This, in turn, requires a more holistic approach that considers all sounds to be (potential) drivers of the diegesis.[20]

What encapsulates the changing landscape of film sound most emphatically is, however, the gradual movement from a vococentric to a noise-centric cinema. Replaced is the classical Hollywood sound aesthetics founded upon a clear demarcation of the singular elements of the soundtrack such that sound effects, dialogue, and music would not be confused and clearly comprehended as pertaining to the different layers of the film. By contrast, the increased convergence between the elements of the soundtrack to the degree that sound effects, environmental sounds, ambient noises, and music often conflate in the filmic soundscape is one of the most noticeable characteristics of the cineacoustic noise aesthetics that has shifted the emphasis from sonic representation to sonic experience.

This development was sparked by the rise of the "sound designer"—associated with figures such as Walter Murch, Ben Burtt, Gary Rydstrom, Randy Thom, and Alan Splet—during the renaissance of film sound in the 1970s. The new title of the sound designer can be seen as a revolt against the compartmentalization of the sound departments, where the work on various sound elements would be conducted in relative isolation from each other. The sound designer instead collaborates with the director, department heads, and screenwriters in creating the overall sonic impression of the film. With the invention of the sound designer, the designing and staging of the filmic soundscape became an occupational profession.[21]

The sound designers of the New Hollywood revolted against the reliance of the major Hollywood studios on the recreation of sound in postproduction, and they did so armed with noises. This was an army of the neglected. As Chion (1994) remarks, "noises, those humble footsoldiers, have remained the outcasts of theory, having been assigned a purely utilitarian and figurative value and consequently neglected" (145).[22] Enhanced by technologies that provided more fine-grained sound reproduction and an increasing number of channels to enclose the spectator in sound, sound designers matched noise with design to create more complex and multilayered soundscapes that no longer merely accompanied the visual representation of space. New sound technologies change the narrative affordance of film and

> allow audiences and story-tellers far greater freedom than ever before: no more just the one source of narrative information, no longer just an image to look at; in its place an increasingly sophisticated intersection of narrative planes where sound provides a truly hemispheric aural environment and not simply support to the image on a rectangular screen. (Sergi 2013, 117)

Advancements in the technology of film sound were then first and foremost utilized to unframe the cinematic space and rearrange it affectively. Comparable to staging or mise-en-scène, sound design invites us to study the sonic scenography of a film. Design and scenography are thus no longer limited to the visual staging of the film through lighting, interior design, costuming, etc. Sounds are no longer just to be recorded but to be composed, arranged, and modified to create the complex acoustic soundscapes of contemporary cinema.

Although the aesthetics of noise has been aided by modern sound technology and thus often been ascribed to contemporary cinema, we find already in the early film theory of Béla Balázs an exploration of the potential of noise for cinema. Balázs saw the potential of the sound film to elevate shapeless noise into an artistic form of expression, signification, and meaning. Whereas his contemporaries were skeptical of the introduction of sound (especially of the "dialogue-film"),[23] Balázs (1953), while also critical of wall-to-wall dialogue, pointed out how sound could enrich the cinematic environment:

> It is the business of the sound film to reveal for us our acoustic environment, the acoustic landscape in which we live, the speech of things and the intimate

whisperings of nature. [. . .] Sensitive lyrical poets always could hear these significant sounds of life and describe them in words. It is for the sound film to let
them speak to us more directly from the screen. (197–98)

Although sound designers continue to complain about an overload of dialogue
in scripts,[24] the soundscapes envisioned by Balázs have materialized in contemporary films. Chion has demonstrated that the cineacoustic spaces prompted by
modern sound technology differ from the fixed, Euclidean spaces of the classical era defined by the visual frame. Thus, the cineacoustic space is not identical
with the visually framed space as constructed by the image. Cineacoustic space
"abounds in detail; it is polyphonic but vague in its outlines and borders; it is,
in other words, acoustic" (73). Sound neither knows Euclidean perspective nor
indicates the outlines of the objects from which it emanates (73). Instead, the
"acoustic field is elastic (in contrast with the fixed edges of the image) and opens
up to ever more polyphony: it dehierarchizes, delinearizes the film" (73).

Modern sound aesthetics no longer commits itself to the early cineacoustic
ideal where "[i]mages that imply sound, along with sounds that suggest images,
took on a high level of importance, and thus weighed heavily in the early development of cinema sound" (Altman 2017, 199). For reasons of both aesthetic
virtue and technological necessity, the classical soundscape tolerated only highly
"motivated" noises (e.g., the noises of a battle scene), and there was a general hostility toward "unnecessary noises."[25] Following Sergi (2002), this aesthetics was
the result of technological limitation, for instance, because the loudspeakers had
been designed principally to reproduce audible speech (108).

Chion (1991) emphasizes the hapticity of the sound afforded to cinema
through Dolby technologies, which was real and precise, clear and sharp in the
high registers and as palpable "as if you were touching it, like the touch of the
skin of a peach, which gives some people the shivers" (69). Resisting the lure of
accrediting to new sound technologies a superior replication of the "real," Chion
argues that "the sound does not attempt to reproduce the real noises of the situation, but to render the physical impact of the blow or the speed of the movement" (71).

If film sound has become less "representational," this is not true only on the
level of the acoustics. Indeed, developments in film sound have reconfigured the
narrative space to the extent that it can no longer meaningfully be understood
as the visual container of the narrative propositions, but far more as the sensorial, tactile, moving, affective, and audible world that affords events to take place
at all.[26] Sound is no longer in the service of a preconstituted diegesis, so it can
be deemed to fall either inside (diegetic) or outside of (nondiegetic); it stretches
its boundaries, portrays, and defines, but also filters and limits, the diegesis.
Spawned by better sound equipment, modern filmmakers began increasingly

to explore the "physical," three-dimensional qualities of sound and encouraged audiences not just to listen to sounds but "feel" them, making the experience of cinematic sound more sensual than ever before (Sergi 2002, 110).

Spawned by the affordances of new sound technologies, the new cinematic sound aesthetics is not only a remolding of the *experience* of the diegesis; it also prompts the replacement of our conceptual tools for understanding that experience by highlighting cinema's affective and material modes of narrative communication.

5.4. Toward an Affective Poetics of Filmic Soundscapes

The major achievement of the notion of the filmic soundscape lies in its capacity not just to accentuate the acoustic dimension of the cinematic space, but to render this space as a lived, embodied narrative environment. The introduction of noise to the cinematic soundscape calls for a remodeling of film theory based on the recognition of the material and affective role of sound. Important thus becomes the highlighting of affective processes as part of the material architecture of the films both in terms of its acoustics but also more generally. Thus, noise offers an ideal conceptual starting point for a more comprehensive delineation of the material-affective poetics of the film experience that this book argues is needed to reconceptualize film narratology.

This is not least the case because the sonic allows us to unfold the entwined nature of the "performative-affective" and the "semiotic" in human experience. Sounds often unite referential (e.g., the sound of thunder), material (e.g., the direct physical impact of a loud thunder), affective (e.g., sensations of excitement, fear, awe, amazement, etc.), and environmental (hostile, inimical, dark, murky, etc.) factors into a unified sonic impression. Instead of separating these heuristically, the notion of the soundscape prepares for an affective poetics that understands the semiotics of film acoustics on the basis of their material and affective production of the diegesis. Even in its purest linguistic form of the dialogue, film sound cannot be reduced to brute code but must be recognized as a form of material-affective communication whose building blocks are rhythmic, dynamic, temporal, tactile, and kinetic sensations.[27]

The task is thus to counter not only the classical narratological neglect of space but also its neglect of the material world and the felt body. Needed is the development of new theories and conceptual tools designed to examine how a work of art organizes and arranges affect (both in relation to the material film and the movements of the spectators' felt bodies). Of central importance to a "poetics of affect"[28] is that the embodied encounter of the affective and the material becomes the most basic building block for the organization of the film, whereas textual film studies was founded upon the denotative propositions of the film text or the mental representations of the fabula in a literary form. Given that cinema as an art form does not trade in representational language as do literary works, the film's representational level is formed on the basis of an enactment of nonlinguistic gestures, facial expressions, intonations, movements, and body language. Representation is thus not the default modality of cinematic artworks; for the cinematic space to be representative of some other place, it must physically enact that place to begin with. Moreover, when we speak of cinematic narratives as *representing* a somewhere and a something else, we must remember that we are not assuming a conception of representation based on the arbitrary relation between signifier and signified. There is no objective content in film that does not refer back to the motor resonances, embodied perception, feeling, and thinking enacted in the cinematic experience.

Representations neither reside in the audiovisual material as the property of the filmic text nor are stored in our brains as a cognitive representation of the literary propositions of the film:

> The connective tie between the image on the screen and the spectators in the audience can be found neither in the plot, nor in the narrative, but in the capacity to affect other bodies and be affected by them. To understand the interaffective structure in which the technical and the human, the artificial and the organic body are entangled, we need to understand the matter in which both are grounded. This matter—for all cinematic forms of audiovisual images, at least—is movement itself. (Kappelhoff and Lehmann 2019, 214)

Once again, we have returned to the resonant movements between the embodied spectator and the filmic material, this time to develop a theory of narrative space that is more than a static container for the objects, characters, and events of the story and advances instead a dynamic model based on material-affective relations. A recurring theme throughout this book has been to develop a conception of the diegesis as a property that emerges out of the dynamical flow of movements produced in the affective coupling of spectator and film.

This reciprocal flow of movements brings together on the same conceptual plane movements pertaining to actors and objects; the movement-suggestions of the natural and built environment, of facial expressions, of sounds, of sound effects, and of music, along with the rhythms created through editing and montage, camera movements, framings, and staging; as well as the affective involvement of the perceiving body. It is in this fluid dynamogenic of sensory impressions, the arrangements of affect, as well as cognitive operations that the cinematic raw material is enacted into a felt, environmental diegesis. Consequently, from the perspective of an affective poetics, the arrangement of the film refers not only to the audiovisual arrangement of the film but also to how this implies an arrangement of our felt bodily perceptions. The diegesis is thus itself a product of the "flow of movements" between the material film and its embodied spectator.

Sergei Eisenstein, Dziga Vertov, Siegfried Kracauer, Jean Epstein, Béla Balázs, and Edgar Morin are all early pioneers in the exploration of the material-affective mode of cinematic communication, which, they in various ways demonstrated, differed from literary art, because it primarily affects the senses of the spectators, engaging them on the level of physiology before they are able to install a cognitive-analytical distance to the film. Recent decades' work in film sound scholarship has again confronted us with the vital recognition of the affective and material basis of cinematic signification essential for the theoretical framework developed by this this book. Despite the early reservations about film sound, in particular, directed against the "talkies," sound is today indispensable for cinema's kinetic and multisensorial qualities and for understanding how the cinematic diegesis is enacted in embodied perception and cognition. The difficulties sound has posed to textual semiotics might have left it marginalized for years, but it has also demonstrated that cinema does not communicate through an arbitrary and neutral sign system. Instead, sound (and cinema) communicates by being a moving force, an everchanging material process of energy in action.

Consequently, film sound again leads us to the principle that we have argued is true more generally of cinema, namely, that it communicates through "resonance effects" that provoke "in the spectator such kinesthetic responses as muscular reflexes, motor impulses, or the like" (Kracauer 1997, 158). Sonic perception is not a matter of receiving information and processing it like a computer does with measurable data. Sound is instead enacted in the direct, material-affective exposure to sonic reverberations, shifting the perspective from decodification, informational processing, and reading to the realm of sensory experience.[29] Audition is therefore more than the extraction of information from vibrating waves by a disengaged informational system; it is a meaningful engagement between the organism and its material and affective embeddedness in the fluctuations and vibrations of the world. Rethinking the diegesis in environmental terms does not mean throwing out the baby with the bathwater, as Chion (1994) argues would be the case were we entirely to abandon classifications such as onscreen/offscreen or diegetic/nondiegetic (75–80). What we do reject, however, is the assumed primacy of such classifications in favor of a more holistic, atmospheric understanding of the diegesis as the felt environment afforded by audiovisual media.

5.5. The Soundscape as a Media-Anthropological Term

Thus far we have considered the affective and material engagement with cinematic soundscapes without taking their particularly mediated nature into concern. In this section, however, it shall be argued that the notion of the soundscape already implies the existence of mediation. From a media-anthropological perspective it is not enough to ask, "How do we perceive the soundscape?" We must go further and ask instead, "How does the very existence of a soundscape change the conditions of our perception of sound?"

One of the most insightful criticisms of the concept of soundscape has been delivered by Tim Ingold (2007). Following him, it is false to pose the soundscape as a pendant to the landscape, since the latter is not a visual category per se but actually, unlike the soundscape, implies a multisensorial mode of engaging with the world. Our prototypical perception of a landscape is thus not tied to one sensory register; rather, the different sensory systems operate in cooperation and with such overlap of function, that their respective contributions are impossible to tease apart (10). Ingold thus argues that the notion of soundscape cannot describe our everyday, multisensorial, "natural," pretechnological, and unmediated interactions with the world.

However, this does not disqualify the concept of soundscape altogether but renders it into a technical term for describing a particular kind of mediated auditory experience. The notion of soundscape thus no longer describes ordinary, quotidian auditory experience but refers instead to how media operations make possible perceptions and sensory experiences that are not "natural" but reliant on techniques of rendering and extraction. Thus, a landscape is not visual by itself; it becomes visual when it is rendered by techniques such as paining or photography that produce an indirect, mediated modality of visual perception. In becoming an image, the landscape is presented to the viewer in an artificially purified form reduced and adapted to one sensory register. A landscape could then also be *audible*, but to be so it would first have to be rendered by a technique of sound art or recording, such that it can be *played back* within an environment (such as a darkened room) that isolates it from the impact of other sensory stimuli (10).

The notion of the soundscape thus implies that a media-technological intervention has taken place according to which the auditory inputs have become extracted, manipulated, or modified and separated from their original multisensorial environmental context. As Ingold puts it, a soundscape has always been rendered through some technique, whether by the use of audio recordings to extract the sonic dimension of a scene or by analytical methods such as Chion's (1994) "masking method" in which the analyst isolates the auditory from the visual stimuli or vice versa to study their individual impact.[30] If the notion of the soundscape is thus inadequate for understanding non-mediated experience, it appears perfectly suitable for comprehending how cinema conjures up its narrative worlds on the basis of the extraction and reassembling of what Chion has dubbed "sensory isolates," which in the case of the cinema are mediated extractions of aural and visual stimuli.

Chion (2013) proposed the notion of sensory isolates to capture how mediated sensations directed at just one of the senses are taken out of their original multisensory and environmental context (328). In the case of recorded sound, the sound phenomenon is first isolated from its original environment, and the sensations that would normally accompany it create the "sensory isolate." The filmic sound of a rattling train is an acoustic isolate and as such differs from the actual sensation that we would experience if we were actually riding in that train, where the sonic impressions would be accompanied with other sensations such as the kinetic sensation of being jolted (328). In his work on sensory isolates, Chion invokes a broad conception of mediation that is reserved neither for art nor media technologies. In this fashion it even becomes possible to talk of modern windows that filter the exposure of light and regulate temperature and noise as sensory isolates.

It is important to stress that despite its reliance on sensory isolates, the cinematic experience is not restricted to its two sensorial input channels. Indeed, as has been argued extensively here and elsewhere, cinema must be understood as multisensorial and synesthetic.[31] In fact, *because* it relies on sensory isolates, cinema might actively heighten the level of synesthetic crossover. This is because synesthetic activation is more likely to occur when we are concentrating upon only one sensorial modality. When only one or a few senses dominate (as in mediated conditions), the more these senses will begin to implicate other senses, and therefore the more complex and the less "pure" its dominion will become (Connor 2004, 153). As a medium that relies upon visual and auditory sensory isolates, cinema can design and arrange its sonic and visual isolates to optimize the production of multisensorial and affective sensations.[32]

By isolating sound and sight as the sensorial vehicles, cinema thus activates other senses including nociception (pain), thermoception (temperature), the vestibular sense (balance), olfaction (smell), and gustation (taste) through "synesthetic spillover."[33] The sensory isolate of the sound of cracking ice combined with the appropriate visuals of footsteps in the snow will, for instance, activate thermoception, i.e., the sense by which an organism feels temperature. However, we obviously do not *feel* cold in the way we would have, were we actually to traverse a snowy landscape. In relation to this, we need to supplement Chion's notion of sensory isolates with scholarship on the multisensorial nature of (film) experience. Therefore, the particular *media-anthropological* sensation of thermoception in cinema should be understood not on the basis of a stimulus–response model but on the model of sensory isolates plus multisensorial perception. The fragmented sensory isolates are thus experienced not on the basis of individual stimuli but as part of a holistic sense impression such that the Foley artist can turn the sound of bacon frying in a pan into rain and the breaking of a leek into that of a broken bone. As a consequence, sensations that are based on sensory isolates are not identical to those that are not. It is, therefore, possible to experience nociception when exposed to audiovisual material, even if this material does not have the ability to cause actual physical pain (such as that which extreme exposure to sound or light would cause). What we experience is a sensation of pain, rather than pain per se, and no healing process is required afterwards. This might help explain neuroscientific findings of the activation of nociceptive processing when a subject is exposed to visual expressions of pain.[34] Rather than triggering nociception or thermoception on the basis of direct stimulation, multisensorial perception is achieved in the cinema on the basis of visual and auditory isolates. The same goes for cinematic sensations such as olfaction without actual smells, gustation without actual taste, and thermoception without actual exposure to heat or cold.

For this reason, the filmic soundscape is not to be actually situated on the level of the purely auditory dimension of the film. Soundscapes operate on the multisensorial and holistic level of the film (our natural modality of perception is after all based on the conjunction of visual and sonic impressions). The soundscape is thus one of cinema's many gateways to the multisensorial and atmospheric world of the film. The environment conjured up by a film's soundscape is thus not essentially an *acoustic* environment but a mediated, atmospheric environment (potentially) abundant with smells, tactile sensations, sensations of pain, tastes, movements, and temperatures. Tom Tykwer's *Perfume: The Story of a Murderer* (2006), for instance, conjures up a world of olfaction, while films such as *Julie & Julia* (directed by Ephron 2009) target our gustatory sense. In addressing the multisensoriality of the diegesis, we necessarily move from the conceptual plane of the sensory isolates (the sound- and image tracks) to that of the atmospheric or affective arrangement of a film. In other words, we move from Chion's (1994) acoustic "superfield" to the overall, media-generated world of the diegesis (based on multisensorial experience).

For analytical purposes it might be instructive to understand the contribution of the sensory and auditory isolates apart; if, that is, we do not lose sight of the fact that these are conjoined in the cinematic experience to convey a unified atmosphere or affective expression. Moreover, films can exploit the possibility of creating cognitive dissonances, where a mismatch between the sensory isolates conjure up conflicting affective states. One example of such is the combination of classical symphonies or upbeat, joyous pop music with the visual depiction of brutal, explicit violence as in *A Clockwork Orange* (directed by Kubric

1971) or *Reservoir Dogs* (directed by Tarantino 1992) (cf. Kiss and Willemsen 2013). In most cases, however, the sensory isolates work in unison to create a unified overall affective expression such as when bright light and a high pitch unite to express sensorial overload or as when chaotic music and rapid editing conjoin to convey a sensation of rushing, chaos, and stress (cf. Plantinga 2009b on "synesthetic affects").

5.6. Conclusion: Sonic Envelopes in *A Quiet Place*

In the post-apocalyptic horror film, *A Quiet Place* (directed by Krasinski 2018), the Abbots, a family that struggles to stay alive in face of the threat of extraterrestrial predators that are blind but have evolved extreme auditory sensibilities, are among the last surviving members of their species. The predators that have almost caused the extinction of humanity hunt by sound alone, and to survive in this hostile environment, the family must keep quiet at all times. Even the innocent act of playing with a toy, as the opening scene of the film fatally demonstrates, has deadly consequences for the youngest member of the family, Beau Abbott (Cade Wordward). With its sustained moments of silence and its near complete abstention of dialogue, the attention of the audience becomes extremely sensitive to the film's acoustic isolates, its plethora of small sonic details that create an enthralling filmic environment. In *A Quiet Place* sound does not pave the way for the plot; the plot paves the way for sound.

The film exemplifies how sound design in contemporary mainstream cinema has become increasingly invested in the creation of complex, multilayered soundscapes that immerse the audience in the filmic environment while backgrounding verbal communication. As Erik Aadahl, the sound engineer on the film along with Ethan Van der Ryn, explains, "[e]very little sound [of the film] is actually a big sound in a way" (Aadahl in Walden 2018). *A Quiet Place* thus invokes a new "audible technique"—i.e., "a concrete set of limited and related practices of listening and practical orientations towards listening" (Sterne 2003, 91)—designed to let certain aspects of the soundtrack, in this case environmental sounds, ambient noises, sound effects, USOs, and room tone, stand out. In *A Quiet Place*, this technique is employed to create "sonic envelopes."[35] Such envelopes designate shifts in the soundscapes resulting partly from the acoustic practices that the Abbots have developed to minimize the production of sound (e.g., use of sign language; barefoot walking; slow, silent movements; and the construction of soundproof niches for everyday life) and partly from conveying the sensory Umwelt according to the auditory perception of the family's hearing-impaired daughter, Regan Abbott (Millicent Simmonds). The film is thus arranged around sonic envelopes that both convey how the Abbotts have developed sonic techniques that minimalize the production of sounds, in order to survive, and also to narrate the subplot of the film, which thematizes Regan's emotional struggles.

Whereas the film's soundscape is mostly dominated by room tone and other indistinct, atmospheric environmental sounds, the film occasionally shifts to Regan's sonic envelope. Instead of environmental noise, Regan's sonic Umwelt is dominated by the sound of a low hum stemming from her cochlear implant. The film thus operates with two distinct soundscapes designed to carve out an experiential gap between Regan and the rest of her family. Shifting between Regan's sonic envelope and the ecologically situated sonic envelope of the rest of her family not only creates a unique sensation of acoustic space; it also becomes the seat of the film's material-affective communication of Regan's relationship with her father Lee (John Krasinski).

This subplot circles around Regan's guilt and her fear of no longer being loved by her father. Regan is convinced of her responsibility for the death of her youngest brother, Beau, because she gave him the batteries to the toy that made the sound that caused his death. The film expresses the conflict between father and daughter through attuning us affectively to the different sonic envelopes they inhabit. During the film's climax, Regan momentarily loses her implant, and we enter her sonic envelope of complete digital silence, devoid of atmospheric noises and "dead air." This moment of complete silence is a testament to the rootedness of sound in the material world, its rhythms, its intensities, and forces that we momentarily become untethered from. The textual designation of this scene as an instance of "intradiegetic" narration (the scene is focalized through Regan's perspective) is founded upon the film's affective mode of communication, i.e., to the affective-kinesthetic attunement of the embodied spectator to the sonic envelopes of the film's soundscape.

In producing a sensation of detachment through a modification of the auditory resonances that flow between spectator and film, A Quiet Place enacts Regan's feeling of being detached from the material world. Consequently, we are not required to fully abandon inquiries into the narrative and representational nature of film narration, but to anchor these in a media-anthropological and enactive reconceptualization of the diegesis considered no longer as a text but an environment that we must inhabit to reach an understanding of the characters and events of the narrative. At its most basic, cinematic signification is thus not reducible to the "literal" denotation of the filmic text but emerges on the basis of a resonance effect. Cinematic signification thus requires the embodied spectator to partake in the film's orchestrated flows of movements.

Afterword

In the second episode of the fifth season of the television show *Homeland* (Showtime, created by Gansa and Gordon, 2011–2020), a series initially about a CIA agent infiltrating a planned al-Qaeda terrorist attack, the main protagonist Carrie Mathison (Claire Danes) is escorted by a Hezbollah commander through a Syrian refugee camp in Lebanon. Intensifying ambient music is heard on the soundtrack among occasional chattering. The camera is shaky and handheld, momentarily pointing directly at the people of the camp, who stare blankly almost directly at us. The atmosphere is bleak; the tension is nervous. Dressed in a headscarf as she traverses the run-down buildings of the camp captured in dusty, gray tones, Carrie passes by graffiti painted walls. One of them reads in Arabic, "*Homeland* is racist."

In the Summer of 2015, while building the set for the fifth season of *Homeland* at the Babelsberg studio in Berlin, the production team unknowingly commissioned a group of art activists—Heba Yehia Amin, Caram Kapp, and Don Karl, who go by the name "Arabian Street Artists"—to draw graffiti on the studio set for the refugee camp. Caring little about the semantics of the graffiti, which functioned to create that Middle Eastern wartime atmosphere associated with post-9/11 films and television shows, the production team failed to notice that the graffiti commented on the show's stereotypical and antagonistic depiction of the Arab world and Islam. The activists had successfully "hacked" the diegesis of *Homeland* with inscriptions such as "this is not a series," "*Homeland* is racist," "this show is not to be trusted," "this show does not represent the views of the artists, and "*Homeland* is a watermelon" (which in Arabic means something like rubbish) (cf. *BBC News* 2015; Barfield 2015).

What the street artists were calling for was a more differentiated view of the region portraying the complexity of the matter in less simplistic terms (*BBC News* 2015). For them, the lack of attention to the semantics of the Arabic script was evidence of the creators' superficial use of their culture to conjure up the cliché image of the Middle East as a hostile environment. In "hacking" the diegesis, the artists wanted to expose *Homeland*'s superficial, stereotypic, and, in their belief, racist depiction of Middle Eastern culture along with their complete ignorance about the region and its people (cf. Barfield 2015). Against these charges of racism, Claire Danes, in an interview with *The Guardian*, refers to the complexity on the level of the screenplay, emphasizing how, for instance, a Palestinian politician is "making credible, cogent points about the ways that America has failed" and in general points to the show's criticisms of the post-9/11 "War on Terror" (Danes 2020).

However, even if *Homeland* obfuscates Hollywood's historical portrayal of the "evil" Arab by breaking with an "us-versus-them" dramaturgy, the battleground for the activists was the clichéd atrocious, timid, and fearful affective atmosphere that enveloped the series' portrayal of the Middle East. The problem with the depiction of the Middle East was not textual. What the activists revolted against was not the semantics but the continuous reproduction of "Orientalist fear" in Hollywood and popular television shows (cf. Semmerling 2006).[1]

Atmospheres are neither filters onto the narrative content nor sheer backgrounds that can be ignored at will; they determine our bodily valence of being in a place, mediated or not. Western audiovisual culture has mass produced an image of the Middle East such that the region has become veiled in an atmosphere of fear. Regardless of the nuances of the plot, the show's unreflected atmosphere production partakes in the association of one region, culture, and people with negative affective states such as fear, alienation, dread, misery, and suffering.

It is exactly due to their reproducibility that atmospheres become most harmful, and this is an important aspect of cinematic worldmaking that textual film analysis remains oblivious to. Although the ethical complications of the affective arrangement of the diegesis reaches far beyond the limits of this particular book, I hope to have provided some theoretical tools for shifting the terrain of narrative representation onto the material, affective, and environmental forms of filmic communication.

As Antonin Artaud famously declared, cinema acts directly on the gray matter of the brain. It involves a total reversal of values, a complete revolution in optics, perspective, and logic that requires speed but most of all repetition, insistence, and recapitulation. Cinema, this insistently repetitive art form, produces its own reality through rhythms, speeds, and intensities that operate directly on the neuronal and affective level. As Artaud warned, this gives cinema the power of a poison that is harmless and direct, a subcutaneous injection of morphine. It is, however, also in its murky waters that we find its magic (Artaud 1976, 181–82). Rather than being confined to representing the real, cinema produces it by altering and modulating our perceptions, affects, cognitions, and experiences. Cinema comes alive though our visceral and cerebral investments into the flow of its movements, and it is vital that we understand its direct material-affective mode of address to understand how it orchestrates its worlds to regulate, reproduce, or create experiences that go far beyond its text.

Notes

Introduction

1. Note, however that the "black box" studio, the "Black Maria," was invented by Thomas Edison to "defy the dictates of day, night, weather, and location in order to frame the production of artificial environments" (Jacobson 2015, 25). *Dogville* thus plays with the very origins of cinema, something that is further emphasized by the character name Tom Edison (Paul Bettany).
2. Here and in the following, the term "environment" is used in the ecological sense as presupposing the entanglement of animal and world. Importantly, the term "environment" does not simply refer to abstract, objective space, but to the lived space for some organism such that it implies its lifeworld, Umwelt, or milieu.
3. See Canning (2007) for a related reading of how the absence of frames and boundaries implicates the community in the rape of Grace.
4. Noël Burch (1979) was the first to shift attention to the diegesis as a process "whereby spectators experience the diegetic world as environment" rather than regarding it as a "fixed, simple object" (19).
5. Throughout this book, the term "diegesis" does not refer to the Platonic/Aristotelean concept of *diēgēsis* (διήγησις) but to the French term *diégèse*. In English, the French term *diégèse* has been translated into diegesis, and thus it coincides with the term used by Plato in the third book of *The Republic (Politeia)* to describe a particular mode of poetic presentation where the author narrates the story directly and undisguised as opposed to through the characters (i.e., mimesis or imitative representation) (cf. Taylor 2007, 1–2). In Aristotle's further development of these terms, "all narrative is mimesis in the wider sense, the simple or direct narrative (as in voice-over narration in film) is diegetic mimesis, whereas dramatic representations (of actors in a scene, for instance) are, strictly speaking, mimetic mimesis" (Taylor 2007, 2). With the French term *diégèse*, however, Souriau evokes the Greek term διήγησις not in the technical Platonic/Aristotelean sense, but (perhaps too) broadly as meaning simply "account," "story," and "representation." Although this use of the word διήγησις accords with its Old Greek meaning, retrospectively we could have wished that the filmologists had chosen another term that did not collide with that used in the poetics of Plato and Aristotle. As Gérard Genette (1983) has called attention to, it is important not to conflate Souriau's diegesis with Plato/Aristotelean diegesis, even if these two terms overlap in English (17–18). For a criticism of the diegesis, see Mitry (1997, 72). For overviews of the convoluted relation between these two uses of the diegesis, see Fuxjäger (2007) and Castelvecchi (2020).

6. Under the banner of "econarratology," Erin James (2015) argues that narratives are cultural tools that provide experiences of "what it is like" to experience a certain environment in certain contextual settings (e.g., according to a set of cultural beliefs or a subjective perception of the world). Stories then create environments that are not just experienced as such but experienced according to preconfigured viewpoints of, for instance, an individual, a moment in time, or a culture.

7. Bordwell, Thompson, and Staiger's *The Classical Hollywood Cinema* (1985) remains the authority when it comes to defining the classical Hollywood style. According to the authors the basic premise of Hollywood storytelling involves "causality, consequence, psychological motivations, the drive toward overcoming obstacles and achieving goals. Character-centered—i.e., personal or psychological—causality is the armature of the classical story" (13).

8. On the notion of "transmission of affects," see Brennan (2004).

9. It is possible to subdivide the "embodied turn" of film studies into three broad and, at times, overlapping theoretical perspectives: Deleuzian inspired affect theory (e.g., Shaviro 1993; Kennedy 2000; del Rio 2008), film phenomenology (e.g., Sobchack 1992, 2004; Barker 2009; Marks 2000), and cognitive psychological and neuroscientific film theory (e.g., Plantinga 2009b; Grodal 2009; Coëgnarts and Kravanja 2015; Gallese and Guerra 2020).

10. Narrative film theories have traditionally been developed from within the framework of film semiology (e.g., Barthes 1960a; Metz 1966, 1974, 1990), structuralist narratology (Chatman 1978, 1984; Kuhn 2011; Scholes 1985; Verstraaten 2009), cognitive formalism (e.g., Bordwell 1985, 2006, 2008; Branigan 1992, 1984; Thompson 1988), and, most recently, embodied cognition (Coëgnarts and Kravanja 2015; Grishakova and Poulaki 2019; Hven 2017a; Kiss 2015).

11. For this strain of "affect theory," see Massumi (1995, 2002); Clough and Halley (2007); Gregg and Seigworth (2010b); and Shaviro (2016).

12. See in this context the debates around Ruth Leys' "A Turn to Affect: A Critique" (2011a), for instance, Connolly (2011) and Leys (2011b). See also Brinkema (2014).

13. See, for instance, Daniel Yacavone's (2015) neo-Metzian distinction between the "world-in" (denotation) and the "world of" (connotation). Another example is the classical cognitive discourse theoretical proposition of Maarten Coëgnarts (2019) that the nonverbal conveying of meaning in film must be translatable into verbal, propositional, and linguistic form in order to ensure that we are not entering the domain of subjective meanings and interpretation. Consequently, "if we wish to show how films are capable of conveying meaning non-verbally, then it is best to focus on the sort of meaning of which we are certain to a confident degree that it is actually intended to be communicated by the films to the viewer. Situational meanings and plot summarization largely meet this condition and are therefore most appropriately fitted to examine the question of meaning in film" (xx). Within this "embodied" textual model of film experience, nonverbal meaning needs to be translated into "the 'lowest,' *literal* level of meaning, that of straightforward explanation of the plot" (xx, my emphasis) to qualify as a secure basis of cinematic signification.

14. This textualism can also be found in Bordwell's (1991) cognitivist distinction between "referential and explicit meanings" (denotation/diegetic) and "implicit and symptomatic meanings" (connotation/nondiegetic).

15. In *Emotion and the Structure of Narrative Film* (1996/2013), Ed Tan explicates the idea that films contain a textual core of signification with a reference to classic cognitive theories of discourse: "As is customary in theories of the cognition of discourse, we are assuming that the viewer's comprehension of the film narrative begins with the formation of the text base, a propositional representation of the discourse (van Dijk and Kintsch 1983). This text base is the first result of following with understanding the filmic action, which is relatively close to the directly observable surface structure of the film" (197). The in-quote reference is to van Dijk, T. A., and W. Kintsch. (1983). *Strategies of Discourse Comprehension.* San Diego, Calif.: Academic Press.

16. I am here referring to the work of scholars such as Ed Tan (2013), Greg M. Smith (2003), Carl Plantinga (2009b, 2009a, 2010, 2012), Torben Grodal (1999, 2005, 2009), and more recently Miklós Kiss (2015) and Maarten Coëgnarts (2014, 2019; Coëgnarts and Kravanja 2015).

17. "Ecocriticism," "econarratology," and "ecocritical film studies" have also renewed interest in environmental and ecological issues of narrativity. However, more than the environmental nature of mediated storyworlds, what concerns econarratology is "the paired consideration of material environments and their representations and narrative forms of understanding" (James and Morel 2020, 1). This book shares the affinity of these approaches to the manner in which narratives make us aware of the environment through narrative strategies and medialized modes of worldmaking. It also shares with affective ecocriticism the basic acknowledgment of the "powerful role environments themselves play in shaping affective experience, and [its willingness] to identify new affects emerging in our contemporary moment" (Bladow and Ladino 2018, 3). For a selection of this environmental strain of literary and film scholarship, see Glotfelty and Fromm (1996), Herman (2011), Willoquet-Maricondi (2010), James (2015), Ivakhiv (2013), and von Mossner (2017).

18. On the renewed narratological interest in worldmaking, see, for instance, Richard Gerrig (1993), Marie-Laure Ryan (1992, 2004; Bell and Ryan 2019), and David Herman (2013a). On narrative experientiality, see Monika Fludernik (2010), Marco Caracciolo (2014a, 2014b), and Merja Polvinen (2016).

19. Recent attempts to capture the environmental nature of the cinematic dispositif include Francesco Casetti (2015; Buckley, Campe, and Casetti 2019), Antonio Somaini (2016) on Benjamin's media concept, and Inga Pollman (2013, 2018) on Uexküll's notion of Umwelt.

20. Thus, whereas the diegesis does not require narrative events, narrative events require a diegesis. The diegesis is, however, not autonomous from the events that occur in it; thus, the diegesis is shaped by the events (narrative or not) that generate it.

21. On the intellectualism of language-oriented philosophies and the cognitive sciences, see also Mark Johnson (2017, 1–36). Johnson provides two reasons why language-oriented philosophy led to a neglect of the body: "(1) its exclusive focus on language as the object of philosophical analysis turned attention away from anything that was

not linguaform, and (2) it operated with a remarkably impoverished, and scientifically unsound, view of language as entirely conceptual and propositional" (4).

22. While media-anthropology is certainly not anthropocentric, it endorses neither the non-anthropocentrism to be found in the first-generation media-ecological credo that media *determine* the human condition, nor Friedrich Kittler's media-philosophy that wants to get the spirit (Geist) out of humanities (*Geisteswissenschaften*), nor Deleuze's, and in extension Massumi's, non-anthropological philosophy of affect.

23. On the media-philosophy of anthropomedial relations, see Christiane Voss (2010; Voss and Engell 2015a). See also Hven (2016, 2017b).

24. The "surrogate body" is Inga Pollman's suggestion for translating the word *Leihkörper*, which literally brings together the words "loan" and "body" (cf. Voss 2011).

25. We find this argument, for instance, in the literary narratology of Marie-Laure Ryan (2001), who asserts, "Literary texts can thus be either self-reflexive or immersive, or they can alternate between these two stances through a game of in and out—masterfully played in *The French Lieutenant's Woman*—but they cannot offer both experiences at the same time because language behaves like holographic pictures: you cannot see the signs and the world at the same time. Readers and spectators must focus beyond the signs to witness the emergence of a three-dimensional lifelike reality" (284).

Chapter 1

1. The list of the more recent academic discussions concerning the theoretical concept of the diegesis, and its epistemological commitments, includes Aumont and Marie (2001), Boillat (2009), Böhnke (2007), Bunia (2010), Castelvecchi (2020), Cecchi (2010), Fuxjäger (2007), Kassabian (2001, 2013), Knight-Hill (2019), Neumeyer (2009), Jeff Smith (2009), Stilwell (2007), Thanouli (2014), Winters (2010), and Yacavone (2012, 2015).

2. For recent criticisms of the diegesis that target a particular "textual" interpretation of the term, see Cecchi (2010), Kassabian (2013), Knight-Hill (2019), and Winters (2010).

3. In her criticism of the diegesis, Kassabian (2013) refers to the intensification of contemporary mainstream cinema, which has been theorized as "intensified continuity" (Bordwell 2002, 2006, 121–38), "impact aesthetics" (G. King 2000, 99–103), and "accelerationist aesthetics" (Shaviro 2010, 137–40). Recently, Adriano D'Aloia (2021) has convincingly argued that the destabilizing intensification and the stabilizing narrative principles reciprocally feed off one another in contemporary cinema.

4. Important works in this tradition include Metz (1974, 1990), Genette (1983, 1988), Bordwell (1985, 2008), Branigan (1984, 1992), and Gorbman (1980, 1987).

5. For an example of the linguistic metaphor for cognitive functioning, see Fodor (1975). For a recent criticism, see Cuccio and Gallese (2018).

6. On the spatial turn of film studies, see Baschiera and De Rosa (2020).

7. For a comprehensive study of the filmology movement, see Lowry (1985a, 1985b); see also Rodowick (2014, 112–30). For an institutional history of the filmology movement, see Lefebvre (2009). For an introduction to filmology with special attention paid to the contributions of psychology, see Hediger (2003). On the lineage from filmology to narratology, see Kessler (2007). On the relation between filmology and semiology, see Kirsten (2018).

8. On the (media-)anthropology of filmology, see Cohen-Séat and Fougeyrollas (1961) and Hediger (2003). Although the media-anthropology of filmology is more dynamic than that found in most positivist thinking, it would be ill-advised to downplay the general positivist predilection of filmology. As Rodowick (2014) observes, "Every line of Cohen-Séat's discourse is underscored by positivism's confidence in the ability of scientific inquiry to organize research in every social discipline, and to manage society rationally so as to direct the course of human history" (120).

9. See, for instance, Wallon (1947). For an exploration of Wallon's role within the filmology movement, see Guillain (2012).

10. On the filmological vocabulary, see Étienne Souriau (1951, 1953). It should be noted that in her entry for the concept of diégèse in Vocabulaire d'esthétique (1990), Anne Souriau declares that she coined the concept of diégèse. In the lecture introducing the vocabulary, Étienne Souriau does not claim ownership of it but states that it is the result of collaborative research conducted at the institute of filmology.

11. Comprehensive accounts of the filmological vocabulary have been provided by Kessler (1997, 2007), Buckland (2003), Aumont and Marie (2001), and Thanouli (2014)

12. Souriau (1951) writes that the diegesis involves "tout ce qu'on prend en considération comme représenté par le film" (237). I find Souriau's use of the term représenté to be potentially misleading. In the German translation by Frank Kessler, the term Darstellung is used instead of Repräsentation, and it seems to me to capture better the art of cinematic (re)presentation, since it suggests that a film brings forth a diegesis without implying that the diegesis exists outside of the realm of the film, i.e., that it can be "represented."

13. In this sense, the diegesis is inscribed into a long tradition of considering the artwork as a world. In his 1901 inaugural "Oxford Lecture" entitled "Poetry for Poetry's Sake," A. C. Bradley (1911) contended that the artwork's nature is "to be not a part, nor yet a copy, of the real world (as we commonly understand that phrase), but to be a world by itself, independent, complete, autonomous; and to possess it fully you must enter that world, conform to its laws, and ignore for the time the beliefs, aims, and particular conditions which belong to you in the other world of reality" (5).

14. My translation. In the French original, the diegesis is "le genre de réalité supposé par la signification du film."

15. My translation. In the original French version Souriau (1953) writes, "dans l'intelligibilité (comme le dit M. Cohen-Séat) à l'histoire racontée, au monde supposé ou proposé par la fiction du film." As Bunia (2010) has observed, the use of the words "dans l'intelligibilité" could be interpreted as either "what can be understood" or "what can be understood without the use of the senses" (87). The fact that Cohen-Séat (1946) differentiates between cinema-as-art and cinema-as-language by postulating

an intelligible realm of the film (cinema as language) that is isolated from the sensible realm (cinema as art) would suggest that Souriau refers to the latter meaning of the term. Such a reading favors Metz's textual reading of the diegesis as pertaining to the film's discourse in disregard of the spectator's emotional responses. However, as Boillat (2009) argues, Souriau does not appear to have this specific sense in mind, meaning that the "unreferenced reference" to Cohen-Séat rings more like an homage to the founding father of filmology (222, 240 n.9). Moreover, the common translation in English of *dans l'intelligibilité* into *by inference* emphasizes the diegesis as a reality reconstructed by the cognitively equipped spectator. Such an interpretation supports the cognitive-formalist theory of narration based on inference making. Examples of this translation include Gorbman (1987) and Thanouli (2014).

16. For a discussion, see Bunia (2010, 687–89).
17. Boillat (2009) writes, "Le filmologue est donc loin de limiter son étude à la seule immanence du texte (filmique) qui caractérisera l'approche structuraliste des années 1960–1970 puisque, dans le contexte des tentatives de théorisation et des expériences relatives à l'intellection filmique effectuées au sein de l'Institut de filmologie, il ne cesse de faire référence au destinataire de la representation" (222).
18. In the French original, Souriau (1951) defines the diegetic space as "espace reconstitué par la pensée du spectateur" (233).
19. Bordwell (1985), for instance, defines the fabula or story as an "imaginary construct" that "perceivers of narrative create through assumptions and inferences" (49).
20. To get a better comprehension of Souriau's unique philosophy of thought, it is worth quoting this lengthy but wonderful passage from *The Different Modes of Existence*: "Indeed, let us be careful to note that thought cannot be conceived of as the product or result of the activity of a psychical being, which is itself conceived in a réique [thingy] manner, distinct from the assembled thing, and which might be thought's subject or its separate support. Thought has no other support than the very thing that it assembles and feels. In certain respects it is purely impersonal, and we must keep ourselves from conceiving of it as it effectively is in the réique status by introducing into it everything we otherwise understand and know about thought. As it is implied by this status, thought is purely and simply liaison and communication. It is also consciousness, though only if that word is understood in the sense of a phenomenal glow; the view that would have this singular and identical consciousness of existence reduced to the observation that we only speak of it as existing when it is presented as being lucid and present for itself may not in fact be constitutive. In the final analysis, it is above all the systematic cohesion, the liaison, that is essential and constitutive here for the role of thought. We should even ask ourselves whether it is not a matter of a factor, rather than an effect, of thought. Whatever the philosophical importance of this point may be, let us consider only one of its aspects: if there are psychical beings, they are far from being the cause of thought, as it is understood here—they imply it; it is a part of their constitution" (147).
21. On the notion of "instauration," see Souriau (2015), Latour and Stengers (2015), and Noske (2015).

22. Karen Pearlman (2009, 2017, 2019) has done an extraordinary job in theoretically excavating the affective and embodied underpinnings of editing as an art practice defined not only by the shaping and patterning of the film material but also as the cultivation of a feeling for its rhythms and for how a film "moves" its audience.

23. See Roques (1947); see also Lowry (1985a, 17–18).

24. Dufrenne (1973) argues, "In order to understand the world of the aesthetic object, we must grasp it in its opposition but also in its quite limited relationship to the world as strictly represented" (169). Dufrenne connects the expressed world with a corporeal sensibility that can be reduced neither to representation nor to language or words. The expressed world is never static; it is perpetually forming and deforming, and dynamic. For Dufrenne, it is "the expressed world that animates the represented world" (176). The aesthetic object "signifies not only by representing but, through that which it represents, by producing in the perceiver a certain impression" (178). Much of my skepticism toward Metz's textual approach lies in the univocal identification of the diegesis, the world of the film, with the represented world.

25. On film music narratology, see Gorbman (1980, 1987), Heldt (2013), Neumeyer (2009), and Smith (1999).

26. For an important work in this tradition, see Gorbman (1987).

27. On the increased attention to embodied signification within literary cognitive narratology, see, for instance, Fludernik (2010), Caracciolo (2014), Polvinen (2016), Kukkonen and Caracciolo (2014), Herman (2013b), and von Mossner (2017).

28. For a criticism of denotation as the primary meaning of a text, see Barthes (1990, 6–9).

29. On this point, see Rodowick (2014, 160). For a critical inspection of a semiotics founded in the tradition of Saussure and Hjelmslev to implement material and embodied concerns, see Bateman (2019).

30. For a comprehensive overview of the field of film phenomenology, see Hanich and Ferencz-Flatz (2016).

31. For an overview, see Elsaesser and Hagener (2009).

32. On Merleau-Ponty's influence on filmology, see Lowry (1985b, 127–32).

33. In this relation, enactivism discovers in Merleau-Ponty's phenomenology of embodied perception an alternative to the cognitivist position that the world we represent to ourselves is independent of our perceptual cognitive capacities and that the cognitive system we use to conjure up this representation is itself independent of the world it represents (Varela, Thompson, and Rosch 1992, xx).

34. The principle of dynamogenesis was developed by the psychologist James Henry Baldwin (1894), whose pioneer studies on the "motor aspects of sensuous feelings" demonstrated that thinking, knowledge, and consciousness are based on muscular movements, i.e., movements of the felt body. According to this principle, "every state of consciousness tends to realize itself in an appropriate muscular movement" (281, emphasis omitted), such that affective consciousness merges with motor consciousness. In other words, sensations of movements are also affective sensations, such as when we are feeling *uplifted* or *down*, but also the corporeal-material basis of higher cognitive functions.

35. For a discussion, see Carbone (2015, 44–45). On the relation of Merleau-Ponty to structuralism, see Schmidt (1985).
36. For an example of how first-generation cognitive film studies was indebted to classical psychology, see Bordwell (1977, 1989).
37. For an exploration of the anti-cognitivist stance of Merleau-Ponty's phenomenology of perception, see Rousse (2016).
38. For two excellent close readings of *A Page of Madness*, see Burch (1979, 127–36) and Petrić (1983).
39. For the attempt to develop a Deleuzian theory of narrative, see Askin (2017).
40. For a criticism of the internalist position in cognitive film theory and a discussion about mediated "affective niches," see Hven (2019).
41. On the "audience effect," see Hanich (2011, 2018).

Chapter 2

1. It is possible to identify two overall branches of "film atmosphere research": (a) the cognitive-inspired theories of "mood" (e.g., Carroll 2003a; Plantinga 2012; Smith 2003) and (b) phenomenology-inspired theories of *Stimmung*, atmosphere, and mood (e.g., Pollmann 2010; Rhym 2012; Sinnerbrink 2012; Spadoni 2014a, 2014b, 2020; Walton 2018). In addition, the German anthology, *Filmische Atmosphären* (Brunner, Schweintz, and Tröhler 2012) draws upon Schmitz and Böhme in their introduction of the atmosphere concept to cinema; see in particular Hans J. Wulff's (2012) provisional outline for a theory of film atmospheres. One could also point to recent eco-meteorological studies of cinema as a branch of cinematic atmosphere research (e.g., Fay 2014, 2018; Ivakhiv 2013; McKim 2013).
2. I count literature on *Stimmungen*, mood, ambience, character, tone, and aura among the body of atmosphere research as long as both the spatial and the subjective dimensions are taken into concern.
3. Important precursory work on atmosphere includes Ludwig Binswanger (1933), Erwin Straus (1930, 1960, 1965), Martin Heidegger (2006 [1926]), Walter Benjamin (2010 [1935]) Hubertus Tellenbach (1968), Otto F. Bollnow (1941), John Dewey (2005 [1934]), and Maurice Merleau-Ponty (2002 [1945]).
4. See, for instance, Böhme (2016), Hasse (2012), and Thibaud (2011).
5. See, for instance, Clark (2008), Clark and Chalmers (1998), Colombetti (2017), Colombetti and Krueger (2015), Colombetti and Roberts (2015), Hven (2019), Maiese (2016), Thompson (2007), and Varela, Thompson, and Rosch (1992).
6. See, for example, McKim (2013), Fay (2014, 2018), Ivakhiv (2013), and O'Brien (2018).
7. Examples include Anderson and Adey (2011), Bissell (2010), and Breshanan (2012).
8. For an extended criticism of this tendency within classical cognitive film theory, see Hven (2017a).
9. As Allan Casebier (1991) sums up the difference between the narrative (plot) and diegesis, "If you knew just the narrative, you would know what happened, but you

would know neither what the world of the work looked like nor felt like nor how it affected the spectator" (105).

10. The "crate-digger soundtrack" describes a use of music that is catchy and prominently displayed on the film's soundtrack without being so commercially known such that it lends to the movie-watching experience the thrill of pawing through boxes of dusty LPs at a flea market (Berman 2018).

11. The degree to which our emotional and affective experience is scaffolded by other members of the audience has been termed the "audience effect"; see Hanich (2011, 2018). On the scaffolding of emotional experience in cinema, see Hven (2019).

12. Examples include Carroll (2003a), Plantinga (2009b, 2012, 2014), Pollmann (2010), Rhym (2012), Schmetkamp (2017), Sinnerbrink (2012), G.M. Smith (1999, 2003), Spadoni (2014a, 2014b, 2020), and Walton (2018).

13. For an introduction to the concept of "Stimmung" and its role in the history of German aesthetics, see Wellbery (2010)

14. Plantinga (2014) explicates this position as follows: "To claim that a film has a mental or bodily state would be wrong because, obviously enough, a film has no mind or body. As an audiovisual display, it can be used to elicit actual moods in spectators, but literally speaking, it cannot have human moods itself" (146). By reducing moods to human moods, cognitive film theorists conceive the relation between the spectator's "actual" mood and the metaphorical "mood of a film" according to a stimuli–response model, where the film contains mood-cues (stimuli) capable of triggering subjective mood states (response). Exemplary of this line of reasoning is Greg M. Smith's definition of mood as "a preparatory state in which one is seeking an opportunity to express a particular emotion or emotion set. Moods are expectancies that we are about to have a particular emotion, that we will encounter cues that will elicit particular emotions. These expectancies orient us toward our situation, encouraging us to evaluate the environment in a fashion congruent to our mood. Moods influence us to interpret our environment as consisting of emotion-producing cues. A cheerful mood leads one to privilege those portions of one's environment which are consistent with that mood. Moods act as the emotion system's equivalent of attention, focusing us on certain stimuli and not others" (113). According to this model, a film contains no actual moods but only mood-cues, i.e., potential elicitors of human mood states.

15. Internalism characterizes both philosophical cognitivism in the tradition of appraisal theory (Arnold 1960, 1970; Scherer 1999) and affective neuroscience in the neo-Jamesian tradition (e.g., Damasio 1995, 1999; Panksepp 1998). For both, emotions and affects can be understood on the basis of internal, brain- and body-bound mechanisms stimulated in part by environmental factors. Appraisal theory understands emotions as "elicited and differentiated on the basis of a person's subjective evaluation or appraisal of the personal signification of a situation, object, or event" (Scherer 1999, 637), whereas the neo-Jamesian view holds emotions to be "perceptions of changes in our somatic condition" (Prinz 2004, 57). In both cases, as Griffith and Scarantino (2009) have argued in their programmatic article on the situated nature of emotions, "emotions are conceived as internal states or processes and the role of the environment is confined to providing stimuli and receiving actions"

(437). Affective neuroscience often advocates an extreme form of internalism that holds the brain to be the locus of affective phenomena, while reducing everything that takes place outside of the brain to mere "background phenomena" (Colombetti 2017b, 1438).

16. Certain dichotomies are envisioned as completely shut off from each other or as being mutually exclusive. This is, of course, not the case with dichotomies such as mind versus body and emotion versus cognition. An interactionist model (demonstrating that two opposed elements interact) therefore merely reinforces the dichotomy because the notion of "interaction" already presupposes two distinct entities in the first place.

17. For an introduction to situated and scaffolded emotion theory, see Colombetti, Kruger, and Roberts (2018); see also Colombetti (2017a, 2017b), Colombetti and Krueger (2015), Griffiths and Scarantino (2009), and Krueger and Szanto (2016).

18. I am indebted to Colombetti (2017b) for this outline of the situated and scaffolded theory of affect, emotion, and cognition.

19. Though here is not the place for a detailed discussion, I think that Plantinga's (2009b, 132–34) theory about our emotional response to nonrepresentational music provides a good illustration of the shortcoming of cognitive-internalist theories of mood. Following Plantinga there is no cognitive justification for us to respond emotionally to nonrepresentational music, yet the reason we do so is because the music evokes *memories* and *associations*—in other words, mental representational content—and it is only this mental content, rather than the music as such, that is capable of explaining our emotional response to nonrepresentational music. The emotional powers of music thus rest on cognitive forms of mediation such as memories and associations to function. It follows from this proposition that music can only touch us indirectly and that there is no direct link between our bodily and physiological arousal to music and the emotional responses it evokes.

20. On the experience of the edited film as an one of a flow of movement that has been "shaped, limited, and designed into cinematically expressible phrases," see Pearlman (2017, 149). See also Pearlman (2009) and Cutting and Pearlman (2019).

Chapter 3

1. Béla Balázs (1953) thus describes *Berlin* as a film that could "scarcely be used to guide a stranger arriving in Berlin for the first time" and argued that the film, rather, evokes the "memories and residual moods of a traveller leaving that city" (178).

2. For an overview of affect theory, see Clough and Halley (2007) and Gregg and Seigworth (2010b). See also Massumi (2002), Connolly (2002), and Barad (2003). For a critical evaluation of affect theory, see Leys (2011a, 2011b). For affect-theoretical approaches to cinema, see Åkervall (2008), del Rio (2008), Kennedy (2000), and Shaviro (1993, 2010). For a critical assessment of affective film theory, see Brinkema (2014).

3. In this context, Bordwell's cognitive film narratology and poetics have been a major influence, among others, on Murray Smith's (1995) theory of character engagement; Ed S. Tan's (2013), Carl Plantinga's (2001, 2009b), and Greg M. Smith's (2003) respective theories of emotion and mood in cinema; Noël Carroll's (2006) ideas on the connection of emotion and genre; Torben Grodal's (2009) theory of the evolutionary underpinnings of cinematic spectatorship; Coëgnarts and Kravanja's (2015) "cognitive-embodied" theory of cinema; Kiss and Willemsen's (2017) explorations of "impossible puzzle films"; as well as Nannicelli and Taberham's (2014) recent introduction to cognitive media theory.

4. The notion of appraisal was first introduced to modern psychology by Magda Arnold (1960) as an antidote to what was believed to be an overemphasis on the behavioral and physiological aspects of emotion and to account for why similar stimuli could induce different emotional responses. The answer, Arnold suggested, should be found in the different ways individuals evaluate or appraise situations. For Arnold, the process of appraisal was first and foremost what she called a sense judgment; namely, it was "direct, immediate, nonreflective, nonintellectual, automatic, 'instinctive,' intuitive" (175). The specific notion of *cognitive* appraisal was advanced by Richard Lazarus (1960) to evidence how our emotional evaluation of the environment is governed by complex processes of cognition. For Lazarus (1984), appraisal is evidence of the "primacy of cognition" such that "cognitive appraisal is a necessary condition of emotion" (128).

5. In *Narration in the Fiction Film* (1985), a book about "the aspects of film viewing that lead to the construction of the story and its world," Bordwell assumes that "a spectator's comprehension of the films' narrative is theoretically separable from his or her emotional responses" (30)." Later, in *Poetics of Cinema* (2008), Bordwell appears to have refined his position on emotions as he grants that "just as modern cognitive science presupposes that emotions operate in tandem with perception and thought, so I'd readily grant that our time-bound process of building the story is shot through with emotion" (101). Nonetheless, Bordwell structures his theoretical argument around an opposition between "comprehension" and "emotional response." To provide the reader with a sense of how this works, it is necessary to quote Bordwell at length: "By focusing on comprehension as an inferential elaboration, I might seem to be ignoring the role of emotions in responding to narrative. Isn't this a cold, cold theory? But this objection would misunderstand how inquiry works. Consider an analogy. People are often emotional when they speak, but it's legitimate and useful to have a theory of language that focuses on how language is structured for understanding, regardless of what emotions are summoned up by certain sentences. If a wife says to her husband, "Pack up and get out," Chomsky's linguistics has little to say about the anger she may be expressing. Rather, Chomsky's theory concentrates on how syntax makes the sentence intelligible. Different theories pick out different features of the phenomena they try to explain. It would be as unfair to say that "my spectator" feels no emotions as to say that Chomsky's "native speaker" feels none. There's a degree of idealization involved in focusing only on comprehension, but it isn't harmful if we grant that it's only one aspect of our experience of narrative" (93).

Bordwell clearly positions "comprehension" and "inferential elaboration" against the emotions that a narrative or an utterance summons up and the (recognition of) emotions experienced by persons and characters. Given that Bordwell wants to derive a theory of (narrative) comprehension in cinema, his separation of the inferential "picking up" of the basic text and the emotional accompaniment suggests that emotions or affect plays no major role for the viewer's basic comprehension of the cinematic diegesis. By contrast, my argument is that basic comprehension in cinema cannot be reduced to cognitive inferential elaboration and that cinema's ability to move our felt bodies should be regarded as a key component of cinematic communication. Thus, our most basic perception of the cinematic diegesis is atmospheric and necessarily entails an affective component.

6. In order to avoid the (unnecessary) anthropocentrism inherent in this argument, I prefer to speak of the organism when it comes to both (animal) cognition and more mediated environments specifically designed for human consumption.

7. On the two dominant vectors in affect theory, see Gregg and Seigworth (2010a).

8. For more on this connection, see Connolly (2002), who draws on both Massumi and Damasio. For a critical assessment of this relation, see Leys (2011a).

9. See, however, the work of Slaby, Mühlhoff, and Wüschner (2017) on "affective arrangement" for a conceptual tool developed in the tradition of affect theory that to a large extent tackles the problems encountered by first-generation affect theory.

10. Neuroscientists have invented a series of devices and technologies for measuring the affective flow in the body/brain such as galvanic skin response censors, neuroimaging (e.g., functional magnetic resonance imaging [fMRI], positron emission tomography [PET], and magnetoencephalography [MEG]), Doppler ultrasound for measuring blood flow, etc. As William Connolly (2011) rightly points out, however, these observations can only inform us about the affective activity in zones of the brain/body, but they are not able to specify content.

11. Mark B. N. Hansen (2004a) explicitly opposes the present challenge of thinking about human technogenesis to that faced by Deleuze in his time. He writes, "Faced with a massive dematerialization (or virtualization) of social life and a suspension of contact with our media technologies (consider the inhuman temporality of real-time computing), we cultural theorists of today are in a very different position from the one occupied by Deleuze in his time. Far from feeling the need to explode the humanist trappings of a dominant and historically-inherited phenomenology in the name of a radical and, in a certain sense, 'posthuman' experimentalism, we are (or should be) motivated today by the pressing need to preserve some form of contact linking the kinds of embodied beings that we are ('wetware') to the increasingly autonomous technological domain (hardware and also software, to the extent that it is becoming ever more opaque to us, its users). This is precisely the ethical imperative of a thinking that takes human technogenesis—and the co-evolution of the human and technics that informs it—as a fundamental insight" (363).

12. The basic emotion paradigm has also informed cognitive theories of emotion in cinema, such as Ed S. Tan's *Emotion and the Structure of Narrative Film* (1996).

13. See, in this context, the "neurocritical" work of Choudhury and Slaby (2012).

14. Gerard Genette (1982) famously asserted, "One will define narrative without difficulty as the representation of an event or a series of events" (127). Following Gerald Prince (1982), "narrative [. . .] may be defined as the representation of real or fictive events and situations in a time sequence" (1). In a recent introduction to narratology, it is argued what we get in a narrative "are not events as such, but signs, the representation of events" (Landa and Onega 2014, 5).

15. Note that Varela et al. (1992) do not criticize the application value of representation—as a theoretical construct it has indeed proven extremely useful to cognitive science—but its epistemological and ontological validity.

16. Caracciolo (2014a) defines the "experiential background" as "a repertoire of past experiences and values that guides people's interaction with the environment" (4).

17. On the influence of Ludwig Klages on early German avant-garde cinema, see Michael Cowan (2007) and Miriam Hansen (2012).

Chapter 4

1. As Volker Pantenburg (2016) observes, the camera inevitably "confronts us with transitions, flowing developments, gradual and continual shifts that are difficult to describe" (45). He argues that the videographic essay—where the audiovisual medium itself is employed to study films—avoids the immobilization of the moving image on the dissection board: "It seems crucial that the new techniques [of videographic essays] enable movement to be repeated and analysed *as movement*. Only now, it seems to me, can we juxtapose and compare camera movements, locate them historically or arrange them synoptically, discern and describe fleeting, musical qualities like rhythm or rhyme" (51, author's emphasis). Audiovisual essays offer one possible way out of the theoretical impasse that cinematic movement constitutes to the textual analytical modality. Nonetheless, the video essay—for the time being, at least—remains a supplement to the written text, which continues to be the favored medium for theoretical and philosophical reflections and discussions.

2. In a funding application from 1969, experimental film director Michael Snow (1994) ponders on the little attention given to camera movement: "After finishing *Wavelength*, which is in its entirety a single camera movement (a zoom), I realized that the movement of the camera as a separate expressive entity in film is completely unexplored" (53). In one of the first articles to address camera movements specifically, David Bordwell (1977) asserts it to be "one of the most difficult areas for critical analysis" and one that has "usually been considered too elusive to be analyzable" (19). Likewise reflecting upon the difficulties camera movements pose to film studies, Vivian Sobchack (1982) embarks upon how this device has eluded "the descriptive and interpretative grasp of traditional and temporary modes of reflection" (317) to the extent that any textual description of a camera movement always seems markedly different from our actual experience of it. In the first book-length study dedicated to unfolding a taxonomy of the narrative functions of camera movements, Jakob Isak Nielsen (2007) observes that while camera movements "permeate our visual culture

to an unprecedented degree," the literature addressing this specific topic remains considerably sparse (1). More recently, Daniel Morgan (2011) has argued that "despite their prominence within the history of cinema, camera movements have remained surprisingly elusive and marginal in critical work" (127).

3. The phrase "to lay down the path in walking" is taken from the poem "Campos de Castilla" by Antonio Machado and used in the enactivist literature to express how reality is enacted through constant interactions with an environment of affordances. The poem goes as follows: "Wanderer, the road is your / footpath, nothing else; / wanderer there is no pain, / you lay down the path in walking. / In walking you lay down a path." See Varela et al. (1992, 237–54), Thompson (2007, 180), and Noë (2009, 97–128).

4. The transitory, dynamic, and fluid operationality of the moving camera makes it difficult to capture according to atomistic analysis. In this respect, Daniel Morgan (2016) argues, "One of the attractions of thinking about camera movements is that they seem to be an element of cinematic style whose complexity is primary, where something important is missed in attempts that try to explain them by finding a single orienting or grounding point" (244).

5. The camera–eye analogy was particularly important in early Soviet cinema. For an overview and history of the camera–eye analogy, see Quendler (2017); for a discussion, see Turvey (1999).

6. The reference is to Hermann Schmitz's term *Bewegungssuggestionen* ("movement suggestions") that describes how even "static" entities such as architectural buildings or landscapes come charged with movement suggestions capable of modulating the felt body through its height, expansiveness, narrowness, vastness, darkness, etc. See, for instance, Schmitz (2009, 2011, 2016a).

7. For a discussion of how filmic perception has been understood according to internal, innate mechanisms, see Rhym (2018) and Hven (2019).

8. For critical reviews of the film/mind analogy, see Noël Carroll (1988) and Wicclair (1978).

9. For an overview of Münsterberg's contributions to cognitive psychological theories of films, see Baranowski and Hecht (2017).

10. An inferential theory of motion perception has most noticeably been employed to film theory and camera movement in Bordwell's article "Camera Movements and Cinematic Space" (1977). The main idea is that we "read" the camera movement (or, rather, "the camera movement effect") on the basis of the visual cues of the film. For Bordwell, what follows from "reading" the cues is a powerful kinesthetic sensation of self-movement: "Under normal circumstances it is virtually impossible to perceive those screen events as merely a series of expanding, contracting, labile configurations. The cues overwhelmingly supply a compelling experience of moving through space" (23).

11. "New Look psychology" refers to a movement in psychology in the 1950s that studied how our beliefs and values impact visual perception, even perception of so-called neutral stimuli, such that our background knowledge and prior experience co-determine the nature of the perceived (cf. Bruner, Goodnow, and George 1956).

12. Note, however, that Bordwell has since grown more agnostic on these issues, pre-
ferring to talk of our "folk-psychology," which has the advantage that "we don't
have to worry about whether it's true; what matters is that filmmakers invoke it
and film viewers follow their lead" (Bordwell 2011, sec. 4). Obviously, this does not
amount to a neutral position, and the many cognitive-inferential assumptions laid
out in Bordwell's early scholarship simply persist in later works even if they are no
longer explicitly outspoken or justified theoretically.

13. For an exploration of the convergences between Merleau-Ponty's philosophy of
embodied perception and Gibsonian ecological psychology, see Heft (1989).

14. On the cinematic externalization of dreamlike states, see Baudry (1981b, 1981a) and
Metz (1975). On the cinematic externalization of embodied perception, see Sobchack
(1982, 1992, 2004), Barker (2009), and Laura U. Marks (2000).

15. Note that even the still camera presents a form of movement in absentia. Moreover,
cinematic motion is, of course, irreducible to the movement of the camera but
comprises many forms of movement, many of which are not related to the camera
(e.g., editing rhythms or music).

16. Examples of first-generation ecological film studies include J. Anderson (1996, 2003),
B. Anderson and J. Anderson (2007), and Cutting (2007).

17. Warren (1984) has pointed out that affordances do not change with the need or state
of the perceiver. In this regard, it differs from Uexküll's concept of Umwelt.

18. See Gibson (1960) for a criticism of the stimulus–response; see Gibson (1966, 266–
86) for a discussion of perception as active and direct information pickup; for his
anti-cognitivism, see Gibson (2015, 139).

19. Thus, a lineage from the ecology of perception to multisensorial or synesthetic theories of film can be drawn. For an overview, see Laine and Strauven (2009).

20. On the multisensorial film experience, see also Antunes (2016).

21. See Marta Braun (2010, 133–58).

22. In his article on camera movements and viewpoint, Daniel Morgan (2016) criticizes
a large part of modern film studies for buying into the "epistemological fantasy" that
we are actually in the diegesis as the conceptual bedrock of their theories. For him,
the interesting aspect lies in how cinema mediates its reality in the process of its creation: "nothing is stable, not even the line between the world of the film and the world
in which it was made" (241).

23. Following Rizzolatti and Fabbri-Destro (2010), canonical neurons are "considered
the neural substrate of the mechanism through which object affordances are translated into motor acts" (223).

24. For accounts that bring neuroscience and the Gibsonian theory of affordances together, see Bach, Nicholson, and Hudson (2014) and de Wit et al. (2017).

25. On the relation of mirror neurons to our emotional and empathic appreciation of
art, see Gallese and Freeberg (2007). For a counterargument, see Sheets-Johnstone
(2012).

26. For instance, Rizzolatti and Arbib (1998) draw on mirror neurons to argue that
"human language (as well as some dyadic forms of primate communication) evolved

from a basic mechanism that was not originally related to communication: the capacity to recognize actions" (193).

27. On the role of the discovery of mirror neurons for the advancement of research on empathy, see Goldie and Coplan (2011).

28. This theory grew out of an initial collaboration with cognitivist philosopher and simulation theorist Alvin Goldman; see Gallese and Goldman (1998). See also Gallese (2005, 2011, 2016), Gallese and Sinigaglia (2011), and Goldman (1989, 1992, 2006).

29. On the affinities of ES and the embodied phenomenology of Merleau-Ponty, see Gallese and Guerra (2020, 24, 46, 79).

30. For a discussion of the ethics of camera movements, see Morgan (2011).

31. On the inadequacies of the differentiation between "bottom-up" versus "top-down" processes, see Thompson and Varela (2001).

32. The Trinity stabilization rig is "a unique hybrid rig that combines traditional mechanical camera stabilization with gimbal technology to give the camera arm an incredible range of movements not possible with a Steadicam" (O'Falt 2020).

33. Gallese appears to gesture in this direction when he writes, "Establishing a connection with a building, a room, or an architectural element might imply, therefore, a spontaneous simulation of the motor acts and emotions evoked by those spaces and those objects" (Gallese in Canepa et al. 2019). I take this statement to draw on an expanded or, at least, more generalized conception of embodied simulation—fueled by, but not restricted to mirror neuron activation—that would warrant a more liberated methodological approach than that governing *The Empathic Screen*. Thus, our exposure to a landscape, a building, a song, or an abstract painting might not involve representational content that warrants the activation of a "mirroring" or "simulative" process (as when an animal grasps out for a banana). Yet, it may give rise to motor resonances, motor suggestions, and an attunement of the movements of the organism to that of a nonrepresentational artwork, a musical composition, or the build environment.

Chapter 5

1. Founded in 1948 in France by Pierre Schaefer, musique concrète is a movement that used then-modern portable recording devices and electronic acoustics to create musical compositions, at times by using "recorded" environmental noises. Whereas Schaeffer made music out of noise, John Cage, another prominent figure of the musique concrète, regarded noise, indeed all sound, as a form of music or "organized sound." In a seminal essay, Cage (1961) presents a reappraisal of noise: "wherever we are, what we hear is mostly noise. When we ignore it, it disturbs us. When we listen to it, we find it fascinating" (3). Among the pioneer filmmakers to draw inspirations from musique concrète are Michelangelo Antonioni (cf. Nardelli 2010), Krzysztof Kieślowski (cf. Kickasola 2012), and Gus Van Sant (cf. Kulezic-Wilson 2012). Given the musicality of many mainstream sound effects, musique concrète is today no longer reserved for more experimental filmmakers.

2. For a discussion of the diegesis as anchored acoustically and not just visually, see Whittington (2007, 115–26).
3. On philosophy's historic inability to attend to the essence of sound, see Cox (2011).
4. Following Yi-Fu Tuan (2001), it is now common practice to separate the notion of space (abstract and undifferentiated) and place (inhabited, felt, valued, designated). Designated narrative spaces can thus be regarded as places with a distinct phenomenal and felt character. In relation to the phenomenal character of space, see Gaston Bachelard on the "Poetics of Space" (Bachelard 1994). On the distinction of space and place in relation to cinema, see Wollen (1980).
5. Critical assessments on the narratological privileging of time over space can, for instance, be found in Friedman (1993, 2005), Parker (2016), Phelan and Rabinowitz (2012), and Ryan (2014).
6. In similar veins, Peter Brooks (1984) maintains that plot "develops its propositions only through temporal sequence and progression" and, a little further down the text, that "plot is the principal ordering force of those meanings that we try to wrest from human temporality" (xi). H. Porter Abbott (2002) famously regarded narrative to be the method of our species for the organization of time (3). As Gabriel Zoran (1984) bluntly states, "the dominance of the time factor in the structuring of the narrative text remains an indisputable fact" (310).
7. Other noticeable exceptions include the work of Gabriel Zoran (1984), David Herman (2002), Marie-Laure Ryan (2014a), and Joshua Parker (2016). In parallel to the narratological tradition, we might point to the work of Mikhail Bakhtin (1981) and Yuri Lotman (1977).
8. See, for instance, Cresswell (2004), de Certeau (1984), Lefebvre (1991), Soja (1989), and Tuan (2001).
9. Chatman does not, however, devaluate description or disregard it as inferior to narration. As he writes in *Coming to Terms: The Rhetoric of Narrative in Fiction and Film* (1990), "Description has a logic of its own, and it is unreasonable to belittle it because it does not resemble the chrono-logic of Narration" (24).
10. For a recent rethinking of description in cinema, see Poulaki (2011, 140–56).
11. On the use of soundscape as an aesthetic category that highlights the use of noise or ambience, see Chion (1994), Sergi (2006), and M.S. Ward (2015).
12. In drawing attention to the ontological premises of sound as borderless, in flux, creating its own dimensions, as anti-pictorial, we must be careful not to resort to what Jonathan Sterne (2003) has termed the "audiovisual litany" (14–19; cf. Sterne 2012, 9–10). The audiovisual litany is first and foremost defined by the supposed ontological gap between vision and audition. Among the assumptions of this litany are: "hearing is spherical, vision is directional; hearing immerses its subject, vision offers a perspective; sounds come to us, but vision travels to its object; hearing is concerned with interiors, vision is concerned with surfaces; hearing involves physical contact with the outside world, vision requires distance from it; hearing places us inside an event, seeing gives us a perspective on the event; hearing tends toward subjectivity, vision tends toward objectivity; hearing brings us into the living world, sight moves us toward atrophy and death; hearing is about affect, vision is about intellect; hearing is a

primarily temporal sense, vision is a primarily spatial sense; hearing is a sense that immerses us in the world, vision is a sense that removes us from it" (15). I believe it is possible to distinguish some qualities of sound (e.g., as borderless and in flux) without buying into the schematic antagonisms between sound and vision of the audiovisual litany. One way of avoiding the binary logic of the audiovisual litany is not to consider the diegesis as made up of visual and auditory components but to conceive it in multisensorial, atmospheric terms instead.

13. For a discussion, see Flückiger (2017, 302–3).

14. For a particularly pronounced example of the visual bias in film studies, see Daniel Percheron's article "Sound in Cinema and Its Relation to Image and Diegesis" (1980). For a defense of the visual bias from the perspective of semiology, see Metz (1980a), and from that of cognitivism, see Branigan (2002).

15. On the roots of the visual bias against sound phenomena in philosophy, see Cox (2011).

16. The McGurk effect describes the cross-modal effect, whereby visual information influences auditory perception in speech perception, particularly in relation to the movements of the speaker's lips, such that what we "hear" depends on our visual input. In this way, we "hear lips" and "see voices"; see McGurk and McDonald (1976). On the specific *audiovisual* nature of cinematic expression, see Bakels (017).

17. On the environmental qualities of cinematic rain, see McKim (2013, 91–133).

18. On the notion of USOs, see Flückiger (2009, 156–58; 2017, 126–30). According to a survey conducted by Flückiger (2017), 20% of all perceptible sound elements in contemporary action and science fiction films are USOs.

19. In an interview with Vincent LoBrutto (1994), Ben Burtt explains, "from 1930 to 1965, when the studio system was dominant, each of those studios had its own department [. . .] [I]t's very easy to distinguish the style of each studio. Just in watching a show and listening for a few moments, I can tell you whether it was Fox or Paramount or Warner Brothers. [. . .] You can particularly tell by the sound effects, because each studio had a library and sound like gunshots, face punches, thunderclaps, and horse whinnies that would reoccur in film after film. Each of the studios had very distinctive sounds. From listening to films as a child, I had become very aware of the sound styles of the studios" (139).

20. For a discussion on the changing relation of diegesis and sound, see Michel Chion (1994, 2009), Lisa Coulthardt (2012, 2013), Kevin J. Donnelly (2014), Andrew Knight-Hill (2019), Danijela Kulezic-Wilson (2015, 2019), Liz Green (2016), James Wierzbicki (2012), Gianluca Sergi (2002, 2004, 2006), and Ben Winters (2010, 2012).

21. It is widely accepted that the title of "sound designer" was invented as a workaround to endorse the work of Walter Murch on *Apocalypse Now* (1979), where he was involved in all aspects of the film's audio track, including dialogue and sound effects through to rerecording in the postproduction mixing. As Coppola recalls, "We wanted very much to credit Walter for his incredible contribution—not only for *The Rain People* [Coppola 1969], but for all the films he was doing. But because he wasn't in the union, the union forbade him getting the credit as sound editor—so Walter said, 'Well, since they won't give me that, will they let me be called "sound designer?"' We said, 'We'll

try it—you can be the sound designer' . . . I always thought it was ironic that 'Sound Designer' became this Tiffany title, yet it was created for that reason. We did it to dodge the union constriction" (Coppola in Ondaatje 2002, 53).

22. In fact, noises were always central to cinema; however, with the rise of new sound technologies it can be argued that noises went from being the unintended side effects of the cinematic machinery to be an intended aesthetic device used to enhance the cinematic illusion. Not surprisingly, not everyone was all praiseful of this cinematic evolution. Mary Ann Doane (1980) complains, "technical advances in sound recording (such as the Dolby system) are aimed at diminishing the noise of the system, concealing the work of the apparatus, and thus reducing the distance perceived between the object and its representation" (35).

23. In fact, most supposed critics of the *sound* film were actually arguing against the *talking* film. See, for instance, Arnheim (1957).

24. See, for instance, Randy Thom (1999, 2007).

25. A concise expression of how early critics both recognized the necessity of sound effects and advised practitioners not to overuse them can be found in Stephen W. Bush's telling article, "When 'Effects' A re Unnecessary Noises," from 1911. In this article, Bush proclaims, "effects to help the picture must be few, simple and well rehearsed for each separate and particular picture," and continues to advise the "worker beyond the screen" to study each picture by itself such that the sound effects produced "have a psychological bearing on the situation as depicted on the screen" (690). Sound effects when thus properly used can "help a picture immensely" (690). See, in this context, Bottomore (2001).

26. This development is expressed in the change of the title of Marie-Laure Ryan's edited collection *Narrative across Media: The Languages of Storytelling* (2004) to her *Storyworlds across Media: Towards a Media-Conscious Narratology* (2014b; edited together with Jan-Noël Thon). The change in title points not only to the shift in thinking narratives not as series of events but as worlds, but also to the shift from transmedial "language" to "media-consciousness." The authors themselves remark, "The replacement of 'narrative' with 'storyworld' acknowledges the emergences of the concept of 'world' not only in narratology but also on the broader cultural scene" (Ryan and Thon 2014a, 1).

27. In *The Spirit of Film*, Balázs (2011) argued that film would be able to capture the small utterances that the theater audience were unable to hear: "what makes the greatest impression on us is what is closest at hand and quite, quite faint. Not the clear, logical sentence or the formally sung song, in other words, but the fading sigh, the sound of breath, the stifled sob. The sound that is indeterminate, even in its own interior nature. The faintest possible human sound, like the note from a loose piano string" (195). Cinema would thus be able to paint "spoken landscapes" such that in film "what attracts our interest is less what a person says than the sound of his voice. In dialogue, too, what is decisive is not the content, but the acoustic, sensuous impression" (195).

28. On the notion of "poetics of affect," see Kappelhoff (2018) and Kappelhoff and Lehmann (2019).

29. For an enactive theory of mediated sound, see Lisa Schmidt (2011).
30. The "masking method" is an analytical mode for studying film suggested by Chion (1994), who recommends that "in order to observe and analyze the sound-image structure of a film we may draw upon a procedure I call the *masking method*. Screen a given sequence several times, sometimes watching sound and image together, sometimes masking the image, sometimes cutting out the sound. This gives you the opportunity to hear the sound as it is, and not as the image transforms and disguises it; it also lets you see the image as it is, and not as sound recreates it. In order to do this, of course, you must train yourself to really see and really hear, without projecting what you already know onto these perceptions" (187).
31. On the synesthetic or multisensorial nature of the film experience, see Antunes (2016), Barker (2008, 2009), Laine and Strauven (2009), Marks (2000, 2002), and Sobchack (2004).
32. On the use of sensory isolates to create "affective niches," see Hven (2019).
33. On the thermoceptive, nociceptive, and vestibular sensations of cinema, see Luis Rocha Antunes (2016).
34. According to this research on nociceptive processing, "[W]itnessing body limbs threatened or stimulated by a painful agent, observing facial expressions of pain, or simply viewing visual cues signaling pain in others activates parts of the cortical signature normally associated with pain perception and referred to as the 'pain matrix'" (Vachon-Presseau et al. 2011, 1525).
35. As Erik Aadahl explains, "Very early on we decided we wanted to try to create a 'sonic envelope,' as John [Krasinski] termed it, for Regan's points of view. In close-up with her character, we switch to her sonic perspective and that was something that we experimented with and stumbled upon pretty early on" (Aadahl in Walden 2018).

Afterword

1. On Hollywood's xenophobic portrayal of Arabs, Islam, and the Middle East, see Shaheen (2001), Semmerling (2006), and Bayraktaroğlu (2018).

Bibliography

Abbott, H. Porter. 2002. *The Cambridge Introduction to Narrative*. Cambridge: Cambridge University Press.

Åkervall, Lisa. 2008. "Cinema, Affect and Vision." *Rhizomes* (16, Summer). http://www.rhizomes.net/issue16/akervall.html.

Allen, Graham. 2003. *Roland Barthes. Routledge Critical Thinkers*. New York and London: Routledge.

Altman, Rick. 2017. "The Early Cinema Soundscape." In *The Routledge Companion to Screen Music and Sound*, edited by Miguel Mera, Ronald Sadoff, and Ben Winters, 190–200. New York: Routledge.

Anderson, Ben. 2009. "Affective Atmospheres." *Emotion, Space and Society* 2 (2): 77–81.

Anderson, Ben, and Peter Adey. 2011. "Affect and Security: Exercising Emergency in 'UK Civil Contingencies.'" *Environment and Planning D: Society and Space* 29 (6): 1092–1109. https://doi.org/10.1068/d14110.

Anderson, Joseph. 1996. *The Reality of Illusion: An Ecological Approach to Cognitive Film Theory*. Carbondale: Southern Illinois University Press.

Anderson, Joseph. 2003. "Moving through the Diegetic World of the Motion Picture." In *Film Style and Story: A Tribute to Torben Grodal*, edited by Lennard Højbjerg and Peter Schepelern, 11–21. Copenhagen: Museum Tusculanum Press.

Anderson, Joseph D., and Barbara Fisher Anderson, eds. 2007. *Moving Image Theory: Ecological Considerations*. Carbondale: Southern Illinois University Press.

Anderson, M. L., and G. Rosenberg. 2008. "Content and Action: The Guidance Theory of Representation." *Journal of Mind and Behavior* 29 (1–2): 55–86.

Andrew, Dudley. 1976. *The Major Film Theories: An Introduction*. London; Oxford; New York: Oxford University Press.

Andrew, Dudley. 1985. "The Neglected Tradition of Phenomenology in Film Theory." In *Movies and Methods*, edited by Bill Nichols, 625–632. Vol. 2. Berkeley: University of California Press.

Antunes, Luis Rocha. 2012. "The Vestibular in Film: Orientation and Balance in Gus van Sant's Cinema of Walking." *Essays in Philosophy* 13 (2): 522–49.

Antunes, Luis Rocha. 2016. *The Multisensory Film Experience: A Cognitive Model of Experiential Film Aesthetics*. Bristol, U.K.; Chicago: Intellect.

Aristotle. 2008. *Physics*. Translated by Robin Waterfield. Oxford; New York: Oxford University Press.

Arnheim, Rudolf. 1957. "A New Laocoön: Artistic Composites and the Talking Film (1936)." In *Film as Art*, 199–230. Berkeley; Los Angeles; London: University of California Press.

Arnold, Magda B. 1960. *Emotion and Personality*. New York: Columbia University Press.

Arnold, Magda B. 1970. *Feelings and Emotions*. San Diego, Calif.: Academic Press.

Artaud, Antonin. 1976. *Antonin Artaud, Selected Writings*. Edited by Susan Sontag. Translated by Helen Weaver. New York: Farrar, Straus and Giroux, Inc.

Askin, Ridvan. 2017. *Narrative and Becoming*. Edinburgh: Edinburgh University Press.

Attali, Jacques. 2009. *Noise: The Political Economy of Music*. 10th printing. Minneapolis; London: University of Minnesota Press.

Attridge, Derek. 1997. "Roland Barthes's Obtuse, Sharp Meaning and the Responsibilities of Commentary." In *Writing the Image after Roland Barthes*, edited by Jean-Michael Rabaté, 77–89. Philadelphia: University of Pennsylvania Press.

Aumont, Jacques, and Michel Marie. 2001. "Diégèse." In *Dictionnaire théorique et critique du cinéma*, 51–52. Paris: Nathan.

Bach, Patric, Toby Nicholson, and Matthew Hudson. 2014. "The Affordance-Matching Hypothesis: How Objects Guide Action Understanding and Prediction." *Frontiers in Human Neuroscience* 8 (254): 1–13. https://doi.org/10.3389/fnhum.2014.00254.

Bachelard, Gaston. 1994. *The Poetics of Space: The Classic Look at How We Experience Intimate Spaces*. Translated by Maria Jolas. Boston: Beacon Press.

Badley, Linda. 2010. *Lars von Trier*. Urbana: University of Illinois Press.

Bakels, Jan-Hendrik. 2017. *Audiovisuelle Rhythmen. Filmmusik, Bewegungskomposition und die dynamische Affizierung des Zuschauers*. Cinepoetics 3. Berlin; Boston: De Gruyter.

Bakhtin, Mikhail M. 1981. *The Dialogic Imagination: Four Essays*. Edited by Michael Holquist. Translated by Caryl Emerson and Michael Holquist. Austin: University of Texas Press.

Balázs, Béla. 1953. *Theory of Film (Character and the Growth of a New Art)*. Translated by Edith Bone. London: Dennis Dobson Ltd.

Balázs, Béla. 2011. *Béla Balázs: Early Film Theory: Visible Man and the Spirit of Film*. Edited by Erica Carter. Translated by Rodney Livingstone. New York; Oxford: Berghahn Books.

Baldwin, James Mark. 1894. *Handbook of Psychology: Feeling and Will*. New York: Henry Holt and Company.

Barad, Karen. 2003. "Posthumanist Performativity: Toward an Understanding of How Matter Comes to Matter." *Signs: Journal of Women in Culture and Society* 28 (3): 801–31.

Baranowski, Andreas, and Heiko Hecht. 2017. "100 Years of Photoplay: Hugo Münsterberg's Lasting Contribution to Cognitive Movie Psychology." *Projections: The Journal for Movies and Mind* 11 (2): 1–21. https://doi.org/10:3167/proj.2017.110202.

Barfield, Tom. 2015. "Why Berlin Graffiti Artists Hacked 'Racist' Homeland." *The Local*. October 15, 2015. https://www.thelocal.de/20151015/berlin-graffiti-artists-sabotage-racist-homeland.

Barker, Jennifer M. 2008. "Out of Sync, Out of Sight: Synaesthesia and Film Spectacle." *Paragraph* 31 (2): 236–51. https://doi.org/10.3366/E0264833408000229.

Barker, Jennifer M. 2009. *The Tactile Eye: Touch and the Cinematic Experience*. Berkeley: University of California Press.

Barrett, Lisa Feldman, and Moshe Bar. 2009. "See It with Feeling: Affective Predictions during Object Perception." *Philosophical Transactions of the Royal Society B: Biological Sciences* 364 (1521): 1325–34. https://doi.org/10.1098/rstb.2008.0312.

Barthes, Roland. 1960a. "Le problème de la signification au cinéma." *Revue internationale de filmologie* 32/33: 83–89.

Barthes, Roland. 1960b. "Les 'unités' traumatiques au cinéma: principes de recherche." *Revue internationale de filmologie* 34: 13–21.

Barthes, Roland. 1972. "The Structuralist Activity." In *Critical Essays*, translated by Richard Howard, 213–20. Evanston, Ill.: Northwestern University Press.

Barthes, Roland. 1975. "An Introduction to the Structural Analysis of Narrative." Translated by Lionel Duisit. *New Literary History* 6 (2, On Narrative and Narratives): 237–72.

Barthes, Roland. 1977a. "The Rhetoric of the Image." In *Image-Music-Text*, translated by Stephen Heath, 32–51. London: Fontana Press.

Barthes, Roland. 1977b. "The Third Meaning: Research Notes on Some Eisenstein Stills." In *Image-Music-Text*, translated by Stephen Heath, 52–68. London: Fontana Press.

Barthes, Roland. 1981. *Camera Lucida*. Translated by Richard Howard. New York: Hill & Wang.

Barthes, Roland. 1990. *S\Z: An Essay*. Translated by Richard Miller. Paperback. Malden, MA; Oxford; Melbourne; Berlin: Wiley-Blackwell.

Baschiera, Stefano, and Miriam De Rosa. 2020. "Introduction." In *Film and Domestic Space: Architectures, Representations, Dispositif*, edited by Stefano Baschiera and Miriam De Rosa, 1–15. Edinburgh: Edinburgh University Press.

Bateman, John A. 2019. "Multimodality and Materiality: The Interplay of Textuality and Texturality in the Aesthetics of Film." *Poetics Today* 40 (2): 235–68. https://doi.org/10.1215/03335372-7298536.

Baudry, Jean-Louis. 1981a. "Ideological Effects of the Basic Cinematographic Apparatus." In *Apparatus*, edited by Theresa Hak Kyung Cha, 25–40. New York: Tanam Press.

Baudry, Jean-Louis. 1981b. "The Apparatus." In *Apparatus*, edited by Theresa Hak Kyung Cha, 41–62. New York: Tanam Press.

Bayraktaroğlu, Kerem. 2018. *The Muslim World in Post-9/11 American Cinema: A Critical Study, 2001–2011.* Jefferson, N.C.: McFarland & Company, Inc.

BBC News. 2015. "Artists Write 'Homeland Is Racist' Graffiti on Set." *BBC News*. October 15, 2015. Sec. US & Canada. https://www.bbc.com/news/world-us-canada-34536434.

Bell, Alice, and Marie-Laure Ryan, eds. 2019. *Possible Worlds. Theory and Contemporary Narratology*. Lincoln; London: University of Nebraska Press.

Benjamin, Walter. 2010. "The Work of Art in the Age of Technical Reproducibility." Translated by Michael W. Jennings. *Grey Room* 39 (Spring): 11–37.

Bergson, Henri. 1991. *Matter and Memory*. Translated by Nancy Margaret Paul and William Scott Palmer. 8th Printing. New York: Zone Books.

Berman, Judy. 2018. "How Wes Anderson Perfected the Music-Nerd Soundtrack." *Pitchfork*. March 21, 2018. https://pitchfork.com/features/article/how-wes-anderson-perfected-the-music-nerd-soundtrack/.

Bille, Mikkel, Peter Bjerregaard, and Tim Flohr Sørensen. 2015. "Staging Atmospheres: Materiality, Culture, and the Texture of the In-Between." *Emotion, Space and Society* 15 (May): 31–38. https://doi.org/10.1016/j.emospa.2014.11.002.

Binswanger, Ludwig. 1933. "Das Raumproblem in der Psychopathologie." *Zeitschrift für die gesamte Neurologie und Psychiatrie* 145 (1): 598–647.

Birdsdall, Carolyn. 2012. *Nazi Soundscapes: Sound, Technology and Urban Space in Germany, 1933–1945*. Amsterdam: Amsterdam University Press.

Bissell, David. 2010. "Passenger Mobilities: Affective Atmospheres and the Sociality of Public Transport." *Environment and Planning D: Society and Space* 28 (2): 270–89. https://doi.org/10.1068/d3909.

Blackman, Lisa. 2012. *Immaterial Bodies: Affect, Embodiment, Meditation*. Los Angeles; London; New Delhi; Singapore; Washington, DC: SAGE Publications Ltd.

Bladow, Kyle, and Jennifer Ladino. 2018. "Toward an Affective Ecocriticism: Placing Feeling in the Anthropocene." In *Affective Ecocriticism: Emotion, Embodiment,*

Environment, edited by Kyle Bladow and Jennifer Ladino, 1–22. Lincoln: University of Nebraska Press.

Böhme, Gernot. 1993. "Atmosphere as the Fundamental Concept of a New Aesthetic." Translated by David Roberts. *Thesis Eleven* 36 (1): 113–26.

Böhme, Gernot. 2013. *Atmosphäre: Essays zur neuen Ästhetik*. Berlin: Suhrkamp Verlag.

Böhme, Gernot. 2014a. "The Theory of Atmospheres and Its Applications." Translated by Andreas-Christian Engels-Schwarzpaul. *Interstices: Journal of Architecture and Related Arts* 15 (1): 92–99.

Böhme, Gernot. 2014b. "Urban Atmospheres: Charting New Directions for Architecture and Urban Planning." In *Architectural Atmospheres: On the Experience and Politics of Architecture*, edited by Christian Borch, 42–59. Basel: Birkhäuser.

Böhme, Gernot. 2016. *The Aesthetics of Atmospheres*. Edited by Jean-Paul Thibaud. London: Routledge, Taylor & Francis Group.

Böhnke, Alexander. 2007. "Die Zeit der Diegese." *montage/av* 16 (2): 93–104.

Boillat, Alain. 2009. "La 'diégèse' dans son acception filmologique. Origine, postérité et productivité d'un concept." *Cinémas Revue d'études cinématographiques* 19 (2–3): 217–45.

Bollnow, Otto Friedrich. 1941. *Das Wesen der Stimmungen*. Frankfurt am Main: V. Klostermann.

Bordwell, David. 1977. "Camera Movements and Cinematic Space." *Ciné-Tracts* 1 (2): 19–25.

Bordwell, David. 1985. *Narration in the Fiction Film*. Madison: University of Wisconsin Press.

Bordwell, David. 1989. "A Case for Cognitivism." *IRIS* 9: 11–40.

Bordwell, David. 1991. *Making Meaning: Inference and Rhetoric in the Interpretation of Cinema*. First Harvard University Press paperback edition. Cambridge, Mass: Harvard University Press.

Bordwell, David. 2002. "Intensified Continuity: Visual Style in Contemporary American Film." *Film Quarterly* 55 (3): 16–28.

Bordwell, David. 2006. *The Way Hollywood Tells It: Story and Style in Modern Movies*. Berkeley; Los Angeles; London: University of California Press.

Bordwell, David. 2008. *Poetics of Cinema*. New York: Routledge.

Bordwell, David. 2011. "Common Sense + Film Theory = Common-Sense Film Theory?" *David Bordwell's Website on Cinema* (blog). May 2011. http://www.davidbordwell.net/essays/commonsense.php.

Bordwell, David. 2020. "Brains, Bodies, and Movies: Ways of Thinking about the Psychology of Cinema." *Observations on Film Art* (blog). April 29, 2020. http://www.davidbordwell.net/blog/2020/04/29/brains-bodies-and-movies-ways-of-thinking-about-the-psychology-of-cinema/.

Bordwell, David, Janet Staiger, and Kristin Thompson. 1985. *The Classical Hollywood Cinema: Film Style and Mode of Production to 1960*. New York: Columbia University Press.

Bottomore, Stephen. 2001. "The Story of Percy Peashaker: Debates about Sound Effects in the Early Cinema." In *The Sounds of Early Cinema*, edited by Richard Abel and Rick Altman, 129–42. Bloomington and Indianapolis: Indiana University Press.

Bradley, Arthur Cecil. 1911. "Poetry for Poetry's Sake." In *Oxford Lectures on Poetry*, 3–34. London: Macmillan.

Branigan, Edward. 1984. *Point of View: A Theory of Narration and Subjectivity in Classical Film*. Berlin; New York; Amsterdam: Mouton Publishers.

Branigan, Edward. 1986. "Diegesis and Authorship in Film." *IRIS* 7 (Special Issue Cinema and Narration 1): 37–54.

Branigan, Edward. 1992. *Narrative Comprehension and Film*. London; New York: Routledge.

Branigan, Edward. 2002. "Sound, Epistemology, Film." In *Film Theory and Philosophy*, edited by Richard Allen and Murray Smith, 96–125. Oxford: Clarendon Press.

Branigan, Edward. 2006. *Projecting a Camera: Language-Games in Film Theory*. London; New York: Routledge.

Braun, Marta. 2010. *Eadweard Muybridge*. London: Reaktion Books.

Brémond, Claude. 1964. "Le message narratif." *Communications* 4 (special issue: "Recherches sémiologiques"): 4–32.

Brennan, Teresa. 2004. *The Transmission of Affect*. Ithaca; London: Cornell University Press.

Bresnahan, Keith. 2012. "Day for Night: Staging 'Nature' in the Contemporary Interior." *Interiors* 3 (1–2): 85–105. https://doi.org/10.2752/204191212X13232577462619.

Brinkema, Eugenie. 2014. *The Forms of the Affects*. Durham; London: Duke University Press Books.

Brooks, Peter. 1984. *Reading for the Plot: Design and Intention in Narrative*. New York: Vintage.

Bruner, J. S., J. J. Goodnow, and A. George. 1956. *A Study of Thinking*. New York: John Wiley & Sons.

Brunner, Philipp, Jörg Schweintz, and Margit Tröhler, eds. 2012. *Filmische Atmosphären*. Zürcher Filmstudien. Marburg: Schüren.

Buckland, Warren. 2003. *Cognitive Semiotics of Film*. Cambridge, Mass.; London: Cambridge University Press.

Buckley, Craig, Rüdiger Campe, and Francesco Casetti, eds. 2019. *Screen Genealogies: From Optical Device to Environmental Medium*. Amsterdam: Amsterdam University Press.

Bunia, Remigius. 2010. "Diegesis and Representation: Beyond the Fictional World, on the Margins of Story and Narrative." *Poetics Today* 31 (4): 679–720.

Burch, Noël. 1979. *To the Distant Observer: Form and Meaning in the Japanese Cinema*. Edited by Annette Michelson. Berkeley; Los Angeles: University of California Press.

Burch, Noël. 1982. "Narrative/Diegesis—Thresholds, Limits." *Screen* 23 (2.1): 16–33.

Bush, Stephen W. 1911. "When 'Effects' Are Unnecessary Noises." *Moving Picture World* September: 690.

Cage, John. 1961. *Silence: Lectures and Writings*. Hanover, N.H.: Wesleyan University Press.

Canepa, Elisabetta, Valter Scelsi, Anna Fassio, Laura Avanzino, Giovanna Lagravinese, and Carlo Chiorri. 2019. "Atmospheres: Feeling Architecture by Emotions. Preliminary Neuroscientific Insights on Atmospheric Perception in Architecture." *Ambiances. Environnement Sensible, Architecture et Espace Urbain*, 5 (December): 1–29. https://doi.org/10.4000/ambiances.2907.

Canning, Elaine. 2007. "Destiny, Theatricality and Identity in Contemporary European Cinema." *New Cinemas: Journal of Contemporary Film* 4 (3): 159–71.

Caracciolo, Marco. 2014a. *The Experientiality of Narrative: An Enactivist Approach*. Berlin; Boston: De Gruyter.

Caracciolo, Marco. 2014b. "Narrative Experientiality." In *The Living Handbook of Narratology*, edited by Peter Hühn, Jan Christoph Meister, John Pier, and Wolf Schmid, 1–9. Germany: Walter de Gruyter. https://www.lhn.uni-hamburg.de/node/102.html.

Carbone, Mauro. 2015. *The Flesh of the Images: Merleau-Ponty between Painting and Cinema*. Translated by Marta Nijhuis. Albany: State University of New York Press.

Carmona, Carlos Ruiz. 2017. "The Role and Purpose of Film Narration." *Journal of Science and Technology of the Arts* 9 (2-Special Issue: Narrative and Audiovisual Creation): 7–16.

Carpenter, Edmund. 1973. *Eskimo Realities*. New York: Holt, Rinehart and Winston.

Carroll, Beth. 2016. *Feeling Film: A Spatial Approach*. London: Palgrave Macmillan.

Carroll, Noël. 1988. "Film/Mind Analogies: The Case of Hugo Munsterberg." *The Journal of Aesthetics and Art Criticism* 46 (4): 489–99.

Carroll, Noël. 1990. *The Philosophy of Horror, or Paradoxes of the Heart*. New York; London: Routledge.

Carroll, Noël. 1996. *Theorizing the Moving Image*. Cambridge; New York: Cambridge University Press.

Carroll, Noël. 2003a. "Art and Mood: Preliminary Notes and Conjectures." *The Monist* 86 (4): 521–55.

Carroll, Noël. 2003b. "On Being Moved by Nature: Between Religion and Natural History." In *Beyond Aesthetics: Philosophical Essays*, paperback, 368–84. Cambridge, Mass.: Cambridge University Press.

Carroll, Noël. 2006. "Film, Emotion, and Genre." In *Philosophy of Film and Motion Pictures: An Anthology*, edited by Noël Carroll and Jinhee Choi, 217–33. Malden, Mass.; Oxford: Blackwell Publishers.

Casebier, Allan. 1991. *Film and Phenomenology: Toward a Realist Theory of Cinematic Representation*. New York: Cambridge University Press.

Casetti, Francesco. 2015. *The Lumière Galaxy: Seven Key Words for the Cinema to Come*. Film and Culture. New York: Columbia University Press.

Castelvecchi, Stefano. 2020. "On 'Diegesis' and 'Diegetic': Words and Concepts." *Journal of the American Musicological Society* 73 (1): 149–71.

Cecchi, Alessandro. 2010. "Diegetic versus Nondiegetic: A Reconsideration of the Conceptual Opposition as a Contribution to the Theory of Audiovision." *World of Audiovision*. http://www-5.unipv.it/wav/pdf/WAV_Cecchi_2010_eng.pdf.

Certeau, Michel de. 1984. *Practice of Everyday Life*. Translated by Steven Rendall. Berkeley; Los Angeles; London: University of California Press.

Certeau, Michel de. 1988. *The Practice of Everyday Life*. Translated by Steven Rendall. First paperback edition. Berkeley; Los Angeles; London: University of California Press.

Chatman, Seymour. 1978. *Story and Discourse: Narrative Structure in Fiction and Film*. Ithaca, N.Y.; London: Cornell University Press.

Chatman, Seymour. 1984. "What Is Description in the Cinema?" *Cinema Journal* 23 (4): 4–11.

Chatman, Seymour. 1990. *Coming to Terms: The Rhetoric of Narrative in Fiction and Film*. Ithaca, N.Y.; London: Cornell University Press.

Chatman, Seymour. 1992. "What Novels Can Do That Films Can't (and Vice Versa)." In *Film Theory and Criticism: Introductory Readings*, 4th ed., edited by Gerald Mast, Marshall Cohen, and Leo Braudy, 403–19. New York and Oxford: Oxford University Press.

Chemero, Anthony. 2003. "An Outline of a Theory of Affordances." *Ecological Psychology* 15 (2): 181–95.

Chion, Michel. 1991. "Quiet Revolution . . . and Rigid Stagnation." Translated by Ben Brewster. *October* 58 (1): 69–80. https://doi.org/10.2307/778798.

Chion, Michel. 1994. *Audio-Vision: Sound on Screen.* Translated by Claudia Gorbman. New York: Columbia University Press.

Chion, Michel. 2009. *Film, a Sound Art.* New York: Columbia University Press.

Chion, Michel. 2013. "The Sensory Aspects of Contemporary Cinema." In *The Oxford Handbook of New Audiovisual Aesthetics,* edited by Claudia Gorbman, John Richardson, Carol Vernallis, 325–330. New York and Oxford: Oxford University Press.

Choudhury, Suparna, and Jan Slaby, eds. 2012. *Critical Neuroscience: A Handbook of the Social and Cultural Contexts of Neuroscience.* Malden, Mass.; Oxford: Wiley-Blackwell.

Clark, Andy. 2000. *Mindware: An Introduction to the Philosophy of Cognitive Science.* New York: Oxford University Press.

Clark, Andy. 2008. *Supersizing the Mind: Embodiment, Action, and Cognitive Extension.* Oxford: Oxford University Press.

Clark, Andy, and David J. Chalmers. 1998. "The Extended Mind." *Analysis* 58 (1): 7–19.

Clough, Patricia Ticineto. 2007. "Introduction." In *The Affective Turn: Theorizing the Social,* edited by Patricia Ticineto Clough and Jean Halley, 1st edition, 1–33. Durham, N.C.: Duke University Press Books.

Clough, Patricia Ticineto, and Jean Halley, eds. 2007. *The Affective Turn: Theorizing the Social.* 1st edition. Durham, N.C.: Duke University Press Books.

Coëgnarts, Maarten, and Peter Kravanja. 2014. "Metaphor, Bodily Meaning, and Cinema." *Image [&] Narrative* 15 (1): 1–4. http://www.imageandnarrative.be/index.php/ima genarrative/issue/view/37.

Coëgnarts, Maarten. 2019. *Film as Embodied Art: Bodily Meaning in the Cinema of Stanley Kubrick.* Boston: Academic Studies Press.

Coëgnarts, Maarten, and Peter Kravanja, eds. 2015. *Embodied Cognition and Cinema.* Leuven: Leuven University Press.

Cohen-Séat, Gilbert. 1946. *Essai sur les principes d'une Philosophie du cinéma.* Paris: Presses Universitaires de France.

Cohen-Séat, Gilbert, and Pierre Fougeyrollas. 1961. *L'Action sur l'homme: cinéma et télévision.* Paris: Editions Denoel.

Colombetti, Giovanna. 2007. "Enactive Appraisal." *Phenomenology and the Cognitive Sciences* 6 (4): 527–46. https://doi.org/10.1007/s11097-007-9077-8.

Colombetti, Giovanna. 2014. *The Feeling Body: Affective Science Meets the Enactive Mind.* Cambridge, Mass.; London: MIT Press.

Colombetti, Giovanna. 2017a. "Enactive Affectivity, Extended." *Topoi* 36 (3): 445–55.

Colombetti, Giovanna. 2017b. "The Embodied and Situated Nature of Moods." *Philosophia* 45 (4): 1437–51. https://doi.org/10.1007/s11406-017-9817-0.

Colombetti, Giovanna, and Joel W. Krueger. 2015. "Scaffoldings of the Affective Mind." *Philosophical Psychology* 28 (8): 1157–76. https://doi.org/10.1080/09515 089.2014.976334.

Colombetti, Giovanna, Joel Kruger, and Tom Roberts. 2018. "Editorial: Affectivity beyond the Skin." *Frontiers in Psychology* 9 (1307): 1–2.

Colombetti, Giovanna, and Tom Roberts. 2015. "Extending the Extended Mind: The Case for Extended Affectivity." *Philosophical Studies* 172 (5): 1243–63. https://doi.org/ 10.1007/s11098-014-0347-3.

Connolly, William E. 2002. *Neuropolitics: Thinking, Culture, Speed*. Minneapolis; London: University of Minnesota Press.

Connolly, William E. 2011. "Critical Response I: The Complexity of Intention." *Critical Inquiry* 37 (4): 791–98.

Connor, Steven. 2004. "Edison's Teeth: Touching Hearing." In *Hearing Cultures: Essays on Sound, Listening and Modernity*, edited by Veit Erlmann, 153–72. Oxford; New York: Berg.

Costall, Alan. 1995. "Socializing Affordances." *Theory & Psychology* 5 (4): 467–81.

Coulthard, Lisa. 2012. "Haptic Aurality: Resonance, Listening and Michael Haneke." *Film-Philosophy* 16 (1): 16–29.

Coulthard, Lisa. 2013. "Dirty Sound: Noise in New Extremism." In *Oxford Handbook of Sound and Image in Digital Media*, edited by Amy Herzog, Brian Richardson, and Carol Vernallis, 115–26. New York: Oxford University Press.

Cowan, Michael. 2007. "The Heart Machine: 'Rhythm' and Body in Weimar Film and Fritz Lang's Metropolis." *Modernism/Modernity* 14 (2): 225–48.

Cowan, Michael. 2014. *Walter Ruttmann and the Cinema of Multiplicity*. Film Culture in Transition. Amsterdam: Amsterdam University Press.

Cox, Christoph. 2011. "Beyond Representation and Signification: Toward a Sonic Materialism." *Journal of Visual Culture* 10 (2): 145–61. https://doi.org/10.1177/14704 12911402880.

Cresswell, Tim. 2004. *Place: A Short Introduction*. Malden, Mass.; Oxford; Victoria: Wiley-Blackwell.

Cuccio, Valentina, and Vittorio Gallese. 2018. "A Peircean Account of Concepts: Grounding Abstraction in Phylogeny through a Comparative Neuroscientific Perspective." *Philosophical Transactions of the Royal Society B* 373 (1752): 1–10. https://doi.org/ 10.1098/rstb.2017.0128.

Culler, Jonathan. 2001. *The Pursuit of Signs: Semiotics, Literature, Deconstruction*. Routledge Classics. London; New York: Routledge.

Cutting, James E. 2007. "Perceiving Scenes in Film and in the World." In *Moving Image Theory: Ecological Considerations*, edited by Joseph D. Anderson and Barbara Fisher Anderson, 9–27. Carbondale: Southern Illinois University Press.

Cutting, James E., and Karen Pearlman. 2019. "Shaping Edits, Creating Fractals." *Projections* 13 (1): 1–22. https://doi.org/10.3167/proj.2019.130102.

D'Aloia, Adriano. 2021. *Neurofilmology of the Moving-Image: Gravity and Vertigo in Contemporary Cinema*. Amsterdam: Amsterdam University Press.

D'Aloia, Adriano, and Ruggero Eugeni. 2014. "Neurofilmology: An Introduction." *Cinéma & Cie* XIV (22–23): 9–26.

Damasio, Antonio. 1995. *Descartes' Error: Emotion, Reason, and the Human Brain*. New York: Penguin Books.

Damasio, Antonio. 1999. *The Feeling of What Happens: Body and Emotion in the Making of Consciousness*. London: Vintage.

Damasio, Antonio. 2003. *Looking for Spinoza: Joy, Sorrow, and the Feeling Brain*. London: William Heinemann.

Danes, Claire. 2020. "Claire Danes on the End of Homeland: "'It was so nice to play such a badass.'" Interview by David Smith. *The Guardian*. April 5, 2020. https://www.theg uardian.com/tv-and-radio/2020/apr/05/claire-danes-on-the-end-of-homeland-it-was-so-nice-to-play-such-a-badass.

Deleuze, Gilles. 2000. "The Brain Is the Screen: An Interview with Gilles Deleuze." In *The Brain Is the Screen: Deleuze and the Philosophy of Cinema*, edited by Gregory Flaxman, translated by Marie Therese Guirgis, 365–74. Minneapolis: University of Minnesota Press.

Deleuze, Gilles. 2004. *Difference and Repetition*. Translated by Paul Patton. London: Continuum.

Deleuze, Gilles. 2005. *Cinema 2: The Time-Image*. Translated by Hugh Tomlinson and Barbara Habberjam. London: Continuum.

Deleuze, Gilles, and Felix Guattari. 1994. *What Is Philosophy?* Translated by Hugh Tomlinson and Graham Burchell. New York: Columbia University Press.

Dewey, John. 1980. *Art as Experience*. 23rd Impression. New York: Perigree.

Di Pellegrino, Giuseppe, Luciano Fadiga, Leonardo Fogassi, Vittorio Gallese, and Giacomo Rizzolatti. 1992. "Understanding Motor Events: A Neurophysiological Study." *Experimental Brain Research* 91 (1): 176–80.

Doane, Mary Ann. 1980. "The Voice in the Cinema: The Articulation of Body and Space." *Yale French Studies* 60 (Cinema/Sound): 33–50.

Donnelly, Kevin J. 2014. *Occult Aesthetics: Synchronization in Sound Film*. Oxford; New York: Oxford University Press.

Dufrenne, Mikel. 1973. *Phenomenology of the Aesthetic Experience*. Translated by Edward S. Casey. Evanston, Ill.: Northwestern University Press.

Duncan, Seth, and Lisa Feldman Barrett. 2007. "Affect Is a Form of Cognition: A Neurobiological Analysis." *Cognition & Emotion* 21 (6): 1184–1211. https://doi.org/10.1080/02699930701437931.

Durham Peters, John. 2015. *The Marvelous Clouds: Toward a Philosophy of Elemental Media*. Chicago; London: The University of Chicago Press.

Ellis, Rob, and Mike Tucker. 2000. "Micro-Affordances: The Potentiation of Components of Actions by Seen Objects." *British Journal of Psychology* 91: 451–71.

Elsaesser, Thomas. 2004. "The New Film History as Media Archaeology." *Cinémas: Journal of Film Studies* 14 (2–3): 75–117.

Elsaesser, Thomas, and Malte Hagener. 2009. *Film Theory: An Introduction through the Senses*. 1st edition. New York: Routledge.

Engell, Lorenz, and Bernhard Siegert. 2013. "Editorial." Edited by Lorenz Engell and Bernhard Siegert. *Zeitschrift für Medien- und Kulturforschung* 4 (1, Schwerpunkt Medienanthropologie): 5–10.

Engell, Lorenz, and Bernhard Siegert. 2017. "Editorial." Edited by Lorenz Engell and Bernhard Siegert. *Zeitschrift für Medien- und Kulturforschung* 8 (2, Schwerpunkt Operative Ontologien): 5–10.

Escriván, Julio d'. 2009. "Sound Art (?) on/in Film." *Organised Sound* 14: 65–73. https://doi.org/10.1017/S1355771809000090.

Fay, Jennifer. 2014. "Buster Keaton's Climate Change." *Modernism/Modernity* 21 (1): 25–49. https://doi.org/10.1353/mod.2014.0006.

Fay, Jennifer. 2018. *Inhospitable World: Cinema in the Time of the Anthropocene*. New York: Oxford University Press.

Flückiger, Barbara. 2009. "Sound Effects: Strategies for Sound Effects in Film." In *Sound and Music in Film and Visual Media: A Critical Overview*, edited by Graeme Harper, 151–79. New York and London: Bloomsbury Academic.

Flückiger, Barbara. 2017. *Sound Design: Die Virtuelle Klangwelt des Films*. 6th edition. Marburg: Schüren.

Fludernik, Monika. 2009. *An Introduction to Narratology*. London and New York: Routledge.

Fludernik, Monika. 2010. *Towards a "Natural" Narratology*. Reprint. London: Taylor & Francis Ltd.

Fodor, Jerry. 1975. *The Language of Thought*. New York: Crowell.

Fodor, Jerry A. 1983. *The Modularity of Mind: An Essay on Faculty Psychology*. Cambridge, Mass.: MIT Press.

Fodor, Jerry A., and Zenon Walter Pylyshyn. 1981. "How Direct Is Visual Perception? Some Reflections on Gibson's 'Ecological Approach.'" *Cognition* 9 (2): 139–96.

Foucault, Michel. 1980. "Questions on Geography." In *Power/Knowledge: Selected Interviews and Other Writings 1972–1977*, edited by Colin Gordon, translated by Colin Gordon, Leo Marshall, John Mepham, and Kate Soper, 63–77. New York: Pantheon Books.

Foucault, Michel. 1986. "Of Other Spaces." Translated by Jay Miskowiec. *Dicacritics* 16 (1): 22–27.

Friedman, Susan Stanford. 1993. "Spatialization: A Strategy for Reading Narrative." *Narrative* 1 (1): 12–23.

Friedman, Susan Stanford. 2005. "Spatial Poetics and Arundhati Roy's *The God of Small Things*." In *A Companion to Narrative Theory*, edited by James Phelan and Peter J. Rabinowitz, 192–205. Malden, Mass.; Oxford: Blackwell Publishers.

Fuxjäger, Anton. 2007. "Diegese, Diegesis, diegetisch: Versuch einer Begriffsentwirrung." *montage/av* 16 (2): 17–37.

Gallagher, Shaun. 2005. *How the Body Shapes the Mind*. New edition. Oxford; New York: Oxford University Press.

Gallagher, Shaun. 2017. *Enactivist Interventions: Rethinking the Mind*. Oxford; New York: Oxford University Press.

Gallagher, Shaun, and Matthew Bower. 2014. "Making Enactivism Even More Embodied." *Avant* 5 (2): 232–47.

Gallagher, Shaun, and Dan Zahavi. 2012. *The Phenomenological Mind*. 2nd edition. London; New York: Routledge.

Gallese, Vittorio. 2005. "Embodied Simulation: From Neurons to Phenomenal Experience." *Phenomenology and the Cognitive Sciences* 4: 23–48.

Gallese, Vittorio. 2011. "Neuroscience and Phenomenology." *Phenomenology & Mind* 1: 33–48.

Gallese, Vittorio. 2016. "Finding the Body in the Brain: From Simulation Theory to Embodied Simulation." In *Goldman and His Critics*, edited by Brian P. McLaughlin and Hilary Kornblith, 297–314. Hoboken, N.J.: Wiley-Blackwell.

Gallese, Vittorio, Luciano Fadiga, Leonardo Fogassi, and Giacomo Rizzolatti. 1996. "Action Recognition in the Premotor Cortex." *Brain* 119 (2): 593–609. https://doi.org/10.1093/brain/119.2.593.

Gallese, Vittorio, and Alan Freeberg. 2007. "Motion, Emotion and Empathy in Esthetic Experience." *Trends in Cognitive Sciences* 11 (5): 197–203.

Gallese, Vittorio, and Alvin Goldman. 1998. "Mirror Neurons and the Simulation Theory of Mind-Reading." *Trends in Cognitive Sciences* 2 (12): 493–501. https://doi.org/10.1016/S1364-6613(98)01262-5.

Gallese, Vittorio, and Michele Guerra. 2014. "The Feeling of Motion: Camera Movements and Motor Cognition." *Cinéma&Cie* XIV (22/23), 103–112.

Gallese, Vittorio, and Michele Guerra. 2020. *The Empathic Screen: Cinema and Neuroscience*. Translated by Frances Anderson. Oxford: Oxford University Press.

Gallese, Vittorio, and Corrado Sinigaglia. 2011. "What Is So Special about Embodied Simulation?" *Trends in Cognitive Sciences* 15 (11): 512–19. https://doi.org/10.1016/j.tics.2011.09.003.

Gallese, Vittorio, and Hannah Wojciehowski. 2011. "How Stories Make Us Feel: Toward an Embodied Narratology." *California Italian Studies* 2 (1): 1–37.

Genette, Gerárd. 1982. *Figures of Literary Discourse*. Ithaca, N.Y.: Cornell University Press.

Genette, Gerárd. 1983. *Narrative Discourse: An Essay in Method*. Translated by Jane E. Lewin. 1st edition. Ithaca, N.Y.: Cornell University Press.

Genette, Gerárd. 1988. *Narrative Discourse Revisited*. Translated by Jane E. Lewin. Ithaca, N.Y.: Cornell University Press.

Gerrig, Richard. 1993. *Experiencing Narrative Worlds: On the Psychological Activities of Reading*. New Haven, Conn.: Yale University Press.

Gibson, James J. 1947. *Motion Picture Testing and Research*. Classic edition. New York; London: U.S. Army Air Forces Aviation Psychology Program Research Reports, 47.

Gibson, James J. 1960. "The Concept of Stimulus in Psychology." *The American Psychologist* 15 (11): 694–703.

Gibson, James J. 1966. *The Senses Considered as Perceptual Systems*. London: George Allen & Unwin Ltd.

Gibson, James J. 2015. *The Ecological Approach to Visual Perception*. Classic edition. New York; London: Psychology Press.

Glotfelty, Cheryll, and Harold Fromm. 1996. "Introduction: Literary Studies in an Age of Environmental Crisis." In *The Ecocriticism Reader: Landmarks in Literary Ecology*, xv–xxxvii. Athens: The University of Georgia Press.

Goldie, Peter, and Amy Coplan. 2011. "Introduction." In *Empathy: Philosophical and Psychological Perspectives*, ix–xlvii. Oxford: Oxford University Press.

Goldman, Alvin I. 1989. "Interpretation Psychologized." *Mind and Language* 4 (3): 161–85.

Goldman, Alvin I. 1992. "In Defense of the Simulation Theory." *Mind and Language* 7 (1–2): 104–19.

Goldman, Alvin I. 2006. *Simulating Minds: The Philosophy, Psychology, and Neuroscience of Mindreading*. Oxford; New York: Oxford University Press.

Gorbman, Claudia. 1980. "Narrative Film Music." *Yale French Studies* 60 (Cinema/Sound): 183–203. https://doi.org/10.2307/2930011.

Gorbman, Claudia. 1987. *Unheard Melodies: Narrative Film Music*. Bloomington; Indianapolis: Indiana University Press.

Greene, Liz. 2016. "From Noise: Blurring the Boundaries of the Soundtrack." In *The Palgrave Handbook of Sound Design and Music in Screen Media*, edited by Liz Greene and Danijela Kulezic-Wilson, 17–32. Basingstoke, U.K.; New York: Palgrave Macmillan.

Greene, Liz, and Danijela Kulezic-Wilson. 2016. "Introduction." In *The Palgrave Handbook of Sound Design and Music in Screen Media*, edited by Liz Greene and Danijela Kulezic-Wilson, 1–13. Basingstoke, U.K.; New York: Palgrave Macmillan.

Gregg, Melissa, and Gregory J. Seigworth. 2010a. "An Inventory of Shimmers." In *The Affect Theory Reader*, edited by Melissa Gregg and Gregory J. Seigworth, 1–25. Durham, N.C.: Duke University Press Books.

Gregg, Melissa, and Gregory J. Seigworth, eds. 2010b. *The Affect Theory Reader*. Durham, N.C.: Duke University Press Books.

Griffero, Tonino. 2014a. *Atmospheres: Aesthetics of Emotional Spaces*. Translated by Sarah De Sanctis. Farnham Surrey, U.K.: Ashgate.

Griffero, Tonino. 2014b. "Atmospheres and Lived Space." *Studia Phaenomenologicia* XIV (Place, Environment, Atmosphere): 29–51.

Griffero, Tonino. 2014c. "Who's Afraid of Atmospheres (and of Their Authority)?" *Lebenswelt* 4 (1): 193–213.

Griffiths, Paul, and Andrea Scarantino. 2009. "Emotions in the Wild." In *The Cambridge Handbook of Situated Cognition*, edited by Philip Robbins and Murat Aydede, 437–53. Cambridge; New York: Cambridge University Press.

Grishakova, Marina, and Maria Poulaki. 2019. *Narrative Complexity: Cognition, Embodiment, Evolution*. Lincoln: University of Nebraska Press.

Grodal, Torben Kragh. 1999. *Moving Pictures: A New Theory of Film Genres, Feelings, and Cognition*. Oxford; New York: Oxford University Press.

Grodal, Torben Kragh. 2005. "Film Lighting and Mood." In *Moving Image Theory: Ecological Considerations*, edited by Barbara Anderson and Joseph Anderson, 152–63. Carbondale: Southern Illinois University Press.

Grodal, Torben Kragh. 2009. *Embodied Visions: Evolution, Emotion, Culture, and Film*. Oxford; New York: Oxford University Press.

Guillain, André. 2012. "Henri Wallon et la filmologie." *1895. Mille huit cent quatre-vingt-quinze* 66 (Spring): 50–73.

Gumbrecht, Hans Ulrich. 2003. *Production of Presence: What Meaning Cannot Convey*. Stanford, Calif.: Stanford University Press.

Gumbrecht, Hans Ulrich. 2012. *Atmosphere, Mood, Stimmung: On a Hidden Potential of Literature*. Translated by Erik Butler. Stanford, Calif.: Stanford University Press.

Gunning, Tom. 2020. "Nothing Will Have Taken Place—Except Place': The Unsettling Nature of Camera Movement." In *Screen Space Reconfigured*, edited by Susanne O. Sæther and Synne T. Bull, 263–81. Amsterdam: Amsterdam University Press.

Hanich, Julian. 2011. "Die Publikumserfahrung. Eine Phänomenologie der affektiven Zuschauerbeziehungen im Kino." In *Emotionen in Literatur und Film*, edited by Sandra Poppe, 171–91. Würzburg: Königshausen und Neumann.

Hanich, Julian. 2018. *The Audience Effect*. Edinburgh: Edinburgh University Press.

Hanich, Julian, and Christian Ferencz-Flatz. 2016. "What Is Film Phenomenology?" *Studia Phaenomenologica* XVI (Film Phenomenology): 11–61.

Hansen, Mark B. N. 2004a. "Communication as Interface or Information Exchange? A Reply to Richard Rushton." *Journal of Visual Culture* 3 (3): 359–66.

Hansen, Mark B. N. 2004b. *New Philosophy for New Media*. Cambridge, Mass.: MIT Press.

Hansen, Mark B. N. 2006. "Media Theory." *Theory, Culture & Society* 23 (2–3): 297–306. https://doi.org/10.1177/026327640602300256.

Hansen, Miriam Bratu. 2012. *Cinema and Experience: Sigfried Kracauer, Walter Benjamin, and Theodor W. Adorno*. Berkelez, Los Angeles, and London: University of California Press.

Hasse, Jürgen. 2012. *Atmosphären der Stadt: Aufgespürte Räume*. Berlin: Jovis.

Hauskeller, Michael. 1995. *Atmosphären Erleben. Philosophische Untersuchungen zur Sinneswahrnehmung*. Berlin: Akademie Verlag.

Heath, Stephen. 1975. "Film and System: Terms of Analysis (Part I)." *Screen* 16 (1): 7–77. https://doi.org/10.1093/screen/16.1.7.

Hediger, Vinzenz. 2003. "Das Projekt der Filmologie und der Beitrag der Psychologie." *montage AV* 12 (1): 55–71.

Heft, Harry. 1989. "Affordances and the Body: An Intentional Analysis of Gibson's Ecological Approach to Visual Perception." *Journal for the Theory of Social Behaviour* 19 (1): 1–30.

Heidegger, Martin. 1962. *Being and Time*. Translated by John Macquarrie and Edward Robinson. 1st ed. Oxford: Blackwell Publishers.

Heidegger, Martin. 1967. *Sein und Zeit*. 11th ed. Tübingen: Max Niemeyer Verlag.

Heldt, Guido. 2013. *Music and Levels of Narration in Film: Steps across the Border*. Bristol, U.K.; Chicago: Intellect.

Helmholtz, Hermann von. 1867. *Handbuch der physiologischen Optik*. Leipzig: Leopold Voss.

Helmholtz, Hermann von. 2005. *Treatise on Physiological Optics*. Edited by James Powell Cocke Southall. Dover Phoenix. Vol. 3. Mineola, N.Y.: Dover.

Herman, David. 2002. *Story Logic: Problems and Possibilities of Narrative*. Lincoln: University of Nebraska Press.

Herman, David. 2009. *Basic Elements of Narrative*. Malden, Mass.: Wiley-Blackwell.

Herman, David. 2011. "Storyworld/Umwelt: Nonhuman Experiences in Graphic Narratives." *SubStance* 40 (1): 156–81.

Herman, David. 2013a. "Approaches to Narrative Worldmaking." In *Doing Narrative Research*, edited by Molly Andrews, Corinne Squire, and Maria Tamboukou, 176–96. 2nd edition. Sage: London and Los Angeles.

Herman, David. 2013b. *Storytelling and the Sciences of Mind*. Cambridge, Mass: MIT Press.

Hesselberth, Pepita. 2014. *Cinematic Chronotopes: Here, Now, Me*. London: Bloomsbury Academic.

Hjelmslev, Louis. 1961. *Prolegomena to a Theory of Language*. Translated by Francis J. Whitfield. Madison: The University of Wisconsin Press.

Hogan, Patrick Colm. 2012. *Affective Narratology: The Emotional Structure of Stories*. Lincoln: University of Nebraska Press.

Hurley, Susan. 2002. *Consciousness in Action*. 1st edition. Cambridge, Mass.: Harvard University Press.

Hurley, Susan. 2008. "The Shared Circuits Model (SCM): How Control, Mirroring, and Simulation Can Enable Imitation, Deliberation, and Mindreading." *Behavioral and Brain Sciences* 31: 1–58. https://doi.org/10.1017/S0140525X07003123.

Hutto, Daniel D. 2000. *Beyond Physicalism*. Vol. 21. Advances in Consciousness Research. Amsterdam; Philadelphia: John Benjamins Publishing Company.

Hven, Steffen. 2016. "The Cinematic Narrative as 'Anthropomedial Relation.'" (Lecture, The Real of Reality: International Conference on Philosophy and Film, Karlsruhe, November 2–6, 2011). https://zkm.de/de/steffen-hven.

Hven, Steffen. 2017a. *Cinema and Narrative Complexity: Embodying the Fabula*. Film Culture in Transition. Amsterdam: Amsterdam University Press.

Hven, Steffen. 2017b. "Sulla possibilità di una narratologia incarnata e antropomediale." Edited by Michele Guerra. Translated by Simona Busni and Caterina Martino. *Fata Morgana* 31 (Special Issue: Consciousness): 197–209.

Hven, Steffen. 2019. "The Affective Niches of Media." *NECSUS: European Journal of Media Studies* 8 (1, # Emotions): 105–23.

Iñárritu, Alejandro González, and David Fear. 2016. "Into the Woods." *Film Comment* 52 (1): 22–27.

Ingold, Tim. 2007. "Against Soundscape." In *Autumn Leaves: Sound and the Environment in Artistic Practice*, edited by Angus Carlyle, 10–13. Paris: Double Entendre.

Ingold, Tim. 2012. "The Atmosphere." *Chiasmi International* 14: 75–87. https://doi.org/10.5840/chiasmi20121410.

Ingold, Tim. 2015. *Life of Lines*. London; New York: Routledge.

Ivakhiv, Adrian. 2013. *Ecologies of the Moving Image: Cinema, Affect, Nature, Environmental Humanities*. Waterloo, Ont.: Wilfred Laurier University Press.

Jacobson, Brian R. 2015. *Studios before the System: Architecture, Technology, and the Emergence of Cinematic Space*. New York: Columbia University Press.

James, Erin. 2015. *The Storyworld Accord: Econarratology and Postcolonial Narratives*. Lincoln; London: University of Nebraska Press.

James, Erin, and Eric Morel. 2020. "Introduction: Notes toward New Econarratologies." In *Environment and Narrative: New Directions in Econarratology*, edited by Erin James and Eric More, 1–26. Columbus: The Ohio State University Press.

Johnson, Mark. 2017. *Embodied Mind, Meaning, and Reason: How Our Bodies Give Rise to Understanding*. Chicago; London: University of Chicago Press.

Johnson, Mark, and George Lakoff. 2002. "Why Cognitive Linguistics Requires Embodied Realism." *Cognitive Linguistics* 13 (3): 245–63.

Jullier, Laurent. 2009. "'L'esprit, et peut-être même le cerveau . . .' La question psychologique dans la *Revue internationale de filmologie, 1947–1962*." *Cinémas Revue d'études cinématographiques* 19 (2–3): 143–67.

Kappelhoff, Hermann. 2018. *Kognition und Reflexion: Zur Theorie filmischen Denkens*. Cinepoetics 6. Berlin: De Gruyter.

Kappelhoff, Hermann, and Hauke Lehmann. 2019. "Poetics of Affect." In *Affective Societies: Key Concepts*, edited by Jan Slaby, Christian von Scheve, and Hauke Lehmann, 210–19. London; New York: Routledge.

Kassabian, Anahid. 2001. *Hearing Film: Tracking Identifications in Contemporary Hollywood Film Music*. New York; London: Routledge.

Kassabian, Anahid. 2013. "The End of Diegesis as We Know It?" In *The Oxford Handbook of New Audiovisual Aesthetics*, edited by John Richardson, Claudia Gorbman, and Carol Vernallis, 89–106. Oxford; Cambridge, Mass.: Oxford University Press.

Kennedy, Barbara. 2000. *Deleuze and Cinema: Deleuze and the Aesthetic of Sensation*. Edinburgh: Edinburgh University Press.

Kessler, Frank. 1997. "Etienne Souriau und das Vokabular der filmologischen Schule." *Montage AV* 6 (2): 132–39.

Kessler, Frank. 2007. "Von der Filmologie zur Narratologie." *Montage AV* 16 (2): 9–16.

Kickasola, Joseph G. 2012. "Kieślowski's Musique Concrète." In *Music, Sound and Filmmakers: Sonic Style in Cinema*, edited by James Wierzbicki, 61–75. London; New York: Routledge.

Kilner, J. M., and R. N. Lemon. 2013. "What We Know Currently about Mirror Neurons." *Current Biology* 23 (23): 1057–62. https://doi.org/10.1016/j.cub.2013.10.051.

King, Geoff. 2000. *Spectacular Narratives: Hollywood in the Age of the Blockbuster*. Cinema and Society. New York: I.B. Tauris & Co Ltd.

Kirsten, Guido. 2018. "Barthes' Early Film Semiology and the Legacy of Filmology in Metz." In *Christian Metz and the Codes of Cinema. Film Semiology and Beyond*, edited by Margit Tröhler and Guido Kirsten, translated by Anthony Cordingley, 127–44. Amsterdam: Amsterdam University Press.

Kiss, Miklós. 2015. "Film Narrative and Embodied Cognition: The Impact of Image Schemas on Narrative Form." In *Embodied Cognition and Cinema*, edited by Maarten Coëgnarts and Peter Kravanja, 43–61. Leuven: Leuven University Press.

Kiss, Miklós, and Steven Willemsen. 2013. "Unsettling Melodies: A Cognitive Approach to Incongruent Film Music." *Acta Universitatis Sapientiae. Film and Media Studies* 7: 169–83.

Knight-Hill, Andrew. 2019. "Sonic Diegesis: Reality and the Expressive Potential of Sound in Narrative Film." *Quarterly Review of Film and Video* 36 (8): 643–65. https://doi.org/ 10.1080/10509208.2019.1593027.

Kohler, Evelyne, Christian Keysers, M. Alessandra Umiltà, Leonardo Fogassi, Vittorio Gallese, and Giacomo Rizzolatti. 2002. "Hearing Sounds, Understanding Actions: Action Representation in Mirror Neurons." *Science* 297 (5582): 846–48. https://doi.org/10.1126/science.1070311.

Konigsberg, Ira. 1987. "Diegesis." In *The Complete Film Dictionary*, 79. New York; Scarborough, Ont.: New American Library.

Kotler, Philip. 1974. "Atmospherics as a Marketing Tool." *Journal of Retailing* 49 (4): 48–64.

Koyré, Alexandre. 1965. "The Significance of the Newtonian Synthesis." In *Newtonian Studies*, 3–24. London: Chapman & Hall.

Kracauer, Sigfried. 1997. *Theory of Film: The Redemption of Physical Reality*. Princeton, N.J.: Princeton University Press.

Krueger, Joel, and Thomas Szanto. 2016. "Extended Emotions." *Philosophy Compass* 11 (12): 863–78. https://doi.org/10.1111/phc3.12390.

Kuhn, Markus. 2011. *Filmnarratologie: Ein erzähltheoretisches Analysemodell*. Berlin; New York: De Gruyter.

Kukkonen, Karin, and Marco Caracciolo. 2014. "Introduction: What Is the 'Second Generation?'" *Style* 48 (No. 3, Cognitive Literary Study: Second Generation Approaches): 261–74.

Kulezic-Wilson, Danijela. 2012. "Gus Van Sant's Soundwalks and Audio-Visual Musique Concrète." In *Music, Sound and Filmmakers: Sonic Style in Cinema*, edited by James Wierzbicki, 76–88. London; New York: Routledge.

Kulezic-Wilson, Danijela. 2015. *The Musicality of Narrative Film*. Basingstoke, U.K.: Palgrave Macmillan.

Kulezic-Wilson, Danijela. 2019. *Sound Design Is the New Score: Theory, Aesthetics, and Erotics of the Integrated Soundtrack*. New York: Oxford University Press.

Laine, Tarja, and Wanda Strauven. 2009. "The Synaesthetic Turn." *New Review of Film and Television Studies* 7 (3): 249–55. https://doi.org/10.1080/17400300903047029.

Lakoff, George, and Mark Johnson. 1999. *Philosophy in the Flesh: The Embodied Mind and Its Challenge to Western Thought*. New York: Basic Books.

Lakoff, George, and Mark Johnson. 2003. *Metaphors We Live By*. Chicago; London: University of Chicago Press.

Landa, Jose Angel Garcia, and Susanna Onega, eds. 2014. *Narratology: An Introduction*. 1st edition. (Longman Critical Readers). London; New York: Routledge.

Langdale, Allan. 2002. "S(t)imulation of Mind: The Film Theory of Hugo Münsterberg." In *Hugo Münsterberg on Film: The Photoplay—a Psychological Study and Other Writings on Film*, edited by Allan Langdale, 1–41. London; New York: Routledge.

Latour, Bruno. 2011. "Reflections on Etienne Souriau's *Les différents modes d'existence*." In *The Speculative Turn: Continental Materialism and Realism*, edited by Levi Bryant, Nick Srnicek, and Graham Harman, translated by Stephen Muecke, 304–33. Melbourne: Re. Press.

Latour, Bruno, and Isabelle Stengers. 2015. "The Sphinx of the Work." In *The Different Modes of Existence*, edited by Étienne Souriau, translated by Erik Beranek and Tim Howles, 11–90. Minneapolis, Minn.: Univocal Publishing.

Lazarus, Richard S. 1966. *Psychological Stress and the Coping Process*. New York: McGraw Hill.

Lazarus, Richard S. 1982. "Thoughts on the Relation between Emotion and Cognition." *American Psychologist* 37 (9): 1019–24.

Lazarus, Richard S. 1984. "On the Primacy of Cognition." *American Psychologist* 39 (2): 124–29.

Lazarus, Richard S., and Craig A. Smith. 1990. "Emotion and Adaptation." In *Handbook of Personality: Theory and Research*, edited by Lawrence A. Pervin, 609–37. New York: Guilford.

Lefebvre, Henri. 1991. *The Production of Space*. Translated by Donald Nicholson-Smith. Hoboken, N.J.: Wiley-Blackwell.

Lefebvre, Martin. 2009. "L'aventure filmologique: documents et jalons d'une histoire institutionnelle." *Cinémas* 19 (2–3): 59–100. https://doi.org/10.7202/037547ar.

Legrenzi, Paolo, and Carlo Umiltà. 2011. *Neuromania: On the Limits of Brain Science*. Translated by Frances Anderson. Oxford: Oxford University Press.

Lenoir, Tim. 2004. "Foreword." In *New Philosophy for New Media*, edited by Mark B. N. Hansen, xiii–xxvii. Cambridge, Mass.: MIT Press.

Leys, Ruth. 2011a. "A Turn to Affect: A Critique." *Critical Inquiry* 37 (Spring): 434–72.

Leys, Ruth. 2011b. "Affect and Intention: A Reply to William E. Connolly." *Critical Inquiry* 37 (4): 799–805.

LoBrutto, Vincent. 1994. "Ben Burtt." In *Sound-on-Film: Interviews with Creators of Film Sound*, 137–49. Westport, Conn.; London: Praeger.

Lotman, Yuri. 1977. *The Structure of the Artistic Text*. Translated by Ronald Vroon. Ann Arbor: The University of Michigan Press.

Lowry, Edward. 1985a. "Filmology: The History of a Problematic." *Quarterly Review of Film Studies* 10 (1): 7–21.

Lowry, Edward. 1985b. *The Filmology Movement and Film Study in France*. Ann Arbor: The University of Michigan Press.

Lubezki, Emmanuel. 2016. "Grizzly Adventure." *British Cinematographer* (blog). February 8, 2016. https://britishcinematographer.co.uk/emmanuel-lubezki-amc-asc-the-revenant/.

Mace, William M. 2015. "Introduction to the Classical Edition." In *The Ecological Approach to Visual Perception*, edited by James J. Gibson, Classic edition, xvii–xxix. New York; London: Psychology Press.

MacLean, Paul D. 1949. "Psychosomatic Disease and the 'Visceral Brain': Recent Developments Bearing on the Papez Theory of Emotion." *Psychosomatic Medicine* 11 (6): 338–53.

MacLean, Paul D. 1952. "Some Psychiatric Implications of Physiological Studies on Frontotemporal Portion of Limbic System (Visceral Brain)." *Electroencephalography and Clinical Neurophysiology* 4 (4): 407–18.

Maiese, Michelle. 2016. "Affective Scaffolds, Expressive Arts, and Cognition." *Frontiers in Psychology* 7 (359): 807–28. https://doi.org/10.3389/fpsyg.2016.00359.

Malafouris, Lambros. 2013. *How Things Shape the Mind: A Theory of Material Engagement*. Cambridge, Mass.; London: MIT Press.

Marks, Laura U. 2000. *The Skin of Film: Intercultural Cinema, Embodiment, and the Senses*. Durham, N.C.; London: Duke University Press.

Marks, Laura U. 2002. *Touch: Sensuous Theory and Multisensory Media*. Minneapolis; London: University of Minnesota Press.

Massumi, Brian. 1995. "The Autonomy of Affect." *Cultural Critique* 31 (The Politics of Systems and Environments, Part II) (Autumn): 83–109.

Massumi, Brian. 2002. *Parables for the Virtual: Movement, Affect, Sensation*. Durham, N.C.; London: Duke University Press.

McCormack, Derek P. 2008. "Engineering Affective Atmospheres on the Moving Geographies of the 1897 Andrée Expedition." *Cultural Geographies* 15 (4): 413–30.

McGurk, Harry, and John MacDonald. 1976. "Hearing Lips and Seeing Voices." *Nature* 264 (5588): 746–48. https://doi.org/10.1038/264746a0.

McKim, Kristi. 2013. *Cinema as Weather: Stylistic Screens and Atmospheric Change*. New York: Routledge.

Menary, Richard, ed. 2010. *The Extended Mind*. Cambridge, Mass.: MIT Press.

Merleau-Ponty, Maurice. 1991a. *Sense and Non-Sense*. Translated by Hubert L. Dreyfus and Paul A. Dreyfus. Evanston, Ill.: Northwestern University Press.

Merleau-Ponty, Maurice. 1991b. "The Film and the New Psychology." In *Sense and Non-Sense*, translated by Hubert L Dreyfus and Paul A Dreyfus, 48–59. Evanston, Ill.: Northwestern University Press.

Merleau-Ponty, Maurice. 2002. *Phenomenology of Perception [Phénomènologie de La Perception]*. Translated by Colin Smith. London; New York: Routledge.

Metz, Christian. 1966. "La Grande Syntagmatique Du Film Narratif." *Communications* 8 (1, Recherches sémiologiques: l'analyse structurale du récit): 120–24.

Metz, Christian. 1974. *Language and Cinema*. Translated by Donna Umiker-Sebeok. The Netherlands: Mouton & Co.

Metz, Christian. 1975. "The Imaginary Signifier." Translated by Ben Brewster. *Screen* 16 (2): 14–76.

Metz, Christian. 1980a. "Aural Objects." Translated by Georgia Gurrieri. *Yale French Studies* 60 (Cinema/Sound): 24–32.

Metz, Christian. 1980b. "Un profil d'Étienne Souriau." *Revue d'esthétique* 3-4 (L'Art instaurateur): 143–60.

Metz, Christian. 1990. *Film Language: A Semiotics of the Cinema*. Translated by Michael Taylor. Chicago: University of Chicago Press.

Michotte, Albert. 1948. "Le caractère de 'réalité' des projections cinématographiques." *Revue internationale de filmologie* 3-4: 249–61.

Michotte, Albert. 1991a. "The Character of 'Reality' of Cinematographic Projections." In *Michotte's Experimental Phenomenology of Perception*, edited by Georges Thinès, Alan Costall, and George Butterworth, translated by Alan Costall, 197–209. Hove; London: Lawrence Earlbaum Associates, Publishers.

Michotte, Albert. 1991b. "The Emotional Involvement of the Spectator in the Action Represented in a Film: Toward a Theory." In *Michotte's Experimental Phenomenology of Perception*, edited by Georges Thinès, Alan Costall, and George Butterworth, translated by Alan Costall, 209–17. Hove; London: Lawrence Earlbaum Associates, Publishers.

Mitry, Jean. 1997. *The Aesthetics and Psychology of the Cinema*. Translated by Christopher King. Bloomington; Indianapolis: Indiana University Press.

Moholy-Nagy, Laszlo. 1967. *Painting, Photography, Film*. Translated by Janet Seligman. London: Lund Humphries.

Moretti, Franco. 1998. *Atlas of the European Novel 1800-1900*. London; New York: Verso.

Morgan, Daniel. 2011. "Max Ophuls and the Limits of Virtuosity: On the Aesthetics and Ethics of Camera Movement." *Critical Inquiry* 38 (1): 127–63.

Morgan, Daniel. 2016. "Where Are We?: Camera Movements and the Problem of Point of View." *New Review of Film and Television Studies* 14 (2): 222–48.

Morin, Edgar. 1956. *Cinéma ou l'lhomme imaginaire. Essai d'anthropologie*. Paris: Les Éditions de Minuit.

Morin, Edgar. 2005. *The Cinema, or the Imaginary Man*. Translated by Lorraine Mortimer. Minneapolis; London: University of Minnesota Press.

Morin, Edgar. 2007. "Restricted Complexity, General Complexity." In *Worldviews, Science and Us: Philosophy and Complexity*, edited by Carlos Gershenson, Diederik Aerts, and Bruce Edmonds, 5–29. River Edge, N.J.: World Scientific Pub. Co. Inc.

Mossner, Alexa Weik von. 2017. *Affective Ecologies: Empathy, Emotion, and Environmental Narratives*. Columbus: The Ohio State University Press.

Münsterberg, Hugo. 1916. *The Photoplay: A Psychological Study*. London; New York: D. Appleton & Company.

Nannicelli, Ted, and Paul Taberham, eds. 2014. *Cognitive Media Theory*. New York; London: Routledge.

Nardelli, Matilde. 2010. "Some Reflections on Antonioni, Sound and the Silence of *La Notte*." *The Soundtrack* 3 (1): 11–23. https://doi.org/10.1386/st.3.1.11_1.

Neumeyer, David. 2009. "Diegetic/Nondiegetic: A Theoretical Model." *Music and the Moving Image* 2 (1, Spring): 26–39.

Neumeyer, David. 2015. *Meaning and Interpretation of Music in Film*. Bloomington; Indianapolis: Indiana University Press.

Nielsen, Jakob Isak. 2007. "Camera Movement in Narrative Cinema: Towards a Taxonomy of Functions." PhD diss., Aarhus University. pure.au.dk/portal/files/52113417/Camera_Movement_0910.pdf.

Noë, Alva. 2009. *Out of Our Heads: Why You Are Not Your Brain and Other Lessons from the Biology of Consciousness*. New York: Hill and Wong.

Noske, Catherine. 2015. "Towards an Existential Pluralism: Reading through the Philosophy of Etienne Souriau." *Cultural Studies Review* 21 (1): 34–57.

O'Brien, Adam. 2018. *Film and the Natural Environment: Elements and Atmospheres*. London; New York: Wallflower Press.

O'Falt, Chris. 2020. "How '1917' Showcases the Future of Camera Stabilization and Movement." *IndieWire* (blog). February 1, 2020. https://www.indiewire.com/2020/02/1917-roger-deakins-camera-movement-stabilization-arri-trinity-1202207817/.

Ondaatje, Michael. 2002. *The Conversations: Walter Murch and the Art of Editing Film*. New York: Knopf.

Othold, Tim, and Christiane Voss. 2015. "From Media Anthropology to Anthropomediality." *Anthropological Notebooks* 21 (3): 75–82.

Pallasmaa, Juhani. 2014. "Space, Place, and Atmosphere: Peripheral Perception in Existential Experience." In *Architectural Atmospheres: On the Experience and Politics of Architecture*, edited by Christian Borch, 18–41. Basel: Birkhäuser.

Panksepp, Jaak. 1998. *Affective Neuroscience: The Foundations of Human and Animal Emotions*. Oxford; New York: Oxford University Press.

Pantenburg, Volker. 2016. "Videographic Film Studies and the Analysis of Camera Movement." Translated by Michael Turnbull. *NECSUS: European Journal of Media Studies* Spring 5 (1): 41–58.

Parker, Joshua. 2016. "Conceptions of Place, Space and Narrative: Past, Present and Future." *Amsterdam Journal for Cultural Narratology* 7–8 (Autumn 2012/Autumn 2014): 74–101.

Pearlman, Karen. 2009. *Cutting Rhythms: Shaping the Film Edits*. Burlington, Mass.: Focal Press.

Pearlman, Karen. 2017. "Editing and Cognition beyond Continuity." *Projections* 11 (2). https://doi.org/10.3167/proj.2017.110205.

Pearlman, Karen. 2019. "On Rhythm in Film Editing." In *The Palgrave Handbook of the Philosophy of Film and Motion Pictures*, edited by Noël Carroll, Laura Teresa Di Summa-Knoop, and Shawn Loht, 143–63. Cham, Switzerland: Palgrave Macmillan.

Percheron, Daniel. 1980. "Sound in Cinema and Its Relationship to Image and Diegesis." Translated by Marcia Butzel. *Yale French Studies* 60: 16–23. https://doi.org/10.2307/2930001.

Pessoa, Luiz. 2008. "On the Relationship between Emotion and Cognition." *Nature Reviews Neuroscience* 9 (2): 148–58.

Pessoa, Luiz. 2013. *The Cognitive-Emotional Brain: From Interaction to Integration.* Cambridge, Mass.; London: MIT Press.

Petrić, Vlada. 1983. "*A Page of Madness.* A Neglected Masterpiece of the Silent Cinema." *Film Criticism* 8 (1, Japanese Cinema): 86–106.

Pezzulo, G. 2011. "Grounding Procedural and Declarative Knowledge in Sensorimotor Anticipation." *Mind and Language* 26 (1): 78–114.

Phelan, James, and Peter J. Rabinowitz. 2012. "Narrative Worlds: Space, Setting, Perspective." In *Narrative Theory: Core Concepts and Critical Debates*, edited by David Herman, James Phelan, Peter J. Rabinowitz, Brian Richardson, and Robyn Warhol, 84–91. Columbus: The Ohio State University Press.

Plantinga, Carl. 1995. "Movie Pleasures and the Spectator's Experience: Toward a Cognitive Approach." *Film and Philosophy* 2 (2): 3–19.

Plantinga, Carl. 2009a. "Emotion and Affect." In *The Routledge Companion to Philosophy and Film*, edited by Carl Plantinga and Paisley Livingstone, 86–96. London; New York: Routledge.

Plantinga, Carl. 2009b. *Moving Viewers: American Film and the Spectator's Experience.* Berkeley; Los Angeles; London: University of California Press.

Plantinga, Carl. 2010. "Affective Incongruity and *The Thin Red Line.*" *Projections* 4 (2): 86–103. https://doi.org/10.3167/proj.2010.040206.

Plantinga, Carl. 2012. "Art Moods and Human Moods in Narrative Cinema." *New Literary History* 43 (3): 455–75. https://doi.org/10.1353/nlh.2012.0025.

Plantinga, Carl. 2014. "Mood and Ethics in Narrative Film." In *Cognitive Media Theory*, edited by Ted Nannicelli and Paul Taberham, 141–57. New York; London: Routledge.

Plantinga, Carl, and Greg M. Smith, eds. 1999. *Passionate Views: Film, Cognition, and Emotion.* Baltimore: Johns Hopkins University Press.

Pollmann, Inga. 2010. "*Kalte Stimmung*, or, the Mode of Mood: Ice and Snow in Melodrama." *Colloquia Germanica* 43 (1–2): 79–96.

Pollmann, Inga. 2013. "Invisible Worlds, Visible: Uexküll's *Umwelt*, Film, and Film Theory." *Critical Inquiry* 39 (4): 777–816. https://doi.org/10.1086/671356.

Pollmann, Inga. 2018. *Cinematic Vitalism: Film Theory and the Question of Life.* Amsterdam: Amsterdam University Press.

Polvinen, Merja. 2016. "Enactive Perception and Fictional Worlds." In *The Cognitive Humanities: Embodied Mind in Literature and Culture*, edited by Peter Garratt, 19–34. London: Palgrave Macmillan.

Poulaki, Maria. 2011. *Before or beyond Narrative? Towards a Complex Systems Theory of Contemporary Films.* PhD diss., University of Amsterdam.

Prince, Gerald. 1982. *Narratology: The Form and Functioning of Narrative.* Berlin: Mouton.

Prinz, Jesse J. 2004. "Embodied Emotions." In *Thinking about Feeling: Contemporary Philosophers on Emotions*, edited by Robert C. Solomon, 44–58. Oxford; New York: Oxford University Press.

Quendler, Christian. 2017. *The Camera-Eye Metaphor in Cinema*. New York: Routledge.

Ramachandran, Vilayanur. 2000. "Mirror Neurons and Imitation Learning as the Driving Force behind the Great Leap Forward in Human Evolution." *Edge*. May 31, 2000. http:// edge.org/conversation/mirror-neurons-and-imitation-learning-as-the-driving-force-behind-the-great-leap-forward-in-human-evolution.

Rauh, Andreas. 2017. "In the Clouds: On the Vagueness of Atmospheres." *Ambiances* 2: 1–16. https://doi.org/10.4000/ambiances.818.

Rhym, John. 2012. "Towards a Phenomenology of Cinematic Mood: Boredom and the Affect of Time in Antonioni's *L'eclisse*." *New Literary History* 43 (3): 477–501.

Rhym, John. 2018. "Historicizing Perception: Film Theory, Neuroscience, and the Philosophy of Mind." *Discourse* 40 (1): 83–109. https://doi.org/10.13110/discou rse.40.1.0083.

Richmond, Scott C. 2010. "Resonant Perception: Cinema, Phenomenology, and the Illusion of Bodily Movement." PhD diss, University of Chicago.

Richmond, Scott C. 2016. *Cinema's Bodily Illusions: Flying, Floating, Hallucinating*. Minneapolis: University of Minnesota Press.

Ricœur, Paul. 1980. "Narrative Time." Translated by Kathleen McLaughlin and David Pellauer. *Critical Inquiry*, On Narrative, 7 (1): 169–90.

Rio, Elena del. 2008. *Deleuze and the Cinemas of Performance: Powers of Affection*. Edinburgh: Edinburgh University Press.

Rizzolatti, Giacomo, and Michael A. Arbib. 1998. "Language within Our Grasp." *Trends in Neurosciences* 21 (5): 188–94.

Rizzolatti, Giacomo, and Laila Craighero. 2004. "The Mirror-Neuron System." *Annual Review of Neuroscience* 27 (1): 169–92. https://doi.org/10.1146/annurev.neuro.27.070 203.144230.

Rizzolatti, Giacomo, and Maddalena Fabbri-Destro. 2010. "Mirror Neurons: From Discovery to Autism." *Experimental Brain Research* 200 (3–4): 223–37.

Rodowick, D. N. 2014. *Elegy for Theory*. Cambridge, Mass.: Harvard University Press.

Rodrigo, Pierre. 2005. "Merleau-Ponty. Du cinéma à la peinture: le 'vouloir-dire' et l'expression élémentaire." In *L'intentionnalité créatrice: Problème de phénoménologie et d'esthétique*, 235–55. Paris: Librairie Philosophique J. VRIN.

Rohrwacher, Alice. 2019. "Alice Rohrwacher: 'We imagine that a good man does good, but it's an illusion.'" Interview by Manuela Lazic. *Little White Lies*. https://manilazic. com/interviews/2019/4/3/alice-rohrwacher-we-imagine-that-a-good-man-does-good-but-its-an-illusion.

Roques, Mario. 1947. "Filmologie." *Revue internationale de filmologie* 1 (1): 5–8.

Rousse, B. Scot. 2016. "Merleau-Ponty and Carroll on the Power of Movies." *International Journal of Philosophical Studies* 24 (1): 45–73.

Rudrum, David. 2005. "From Narrative Representation to Narrative Use: Towards the Limits of Definition." *Narrative* 13 (2): 195–204.

Russolo, Luigi. 1986. "The Art of Noises." In *The Art of Noises: Futurist Manifesto*, translated by Barclay Brown, 23–30. New York: Pendragon Press.

Ryan, Marie-Laure. 1992. *Possible Worlds, Artificial Intelligence, and Narrative Theory*. Bloomington: Indiana University Press.

Ryan, Marie-Laure. 2001. *Narrative as Virtual Reality: Immersion and Interactivity in Literature and Electronic Media*. Baltimore; London: The Johns Hopkins University Press.

Ryan, Marie-Laure. 2004. *Narrative across Media: The Languages of Storytelling*. Lincoln: University of Nebraska Press.

Ryan, Marie-Laure. 2014. "Space." In *The Living Handbook of Narratology*, edited by Peter Hühn, 1–16. Hamburg: Hamburg University Press. http://www.lhn.uni-hamburg.de/article/space.

Ryan, Marie-Laure. 2017. "Narrative." In *A Companion to Critical and Cultural Theory*, edited by Imre Szeman, Sarah Blacker, and Justin Sully, 517–30. Hoboken, N.J.: John Wiley & Sons.

Ryan, Marie-Laure, and Jan-Noël Thon. 2014a. "Storyworlds across Media: Introduction." In *Storyworlds across Media: Toward a Media-Conscious Narratology*, edited by Marie-Laure Ryan and Jan-Noël Thon, 1–21. Lincoln; London: University of Nebraska Press.

Ryan, Marie-Laure, and Jan-Noël Thon, eds. 2014b. *Storyworlds across Media: Toward a Media-Conscious Narratology*. Lincoln; London: University of Nebraska Press.

Ryle, Gilbert. 2009. *The Concept of Mind*. New York: Routledge.

Saussure, Ferdinand de. 1998. *Course in General Linguistics*. Edited by Charles Bally and Albert Sechehaye. Translated by Roy Harris. Reprint edition. Chicago; LaSalle, Ill: Open Court.

Schafer, Raymond Murray. 1977. *The Soundscape: Our Sonic Environment and the Tuning of Our World*. 2nd ed. Rochester, Vt.: Destiny Books.

Scherer, Klaus Rainer. 1999. "Appraisal Theory." In *Handbook of Emotion and Cognition*, edited by Tim Dalglish and Mick Power, 637–63. Chichester, U.K.: John Wiley & Sons.

Schmetkamp, Susanne. 2017. "Gaining Perspectives on Our Life: Moods and Aesthetic Experience." *Philosophia* 45 (4): 1681–95.

Schmidt, James. 1985. *Maurice Merleau-Ponty: Between Phenomenology and Structuralism*. New York: St Martin's Press.

Schmidt, Lisa. 2011. "Sound Matters: Towards an Enactive Approach to Hearing Media." *The Soundtrack* 4 (1): 32–42. https://doi.org/10.1386/st.4.1.33_1.

Schmitz, Hermann. 1998. *Der Leib, der Raum und die Gefühle*. Ostfildern vor Stuttgart: Edition Tertium.

Schmitz, Hermann. 2007. *Freiheit*. Freiburg; München: Verlag Karl Alber.

Schmitz, Hermann. 2009. *Kurze Einführung in die Neue Phänomenologie*. 4th edition. Freiburg; München: Verlag Karl Alber.

Schmitz, Hermann. 2011. *Der Leib*. Berlin; Boston: De Gruyter.

Schmitz, Hermann. 2016a. *Atmosphären*. 2. Freiburg; München: Verlag Karl Alber.

Schmitz, Hermann. 2016b. "Atmospheric Spaces." Translated by Margret Vince. *Ambiances* 2 (Redécouvertes): 1–10.

Scholes, Robert. 1985. "Narration and Narrativity in Film." In *Film Theory and Criticism*, edited by Gerald Mast, Marshall Cohen, and Leo Braudy, 390–403. New York: Oxford University Press.

Schonig, Jordan. 2017. "Cinema's Motion Forms: Film Theory, the Digital Turn, and the Possibilities of Cinematic Movement." PhD diss., University of Chicago.

Semmerling, Tim Jon. 2006. *"Evil" Arabs in American Popular Film*. Austin: University of Texas Press.

Sergi, Gianluca. 2002. "A Cry in the Dark: The Role of Post-Classical Film Sound." In *The Film Cultures Reader*, edited by Graeme Turner, 107–14. London & New York: Routledge, Taylor & Francis Group.

Sergi, Gianluca. 2004. *The Dolby Era: Film Sound in Contemporary Hollywood*. Inside Popular Film. Manchester, U.K.; New York: Manchester University Press.

Sergi, Gianluca. 2006. "In Defence of Vulgarity: The Place of Sound Effects in the Cinema." *Scope: An Online Journal of Film and Television*, no. 5: June 2006. https://www.notting ham.ac.uk/scope/documents/2006/june-2006/sergi.pdf.

Sergi, Gianluca. 2013. "Knocking at the Door of Cinematic Artifice: Dolby Atmos, Challenges and Opportunities." *The New Soundtrack* 3 (2): 107–21.

Shaheen, Jack G. 2001. *Reel Bad Arabs: How Hollywood Vilifies a People*. Brooklyn, N.Y.: Olive Branch Press.

Shaviro, Steven. 1993. *The Cinematic Body*. Vol. 2. Theory out of Bounds. Minneapolis; London: University of Minnesota Press.

Shaviro, Steven. 2010. *Post-Cinematic Affect*. Winchester, U.K. Washington, D.C.: Zero Books.

Shaviro, Steven. 2016. "Affect vs. Emotion." *The Cine-Files*, 10 (Spring). https://www.thec ine-files.com/shaviro2016/.

Sheets-Johnstone, Maxine. 2012. "Movement and Mirror Neurons: A Challenging and Choice Conversation." *Phenomenology and the Cognitive Sciences* 11 (3): 385–401. https://doi.org/10.1007/s11097-011-9243-x.

Sider, Larry. 2004. *Soundscape: The School of Sound Lectures 1998–2001*. New York: Columbia University Press.

Simcovitch, Maxim. 1972. "The Impact of Griffith's *Birth of a Nation* on the Modern Ku Klux Klan." *Journal of Popular Film* 1 (1): 45–54. https://doi.org/10.1080/00472 719.1972.10661639.

Simmel, Georg. 1903. "Die Großstädte und das Geistesleben." In *Die Großstadt. Vorträge und Aufsätze zur Städteaustellung*, edited by Theodor Petermann, 185–206. Dresden: Gehe Stiftung.

Sinnerbrink, R. 2012. "Stimmung: Exploring the Aesthetics of Mood." *Screen* 53 (2): 148–63. https://doi.org/10.1093/screen/hjs007.

Slaby, Jan, Rainer Mühlhoff, and Philipp Wüschner. 2017. "Affective Arrangements." *Emotion Review* 11 (1): 3–12. https://doi.org/10.1177/1754073917722214.

Smith, Greg M. 1999. "Local Emotions, Global Moods, and Film Structure." In *Passionate Views: Film, Cognition, and Emotion*, edited by Carl Plantinga and Greg M. Smith, 103–26. Baltimore, Md.: Johns Hopkins University Press.

Smith, Greg M. 2003. *Film Structure and the Emotion System*. Cambridge: Cambridge University Press.

Smith, Jeff. 1999. "Movie Music as Moving Music: Emotion, Cognition, and Film Score." In *Passionate Views: Film, Cognition, and Emotion*, edited by Carl Plantinga and Greg M. Smith, 146–67. Baltimore, Md: Johns Hopkins University Press.

Smith, Jeff. 2009. "Bridging the Gap: Reconsidering the Border between Diegetic and Nondiegetic Music." *Music, Sound, and the Moving Image* 2 (1): 1–25.

Smith, Murray. 1995. *Engaging Characters: Fiction, Emotion, and the Cinema*. Oxford: Oxford University Press.

Smith, Murray. 1996. "The Legacy of Brechtianism." In *Post-Theory: Reconstructing Film Studies*, edited by David Bordwell and Noël Carroll, 1st edition, 130–48. Madison: University of Wisconsin Press.

Smith, Murray. 2017. *Film, Art, and the Third Culture: A Naturalized Aesthetics of Film.* Oxford: Oxford University Press.

Smith, Murray. 2020. "Foreword: The Neuroscientific Turn." In *The Empathic Screen: Cinema and Neuroscience,* by Vittorio Gallese and Michele Guerra, translated by Frances Anderson, vii–xxiii. Oxford: Oxford University Press.

Snow, Michael. 1994. "La Régione Centrale." In *The Collected Writings of Michael Snow,* edited by Michael Snow and Louise Dompierre, 53–56. Waterloo, Ont.: Wilfrid Laurier University Press.

Sobchack, Vivian Carol. 1982. "Toward Inhabited Space: The Semiotic Structure of Camera Movement in the Cinema." *Semiotica* 41 (1–4): 317–35.

Sobchack, Vivian Carol. 1992. *The Address of the Eye: A Phenomenology of Film Experience.* Princeton, N.J.: Princeton University Press.

Sobchack, Vivian Carol. 1998. "Lounge Time: Postwar Crises and the Chronotype of Film Noir." In *Refiguring American Film Genres: History and Theory,* edited by Nick Browne, 129–70. Berkeley: University of California Press.

Sobchack, Vivian Carol. 2004. *Carnal Thoughts: Embodiment and Moving Image Culture.* Berkeley; Los Angeles; London: University of California Press.

Soja, Edward W. 1989. *Postmodern Geographies: The Reassertion of Space in Critical Social Theory.* London; New York: Verso.

Somaini, Antonio. 2016. "Walter Benjamin's Media Theory: The *Medium* and the *Apparat*." *Grey Room* 62 (Winter): 6–41.

Souriau, Anne. 1990. "Diégèse." In *Vocabulaire d'esthétique,* edited by Étienne Souriau and Anne Souriau, 611–14. Paris: Presses universitaires de France.

Souriau, Étienne. 1943. *Les différents modes d'existence.* Paris: Presses Universitaires de France.

Souriau, Étienne. 1951. "La structure de l'univers filmique et le vocabulaire de la filmologie." *Revue internationale de filmologie* 2 (7–8): 231–40.

Souriau, Étienne. 1953. *L'univers filmique.* Paris: Flammarion.

Souriau, Étienne. 2015. *The Different Modes of Existence.* Translated by Erik Beranek and Tim Howles. Minneapolis, Minn.: Univocal Publishing.

Sousa, Ronald de. 1990. *The Rationality of Emotion.* Cambridge, Mass.; London: MIT Press.

Spadoni, Robert. 2014a. "Carl Dreyer's Corpse: Horror Film Atmosphere and Narrative." In *A Companion to the Horror Film,* edited by Harry M. Benshoff, 151–67. Medford, Mass.: Blackwell.

Spadoni, Robert. 2014b. "Horror Film Atmosphere as Anti-Narrative (and Vice Versa)." In *Merchants of Menace: The Business of Horror Cinema,* edited by Richard Nowell, 109–28. New York; London; New Delhi; Sydney: Bloomsbury Academic.

Spadoni, Robert. 2020. "What Is Film Atmosphere?" *Quarterly Review of Film and Video* 37 (1): 48–75. https://doi.org/10.1080/10509208.2019.1606558.

Sterelny, Kim. 2010. "Minds: Extended or Scaffolded?" *Phenomenology and the Cognitive Sciences* 9 (4): 465–81. https://doi.org/10.1007/s11097-010-9174-y.

Sterne, Jonathan. 2003. *The Audible Past: Cultural Origins of Sound Production.* Durham, N.C.; London: Duke University Press.

Sterne, Jonathan. 2012. "Sonic Imaginations." In *The Sound Studies Reader,* edited by Jonathan Sterne, 1–17. New York; London: Routledge.

Sticchi, Francesco. 2018a. "From Spinoza to Contemporary Linguistics: Pragmatic Ethics in Denis Villeneuve's *Arrival*." *The Canadian Journal of Film Studies/Revue*

Canadienne d'etudes Cinematographiques 27 (2): 48–65. https://doi.org/10.3138/ CJFS.27.2.2018-0003.

Sticchi, Francesco. 2018b. "Inside the 'Mind' of Llewyn Davis: Embodying a Melancholic Vision of the World." *Quarterly Review of Film and Video* 35 (2): 137–52. https://doi. org/10.1080/10509208.2017.1381012.

Sticchi, Francesco. 2018c. "Undoing Male Fantasies and Narrative Reliability in Park Chan-wook's *The Handmaiden*." *Screen Bodies* 3 (2): 61–78. https://doi.org/10.3167/scr een.2018.030205.

Sticchi, Francesco. 2019. *Melancholy Emotion in Contemporary Cinema: A Spinozian Analysis of Film Experience*. New York; London: Routledge.

Stiegler, Bernard. 1998. *Technics and Time, 1: The Fault of Epimetheus*. Vol. 1. 3 vols. Stanford, Calif.: Stanford University Press.

Stilwell, Robynn J. 2007. "The Fantastical Gap between Diegetic and Nondiegetic." In *Beyond the Soundtrack: Representing Music in Cinema*, edited by Daniel Goldmark, Lawrence Kramer, and Richard Leppert, 184–202. Berkeley; Los Angeles; London: University of California Press.

Straus, Erwin. 1930. "Die Formen des Räumlichen: Ihre Bedeutung für die Motorik und die Wahrnehmung." *Nervenarzt* 3: 633–56.

Straus, Erwin. 1960. *Psychologie der menschlichen Welt: Gesammelte Schriften*. Berlin; Heidelberg: Springer Verlag.

Straus, Erwin. 1965. "The Sense of the Senses." *Southern Journal of Philosophy*, Philosophy of Mind, 3 (4): 192–201.

Tallis, Raymond. 2011. *Aping Mankind: Neuromania, Darwinitis, and the Misrepresentation of Humanity*. Durham, U.K.: Acumen.

Tan, Ed S. 1996. *Emotion and the Structure of Narrative Film: Film as an Emotion Machine*. New York: Routledge.

Tan, Ed S. 2013. *Emotion and the Structure of Narrative Film: Film as an Emotion Machine*. New York: Routledge.

Tan, Ed S. 2018. "A Psychology of the Film." *Palgrave Communications* 4 (1): 82. https:// doi.org/10.1057/s41599-018-0111-y.

Taylor, Henri M. 2007. "The Success Story of a Misnomer." *Offscreen* 11 (8–9, Aug./ Sept.): 1–5.

Tellenbach, Hubertus. 1968. *Geschmack und Atmosphäre: Medien menschlichen Elementarkontaktes*. Salzburg: Otto Müller Verlag.

Thanouli, Eleftheria. 2014. "Diegesis." In *The Routledge Encyclopedia of Film Theory*, edited by Edward Branigan and Warren Buckland, 133–37. New York: Routledge.

Thibaud, Jean-Paul. 2003. "Die sinnliche Umwelt von Städten: Zum Verständnis urbaner Atmosphären." In *Die Kunst der Wahrnehmung: Beiträge zu einer Philosophie der sinnlichen Erkenntnis*, edited by Michael Hauskeller, 280–97. Zug, Switzerland: Die Graue Edition.

Thibaud, Jean-Paul. 2011. "The Sensory Fabric of Urban Ambiences." *The Senses and Society* 6 (2): 203–15.

Thibaud, Jean-Paul. 2014. "A Conversation on Atmosphere." In *Architecture and Atmosphere*, edited by Philip Tidwell: 67–76. Espoo, Finland: Tapio Wirkkala-Rut Bryk Foundation.

Thom, Randy. 1999. "Designing a Movie for Sound." *Filmsound.Org* (blog). http://www. filmsound.org/articles/designing_for_sound.htm.

Thom, Randy. 2007. "Acoustics of the Soul." *Offscreen* 11 (8–9). September 2007. https://offscreen.com/view/soundforum_2.

Thompson, Evan. 2007. *Mind in Life: Biology, Phenomenology, and the Sciences of Mind.* Cambridge, Mass.: Harvard University Press.

Thompson, Evan, and Francisco J. Varela. 2001. "Neural Dynamics and Consciousness." *Trends in Cognitive Sciences* 5 (10): 418–25.

Thompson, Kristin. 1977. "The Concept of Cinematic Excess." *Ciné-Tracts* 1 (2): 54–63.

Thompson, Kristin. 1988. *Breaking the Glass Armor: Neoformalist Film Analysis.* Princeton, N.J.: Princeton University Press.

Tikka, Pia. 2008. *Enactive Cinema: Simulatorium Eisensteinense.* Helsinki: University of Art and Design, Helsinki.

Todorov, Tzvetan. 1969. "Structural Analysis of Narrative." Translated by Arnold Weinstein. *NOVEL: A Forum on Fiction* 3 (1): 70–76.

Toop, David. 1995. *Ocean of Sound: Aehter Talk, Ambient Sound and Imaginary Worlds.* London: Serpent's Tail.

Tuan, Yi-Fu. 2001. *Space and Place: The Perspective of Experience.* 8th edition. Minneapolis; London: University of Minnesota Press.

Turvey, Malcolm. 1999. "Can the Camera See? Mimesis in 'Man with a Movie Camera.'" *October* 89 (Summer): 25–50. https://doi.org/10.2307/779138.

Turvey, Malcolm. 2020. "Mirror Neurons and Film Studies: A Cautionary Tale from a Serious Pessimist." *Projections* 14 (3): 21–46. https://doi.org/10.3167/proj.2020.140303.

Vachon-Presseau, Etienne, Marc O. Martel, Mathieu Roy, Etienne Caron, Philip L. Jackson, and Pierre Rainville. 2011. "The Multilevel Organization of Vicarious Pain Responses: Effects of Pain Cues and Empathy Traits on Spinal Nociception and Acute Pain." *Pain* 152 (7): 1525–31. https://doi.org/10.1016/j.pain.2011.02.039.

van Dijk, Teun, and Kintsch, Walter. 1983. *Strategies of Discourse Comprehension.* San Diego, CA: Academic Press.

Varela, Francisco Javier, Evan Thompson, and Eleanor Rosch. 1992. *The Embodied Mind: Cognitive Science and Human Experience.* Cambridge, Mass.: MIT Press.

Verstraaten, Peter. 2009. *Film Narratology.* Translated by Stefan van der Lecq. Toronto; Buffalo; London: University of Toronto Press.

Voss, Christiane. 2010. "Auf dem Weg zu einer Medienphilosophie anthropomedialer Räume." *Zeitschrift für Medien- und Kulturforschung* 2 (Medienphilosophie): 170–84.

Voss, Christiane. 2011. "Film Experience and the Formation of Illusion: The Spectator as 'Surrogate Body' for the Cinema." Translated by Inga Pollmann. *Cinema Journal* 50 (4): 136–50.

Voss, Christiane. 2014a. "Affekt." In *Essays zur Film-Philosophie*, edited by Lorenz Engell, Christiane Voss, Vinzenz Hediger, and Oliver Fahle, 1st edition, 63–116. Film Denken. Paderborn, Germany: Wilhelm Fink.

Voss, Christiane. 2014b. *Der Leihkörper: Erkenntnis und Ästhetik der Illusion.* Film Denken. München: Wilhelm Fink Verlag.

Voss, Christiane, and Lorenz Engell. 2015a. *Mediale Anthropologie.* Schriften des Internationales Kolleg für Kulturtechnikforschung und Medienphilosophie. Paderborn: Wilhelm Fink Verlag.

Voss, Christiane, and Lorenz Engell. 2015b. "Vorwort." In *Mediale Anthropologie*, 7–17. Schriften des Internationales Kolleg für Kulturtechnikforschung und Medienphilosophie. Paderborn, Germany: Wilhelm Fink Verlag.

Walden, Jennifer. 2018. "How *A Quiet Place*'s Essential Sound Was Created." *A Sound Effect* (blog). April 18, 2018. https://www.asoundeffect.com/a-quiet-place-sound/.

Wallon, Henri. 1947. "Qu'est-ce que la filmologie?" *La pensée* 15: 29–34.

Walton, Saige. 2018. "Air, Atmosphere, Environment: Film Mood, Folk Horror and *The VVitch*." *Screening the Past* (43, April). http://www.screeningthepast.com/issue-43-dossier-materialising-absence-in-film-and-media/air-atmosphere-environment-film-mood-folk-horror-and-the-vvitch/.

Ward, Mark S. 2015. "Art in Noise: An Embodied Simulation Account of Cinematic Sound Design." In *Embodied Cognition and Cinema*, edited by Maarten Coëgnarts and Peter Kravanja, 155–86. Leuven: Leuven University Press.

Ward, Meredith C. 2019. *Static in the System: Noise and the Soundscape of American Cinema Culture*. Oakland: University of California Press.

Warren, William H. 1984. "Perceiving Affordances: Visual Guidance of Stair Climbing." *Journal of Experimental Psychology: Human Perception and Performance* 10 (5): 683–703.

Wellbery, David E. 2010. "Stimmung." In *Ästhetische Grundbegriffe: Band 5: Postmoderne—Synästhesie*, edited by Karlheinz Barck, Martin Fontius, Dieter Schlenstedt, Burkhart Steinwachs, and Friedrich Wolfzettel, 703–33. Stuttgart/Weimar: J.B. Metzler.

Margaret, Wetherell. 2012. *Affect and Emotion: A New Social Science Understanding*. London: SAGE Publications.

Whittington, William. 2007. *Sound Design & Science Fiction*. Austin: University of Texas Press.

Wicclair, Mark. 1978. "Film Theory and Hugo Münsterberg's 'The Film: A Psychological Study.'" *The Journal of Aesthetic Education* 12 (3): 33–50.

Wierzbicki, James. 2012. "Sonic Style in Cinema." In *Music, Sound and Filmmakers: Sonic Style in Cinema*, edited by James Wierzbicki, 1–14. London; New York: Routledge.

Willoquet-Maricondi, Paula, ed. 2010. *Framing the World*. University of Virginia Press. http://www.jstor.org.proxy.uchicago.edu/stable/j.ctt6wrgnd.

Wilson, Robert A. 2003. "Individualism." In *The Blackwell Guide to Philosophy of Mind*, edited by Stephen P. Stich and Ted A. Warfield, 256–83. Malden, Mass.; Oxford; Melbourne; Berlin; Blackwell Publishers.

Winters, Ben. 2010. "The Non-Diegetic Fallacy: Film, Music, and Narrative Space." *Music & Letters* 91 (2): 224–44.

Winters, Ben. 2012. "Musical Wallpaper? Towards an Appreciation of Non-Narrating Music in Film." *Music, Sound, and the Moving Image* 6 (1): 39–54. https://doi.org/10.3828/msmi.2012.5.

Wit, Matthieu M. de, Simon de Vries, John van der Kamp, and Rob Withagen. 2017. "Affordances and Neuroscience: Steps towards a Successful Marriage." *Neuroscience and Biobehavioral Reviews* 80 (September): 622–29. https://doi.org/10.1016/j.neubiorev.2017.07.008.

Wollen, Peter. 1980. "Introduction: Place in Film." *Framework: The Journal of Cinema and Media* 13 (Autumn): 25.

Wulff, Hans J. 2012. "Prolegomena zu einer Theorie des Atmosphärischen im Film." In *Filmische Atmosphären*, edited by Philipp Brunner, Jörg Schweintz, and Margit Tröhler, 109–24. Zürcher Filmstudien. Marburg: Schüren.

Yacavone, Daniel. 2012. "Spaces, Gaps, and Levels: From the Diegetic to the Aesthetic in Film Theory." *Music, Sound, and the Moving Image* 6 (1): 21–37.

Yacavone, Daniel. 2015. *Film Worlds: A Philosophical Aesthetics of Cinema.* New York: Columbia University Press.

Yacavone, Daniel. 2016. "Film and the Phenomenology of Art: Reappraising Merleau-Ponty on Cinema as Form, Medium, and Expression." *New Literary History* 47 (1): 159–85.

Zerilli, Linda Marie-Gelsomina. 2015. "The Turn to Affect and the Problem of Judgment." *New Literary History* 46 (2): 261–86.

Zielinski, Siegfried. 2006. *Deep Time of the Media: Toward an Archology of Hearing and Seeing by Technical Means.* Translated by Gloria Custance. Cambridge, Mass.; London: MIT Press.

Zoran, Gabriel. 1984. "Towards a Theory of Space in Narrative." *Poetics Today* 5 (2, The Construction of Reality in Fiction): 309–35.

Index

For the benefit of digital users, indexed terms that span two pages (e.g., 52–53) may, on occasion, appear on only one of those pages.